AGRICULTURE IN THE ERA OF ECONOMIC REFORMS

CHALLENGES AND STRATEGIES FOR DEVELOPMENT

AGRICULTURE IN THE ERA OF ECONOMIC REFORMS

CHALLENGES AND STRATEGIES FOR DEVELOPMENT

Editor

K.K. BAGCHI

ABHIJEET PUBLICATIONS

DELHI – 110 094

ABHIJEET PUBLICATIONS
2/46 Tukhmeerpur Extension
Delhi-110 094
Phone: 011-22960492, 65698474
E-mail: abhijeetpublication@gmail.com

AGRICULTURE IN THE ERA OF ECONOMIC REFORMS

First Published 2011

ISBN 978-93-81136-46-1

PRINTED IN INDIA

Published by J.K. Singh for Abhijeet Publications, Delhi-110 094, Lasertypeset by Gaurav Graphics, New Delhi and Printed at Himanshu Printers, Delhi.

Introduction

K.K. Bagchi

Agricultural sector in India is not performing well for about the entire period of last decade. This period coincides with the introduction of economic reforms in agriculture and adoption of National Agricultural Policy in 2000. The adverse consequences are already visible in different forms. This is a matter of concern to planners, policy makers and citizens in general. It is also an issue of debate whether initiation of economic reforms is responsible for the stagnation of the agricultural sector. In the mean time, due to WTO negotiations and agreements there have been considerable liberalization of imports and exports of agricultural commodities. But developed countries have played their cards cleverly and have taken steps to block agricultural exports from developing countries including India through various loopholes in AOA and allied agreements.

Moreover, due to lack of cost-effectiveness and lack of productivity growth, Indian agriculture is not much competitive in the world market. Prices of agricultural inputs are soaring. Farmers do not get profitable prices for their products. Agriculture has become a non-remunerative and often loss generating occupation to farmers. Incentives currently provided to farmers in different forms are not adequate enough. A major technological breakthrough is the need of the hour to improve productivity. Adequàte institutional and infrastructural facilities including credit, marketing and irrigation facilities are of crucial importance at the present juncture. All these issues have been argued upon in the 23 research papers included in this volume. In addition to identifying the problems and challenges, the contributors have suggested strategies to rectify and improve the situation. In what follows we have presented a synoptic view of the content of each of the studies included in this volume to enable the reader to quickly grasp the essence of them.

Misra and Tiwari have made an attempt to identify the areas of Indian agriculture where reforms are indispensable. According to them, the role of the government by way of public policies, programmes, and investment is going to be extremely important. They are convinced that once the above significant issues are addressed and agricultural functioning opened up to managerial efficiencies, India can manage to emerge as a new agricultural super power through substantial productivity gains. Then only growth of the rural economy will be inclusive – technologically, environmentally and economically.

Sib Ranjan Misra observes that there is widespread concern in the country about the stagnation in agricultural production. This, together with the falling prices of agricultural produce and the rising prices of agricultural inputs, have seriously affected the economy of a large number of farmers. The well-being of millions of families dependent on agriculture for their livelihood is jeopardized. The spate of suicides of farmers in different parts of the country is a stark manifestation of these developments. A large number of people in the farm sector are witnessing serious erosion in their incomes and living standards. Misra hopes that with several favourable factors it is possible to launch bold initiatives in favour of the millions of marginal farmers who have been left out of the mainstream of development.

Balasubramaniyan's study focuses on trends in globalization and the impact of globalization on agricultural growth. He has also compared the growth rates of agricultural and non-agricultural sectors. He maintains that the paradigm of the AOA as conceived in the WTO is not only alien to the kind of peasant farming that prevails in the G-20 countries but also creating a rift among developing economies. The propaganda and myth about trade liberalization was that it would lift India's poor from below poverty line. According to him, the market access rules of WTO are not wiping out poverty, they are wiping out the poor.

Tiwari in his paper has suggested that the replacement of shifting cultivation by wet cultivation and promotion of horticulture and its products need attention to evolve a sustainable strategy of agricultural development taking into account the environmental preservation and micro-agro-climatic condition. He suggests that every effort should be made to protect the poor from the vagaries of market forces. He has also suggests that the stress on human resource development in a desired manner will facilitate integration of local people's participation in new economic enterprises. It will also help the people to take up the challenges of market forces.

Dhandapani's paper deals with the changes in the land use pattern of agricultural sector in general before and after economic reforms and area used for the cultivation of food grains in particular. He has analyzed the trend in the production of food grains and non-food grains and compared the area, production and productive ity of principal crops of Indian agriculture with other countries. He has presented the index number of area, production and yield rate of food grains and non-food grains in India and elucidated the challenges of the agricultural sector in India. He maintains that there is a need for the continuous focus on improving productivity and step-up the growth of allied activities and non-farm activities. He has suggested several strategies for strengthening the agricultural sector.

Suresh Babu's study deals with the Indian agricultural structure and agrarian crisis. He has examined the farmers' suicides and agrarian distress in India during the pre-WTO period and the post-WTO period and concludes by outlining some general strategies as a way to tackle agrarian crisis in a suitable manner. He has concluded that globalization is partly responsible for the present agrarian crisis and farmers' suicides. WTO Agreement on Agriculture has not benefited Indian farmers and Indian economy. The growth rate analysis reveals that there is a sharp decline in growth rate of agricultural sector and growth rates of yield for commodities such as pulses, oil seeds and cotton was negative during the post-WTO period. Babu has suggested several measures to protect the interest of farming community particularly marginal and small farmers.

Tripathy's paper deals with the issues of globalization, crop diversification and agricultural development. He has concluded his study by stating that promoting agricultural diversification towards high-value commodities, doing value-addition through their processing and creating appropriate markets for them can be used as effective measures to alleviate rural poverty, generate rural employment and conserve natural resources in the niche areas.

Singh and Singh in their study has made an attempt to examine the effects of reform measures launched in agriculture in India on food security and suggested remedial measures to make effective food security. They have advocated that PDS should be strengthened and improved by streamlining the administrative machinery. They preach that inflation in food articles can be tackled by creating food chain with neighbouring countries and whole hearted effort should be made to arrest climatic change by afforestation and limiting the emissions of green house gases. However, according to them, the greatest effort should be made to reduce population growth.

Kumar observes that India is one of the few countries which have experimented with a broad spectrum of programmers for improving food security. They feel that India has already made substantial progress in terms of overcoming transient food insecurity by giving priority to self-sufficiency in food grains and through procurement and public distribution of food grains, employment programmers, etc. according to them India needs second Green Revolution to bring food security to its billion plus population to remove distress of farming community and to make its agriculture globally competitive. According to Kumar, though India has solved the problem of food security which is reflected in mounting buffer stocks, but there are millions of food insecure and undernourished people in India. He feels that the limitation is not food supply, but its distribution.

Ramesh has analysed the implications for India's food security due to the implementation of WTO policies. He has done this by analysing the changes in agricultural trade, cropping pattern and production of major crops and net availability of food grains since 1991-92. he has also shown that per capita net availability of food grains is at historical low, casting a doom for domestic food security. Hence, according to him developing countries should be allowed to attain food self-sufficiency which is the necessary condition in attaining food security and at the same time it also provides the necessary purchasing power in the hands of rural households. It needs a new strategy in conformity with the WTO to avoid the impact of this market-oriented production approach. He advocates that the poorest and the women in the rural households, who form the most vulnerable group, should be given alternative livelihood strategies.

Kakali Majumdar apprehends that the changing scenario of global agriculture in the post-WTO regime poses a serious challenge for developing countries like India. Significant fall in the growth rates of agricultural production have been noticed from the pre to post-WTO period. The Agreement on Agriculture (AOA) under WTO laid more emphasis on export as an instrument of growth. However, the share of agriculture export also declined over the years in the post-WTO period. Keeping this aspect in the background Majumdar's paper has given a detailed picture of Indian agriculture with special reference to production and export of Indian food-grains under WTO agreement. She finds that at this juncture it is very much important to take steps to improve the competitiveness of Indian agricultural output. With a contribution of 13 per cent to total export earnings, agri-exports have occupied an important position in Indian external trade. She concludes that the problems of downward trend in exports, sharp year to year fluctuations in net trade etc. raise question marks about the future of WTO in India and also for the other developing countries and seek further discussion or policy prescription on this subject at the international level.

Nayak has commented that liberalization has created several favourable impacts on the agricultural sector of the country. India with its rising population is in an advantageous position to develop its agricultural and allied sectors which are mostly labour intensive. Liberalization has provided ample scope for the modernization and development of the agricultural sector and also to reap the maximum benefit from the increasing scope of agricultural export arising out of the path of globalization adopted.

Jayasankar found that the developed countries have played their cards very cleverly and have taken effective steps to block agricultural exports from developing countries including India through various loopholes in AoA and allied agreements. Therefore, he maintains that to protect the Indian agriculture and Indian farmers from evils of globalization, the Indian agricultural policy needs to be built-up with adequate 'safety-nets'. This is possible only under interventionist policies of the Government.

Punjabi and Rathore have analyzed trade policy making in India in the context of the ongoing negotiations on agricultural trade policy reforms and WTO's impacts in India over the past decade. They opine that India's position on liberalization of trade in agriculture at multilateral trade negotiations is dominated by its protectionist interest expressed in terms of a centered food security rather than liberal interests in gaining market condition. According to them India has a long way to go in integrating its vast agriculture sector into world markets.

Saran and Goyal uphold the view that agriculture forms the backbone of Indian economy. Since independence, India has passed through several phases in agricultural development and most spectacular was the Green Revolution with a sharp increase in agricultural production. They have analyzed the differentials in the productivity of food grains and non-food grains in major states during the period 1965-66 to 1989-90 and 1989-90 to 2004- 05 and the factors responsible for the differential growth in the productivity. The study reveals that the performance of the states in regard to productivity of food grains depends upon fertilizer consumption, irrigation facilities, cropping intensity, high yielding varieties and machinery. Their final conclusion is that the performance of a particular state seems to be determined by the use of multiple rather than one single agricultural input.

Chakrabarti and Bagchi have made an attempt to find out whether the agriculture sector in north-eastern States of India is neglected or not in the post-reform era. They have found that agriculture sector has shown negative trend for most of the northeastern States in terms of contribution in SDP, employment elasticity and growth rate of average productivity. They have also found that the growth of agricultural output in all states has a decreasing trend. One of the reasons behind this fact is falling share of planned outlay on agricultural sector. There is no clear evidence that falling productivity of agriculture sector has become helpful to flourish manufacturing sector. Basically service sector has been benefited from the growth process of all northeastern States in term of income share, employment elasticity and average productivity.

Chakrabarti and Roy Mukherjee have done an evaluative study on problems and prospects of agriculture in the State of Sikkim. They express the view that attention should immediately be given to raise agricultural productivity and production in the State and to do so institutional changes have become imperative. Mere references of high economic growth and high per-capita income otherwise will become misleading and will fail to reflect the true economic status of 60 percent of the work force who earn their living from agriculture. They suggest that serious efforts are to be made to bring more land into cultivation through appropriation of surplus land possessed by big land owners and enough space needs to be created within the economy where surplus agricultural workers can gainfully be employed.

Choudhury's study deals with regional variations in agricultural productivity of West Bengal with a focus on the role of irrigation. He finds that substantial difference in agriculture productivity exists between irrigated and non-irrigated lands in West Bengal. There has been growing disparity in agriculture productivity both inter-state and intra-state. He maintains that such regional imbalances in agriculture performance have serious implications for rural livelihood.

In the study he has not only estimated the level of agriculture development in various districts of West Bengal but also identified the factors that inhibit development in some districts as compared to others. He has constructed a composite index for development of agriculture in the districts and the districts are ranked according to it. He finds that improvement in agriculture infrastructure, especially irrigation infrastructure is required for sustainable development of the agriculture sector. Exploitation of groundwater through proliferation of private water markets is untenable in the long run.

Jeyarani has analyzed the impact of liberalization on economics of pepper cultivation in India before and after liberalization. She observes that though India is the homeland of many spices, productivity of many of the spices are low, when compared to other competing countries. As the international market become increasingly competitive, it is imperative to enhance production and productivity and bring down the cost of cultivation and price of the produce to make Indian spices globally competitive. She preaches that farm mechanization will be profitable since there is shortage of agricultural labour in India and labour has become very costly.

Deshpande has made a review of the performance of agricultural credit in India. Her study reveals that though the overall flow of institutional credit has increased over the years, there are several gaps in the system like inadequate provision of credit to small and marginal farmers, paucity of medium and long-term lending, limited deposit mobilization and heavy dependence on borrowed funds by major agricultural credit purveyor. These have major implications for agricultural development as also the well-being of the farming community. She suggests that efforts are therefore required to address and rectify these issues.

Narasimhan and Sivachithappa have found out the impact of the institutional loan on the socio-economic conditions of the farmers of Mysore district of Karnataka. The study is based on primary data. They have found that majority of the respondents have utilized the finance for productive purposes such as purchase of fertilizers, seeds, land development, purchase of agricultural implements etc. They have also found that economic status of 93.4 per cent respondent's has improved after availing the loan from the institutional sources.

Sivachithappa has made an assessment of the effectiveness of various schemes of the RRBs in the light of a case study of Cauvery Grameena Bank in Mysore district. They have found that the bank officials were keen to extend the facility of (Kishan Credit Cards) KCC to farmers. In most of the places, it is the bank personnel who informed the farmers about the scheme and its benefits. All the respondent farmers indicated that obtaining KCC from banks is very easy. Further, banks are not maintaining any minimum credit limit while issuing cards. Similarly, the banks are not charging any fees on card holders for obtaining KCC. Since the banks are not maintaining any minimum credit limit, the marginal and small cultivators who require small loans are not deprived of KCC facility.

Madival and Sivachithappa's study relates to the evaluation of the role of primary agricultural cooperative credit societies in rural development of Mysore district of Karnataka. They suggest that for more effective functioning of cooperatives, government should recognize that cooperatives are private sector enterprises which are formed and managed by their members and which are not subject to intervention by government authorities in their internal management. In the light of this recognition revision of cooperative legislation should be taken up as a mater of priority. The powers vested in government to direct and supervise cooperatives should be critically reviewed. The overall aim should be to give autonomy to cooperatives. They have concluded the study with the positive note that cooperatives seem to be the only hope to inject strength and accelerate the growth of rural economy and ensure the development of rural areas.

I express my sincere thanks and gratitude to all the contributors for their invaluable contribution to the volume.

Contents

1

Agricultural Reforms in India: Locating the Imperatives

S.K. Mishra & Dewendra Pratap Tiwari

At the time of our gaining independence 1st Prime Minister of India Jawaharlal Nehru said "Everything else can wait but not agriculture." Unfortunately this profound truth is yet to be converted into concrete policies and action on an adequate scale. There have been several policy statements for agriculture during the last sixty two years, including the comprehensive reports of the national commission on agriculture (1976). The last ten years have witnessed a fatigue in the green revolution with the growth rate in food grain production falling bellow population growth. Thus, human numbers are increasing faster than our capacity to make the goal of "Food for All" a reality. A famine of jobs/livelihoods as a result of poor growth of opportunities for employment in the rural non-farm and off-farm sectors is leading to a famine of food at the house hold level. According to the Union Planning Commission, we are off-track in achieving the UN Millennium Development Goal of reducing the number of hungry persons by half by 2015. Our Prime Minister has rightly emphasized the need to double annual food grain from the present 210 million tonnes to 420 million tonnes within the next 10 years. Agricultural growth has decelerated during the last decade. This has led to a decline in real per capita income in rural India in comparison to the rapid growth in urban incomes.

Indian Agriculture is facing stagnation in the era of reforms. The economic reforms initiated in early 1990s not only failed to help agricultural growth but have actually aggravated the situation, in fact, hampering agricultural growth. It must be emphasized here that if farm economics and ecology go wrong, nothing else will go right in agriculture.

The slow down in agriculture growth since the mid 1990s has adversely impacted the livelihood base of the farming community at large. The slow down has occurred in all the sub sectors of agriculture, including livestock and horticultural growth in the immediate past. A large number of proximate and structural factors have contributed to the decline of agriculture.

The biggest challenges before the policy makers; therefore, are how to enhance the agricultural productivity and sustain the livelihood of resource poor marginal and small farmers and generate productive jobs for farm worker. The eleventh plan envisages that the agriculture should grow at least by four percent per annum to achieve the targeted G.D.P. growth rate of 10 percent. One of the challenges for achieving growth during this plan relates to the revival of Indian agriculture. Its growth rate was less than 2 percent in the last decade. Farming is becoming a non-viable activity. Disparities in productivity across regions and crops have persisted.

Estimates given by C.S.O. show that the index of agricultural production (IAP) grew up at the rate of 3.1 percent per annum during the period 1949-50 to 1964-65. This was attributable to high growth rates in both food grains and non food grains production. However, the growth rate of IAP decline to 2.3 percent during 1967-68 to 1980-81. The period between 1981-82 and 1991-92 witnessed a recovery with a 3.4 percent growth rate of the IAP significantly. During the period of 1992-93 and 2005-06, there was a sharp decline in the growth rate of IAP when it dipped down to 1.2 percent. This trend bears testimony to the fact that for the fist time since independence the rate of growth of IAP fell behind the rate of growth of population. There has been a moderate kick up in agricultural growth rate between 2005-06 and 2006-07. How ever, the following observation of the planning commission merits special significance, "not only that the period is too short to reach firm judgment on trends, the prolonged deceleration over several years has meant that despite the improvement; per capita output of cereals, pulses, oilseeds and also of some major vegetables and fruits in 2006-07 remained below 1996-97 levels." (GOI, 2008)

The two major sources of growth in agriculture viz. extension and productivity growth, which served well in the past, are now plagued with some limitations. In recent debate on agricultural development, efforts from every part of economy have been made to improve the agricultural performance through the instruments of technological and institutional innovation, one of the major challenges in agricultural growth. It is argued that any significant technological breakthrough can not be accepted in the near future and hence, one has to depend on the exploitation of the potential of the existing technology. Therefore, an other alternative which may prove to be very useful in this context, at least in the short run, is to move towards diversification into high value crop (GOI, 2006).

The emerging expectations of food, nutrition, employment and environmental protection calls for higher productivity per unit of land, labour, water and other inputs in an equitable and sustainable manner. The current national agriculture strategy aims to attain a growth rate of four percent plus per annum in the agriculture sector. We need a growth that is based on efficient use of resources and conservation of our soil, water and biodiversity; growth with equity that is, growth which is wide spread across regions and different classes of farmers; growth that is demand driven and stabilizes domestic markets and maximizes benefit from exports of agricultural products in the face of global challenges, and growth that is also based on sustainable technology, environmental and economically enabling policies and efficient input use technologies. To this, it is necessary to catch up with the rapidly changing scenario by converting threats into opportunities which not only paves paves way to structural reforms in Indian agriculture but make it imperative.

This paper is an attempt to identify the areas of Indian agriculture where reforms are indispensable. The paper is exploratory from methodological point of view.

The basic objectives of reforms in agriculture in India may be as follows:

First, stepping up agricultural growth to at least four percent per annum to sustain to overall growth rate in GDP at a high rate, say, eight percent.

Second, diversifying agriculture with a view to promote, among other things, the growth of rural non-farm sector such as agro-processing. Thus, facilitating a significant shift of labour force from agriculture to non-agriculture is the need of hour.

Third, increasing application of cost reducing technologies for making agriculture competitive.

Fourth, reducing rural poverty and inequality through broad based growth of agriculture by reducing disparities between different regions and classes of farmers and by strengthening the role of women in family.

Fifth, protecting environment by reversing the ongoing degradation of natural resources like land and water and by preventing the excessive chemicalisation of agriculture.

Reform needed for achieving these objectives are outlined below.

Agriculture Research and Extension

It has not only provided the critical base for India's green revolution but holds the key to future agricultural and rural growth. Indian farmers, despite low literacy rates, have responded to new technologies and also frontier technology like biotechnology. However, it remained underexploited in the country. Agricultural research influences livelihood of two-third of Indian workforce. Majority of them are resource poor and suffer from disguised unemployment (over crowding with marginal productivity). For ncorporating their needs and economic aspirations, research programs is necessary. Apart from assuring adequate funds, government can right track ICAR activity and productivity by continuously supporting a performance enabling environment. On its part, ICAR must redefine its mission, programme, objective and governance framework to inculcate system efficiency, affectivity and relevance.

C.S.O. data shows that in the 1990s and 2000s, there was a decline in the rate of growth of public spending on agricultural research and extension compared to the earlier decades. The growth rate of public spending on agricultural research fell from 6.3 percent in the 1980s to 4.8percent in the 1990s and 2000s. The corresponding figures for agricultural extension were 7 percent in the 1980s and 2 percent the 1990s and 2000s.

There is need to revamp the research, teaching and extension network of the state agriculture universities. Most of the agriculture universities face resource crunch in funding there different research, teaching and extension programs. The central government should exert more administrative influence on these institutions in prioritizing their research, teaching and extension programmes. The funding of these institutions should be increased and linked with time bound objectives and with perception of need based scientific and other man power. The central government should also devise effective system in interlinking the institutes of Indian council of agricultural research (ICAR) and the institute engaged in agriculture research with the state agriculture universities for pooling the resources and scientific expertise in achieving the common objective, keeping in view that the strong research and development base and trained man power should be available in the country within the short term. India has considerable strength in agricultural research and education.

Therefore, the returns from investment in agricultural research and extension in the country can be expected to be very high, relatively quick and assured. The main ingredients of this reform may be:

1. Active involvement of farmers through user group and self help group, and accountability to them.
2. Enabling participation by the privative sector, farmers association and the NGOs to compliment public service by putting in place an independent regulatory body

to which samples can be submitted for quality checks, encompassing inputs like fertilizer, pesticides and seeds.

3. Increasing use of media and information technology including cyber kiosk, to disseminate knowledge on new agricultural practices and the information technology on output and input prices for imposing the effectiveness of agricultural services in general. The use of information technology will reduce the requirement of large number of extension workers at the block level and would indeed complement to a considerable extent, the services rendered by the extension works in remote areas.
4. Building gender concerns in to the system for examples, by meaning the extension services predominantly by the women in hill and tribal areas where farming is managed essentially by women.
5. Capacity building of extension functionaries and farmers, among other means, through distance education.

Credit Reforms

Credit and Insurance are the areas which require reforms. Keeping in view the decline in the profitability of agriculture and increasing farmer's distress and indebtedness, the government may consider providing support to the banking system for reducing the rate of interest for crop loans to 4% during the year of Agricultural Renewal. There is an argument going on for a paradigm shift from micro-finance to livelihood finance, as the access of the poor to micro-finance alone is not likely to alleviate their poverty. There are areas in our country, which have recurrent and frequent droughts/floods etc. which cripple the income of the farmers. The government of India may step into creating an Agricultural-Risk Fund to provide relief to the farmers. The Kisan Credit Card (KCC) is a major innovation in agricultural credit. Crop insurance is covering about 14% of the farmers.

Agricultural credit clearly started to grow after bank nationalization and it has been growing since then. With all the concerns and skepticism expressed, the difficult and continuous changes in institutional credit have indeed borne fruit. Over the years, there has been a significant increase in the access of rural cultivators to institutional credit and, simultaneously, the role of informal agencies, including moneylenders, as a source of credit has declined.

The remarkable feature of agricultural credit extension in India is the widespread network of rural financial institutions (RFCs) following the phase of nationalization of commercial banks in 1969. Large-scale branch expansion was undertaken with a view to creating a strong institutional base in rural areas. At the time of nationalization in 1969, the total number of rural offices of scheduled commercial banks was 1,833, which then increased significantly to 32,115 by March 2005. The number of co-operative institutions creating the agriculture went up from 95,871 in end-June 1980 to over 1,10,000 in 2003. The share of the rural branches of scheduled commercial banks in total increased sharply from 22 per cent in June 1969 to 46 per cent by march 2005.The main story in the expansion of rural credit in the 1980s and 1990s has been the ascendancy of commercial banks, along with RRBs, with a corresponding fall in the share of co operatives.

Report shows that share of non-institutional sources in general and of moneylenders, in particular, in agricultural credit has significantly gone up during the era of structural changes, i.e., after 1991. This is really a matter of serious concern which has to be taken care of by our reform policy.

Land Reforms

Implementation of land reforms varied considerably across regions as land reform is within the purview of the individual states. Success in its implementation has been varied and has depended mostly on the constellation of political forces at the grass roots and the commitment of the government. Kerala and West Bengal, which were the more successful land reforming states in India, implemented the reforms with vigor under a leftist government. West Bengal also vigorously implemented a programme of registration of share cropping tenants, thereby providing them with security and low rents. More than 1.4 million sharecroppers (bargadars) were recorded under "Operation Barga". This was done in collaboration with groups of beneficiaries and with the active assistants of rural formers organizations as "Krishak Sabhas" and Panchayati Raj institutions dominated by poor and middle class peasants.

The implementation of land reforms policies aimed at equity and growth has been patchy across states. While land reforms have led to the expansion in the base of owner cultivators, technological and other changes have led to significant shift in the agrarian structure.

The average farm size is going down and nearly 80% of the farm families belong to the marginal and small farmer categories. Fortunately, the ownership of live stock is more egalitarian. Enhancing small farm productivity and increasing small farm income through crop livestock integrated production system and multiple lively hood opportunities through agro-processing and bio-mass utilization are essential both to meet food production targets and for reducing hunger, poverty and rural unemployment.

In view of the continued pressure of population on land, it may not be advisable to remove, at the present juncture, the ceiling on the ownership of agricultural land that has in general made land market favorable to the small and marginal farmers. Though it can augment their ownership as well as operational holdings, tenancy laws guaranteeing security of tenure and prescribing the rental share have led to the growth to the concealed tenancy that discourages investment by the tenants and also tend torestricts the flow of credit to them. Since such tenants are in any case paying market rents, liberalization of tenancy laws can help increase their employment and income by augmenting their operational holdings, stepping up investment and getting better access to credit and inputs.

Trade Liberalization

In India, Agricultural trade reforms were a point of departure in agricultural policy. It can be argued that this sequence was a natural choice for India since the incentive structure of Indian agriculture was highly distorted at the outset of reforms; the sector was and still is burdened with excessive regulation on private trading and most of the market activities. There is significant potential for growth only if these constraints are removed.

In case of India, liberalization of agricultural trade policy happened to create a series of imbalances by preceding incentive and market reform in the domestic arena. Lowered protection against a backdrop of low international prices increased imports, although in the case of wheat there was already excess supply from domestic production induced by high minimum support price (MSP). While broad-based economic and trade reforms resulted in the new export orientation of the sector and improved the incentive- sum - work of agriculture, they also left the sector more exposed to international competition because of persisting constraint to productivity improvement attempting marketing reforms and removal of regulatory constraint, at least in some of the states, by amending 'Agriculture produce marketing committee Act' although 'Essential Commodities Act' still remains in place.

Post WTO trade liberalization helped India to achieve small increase in agricultural exports; whereas it resulted in sharp and continuous increase in import. This has adversely affected self reliance in agriculture. The foremost reason for this adverse effect is unprecedented decline in international prices, which in turn was caused by attempts by almost all the countries to push exports and continuation of high level of domestic support and export subsidies by OECD countries. As a net exporting country India stand to gain from increase in international prices.

Serious differences persist between three main groups of WTO members, namely, developing countries led by G20, EU and USA on almost all the issues like reduction in domestic support and export subsidies in OECD counties, formula for tariff reduction and special and differential treatment for developing countries on almost all the commitments. Therefore, there is a stalemate which implies that imbalance of UR agreement would continue. This statement has given freedom to the developing countries not to further liberalize their markets. While it is highly desirable to eliminate export subsidies, phase out domestic support and to have separate set of commitments for developed and developing counties; it is also important to recognize that the deadlock is not helping anyone to achieve these goals. India and other developing countries need to put pressure on the developed countries to have some interim agreement to at least reduce domestic support and export subsidies as per their initial offers.

Market Reforms in Indian Agriculture

Agriculture is the single largest industry in India employing nearly 58% of the workforce. It is the largest user of land and water resources. Many of the features of domestic policies were introduced with the objective of protecting farmer's or consumer's interests. Underlying many of the acts and regulations was a deep suspicion about the exploitative role of middle man. In these changed circumstances, many of the prices of legislation are providing dysfuctional, among which the most pernicious is the. "Zoning" provision whereby sale of foodgrains outside a zone was prohibited. Bottle up of the surplus region had facilitated state purchase of grains at a previously announced procurement price.

As V.S. Vyas suggested the main ingredients of a market reforms agenda in agriculture should include the following.

- Establishing the principle of cost recovery in agricultural inputs and phasing out input subsidies by placing a "cap" on existing subsidies while announcing a time bound programme of phasing out and assuring the efficient operation of input supplying agencies.
- Thoroughly revising the agricultural price support system by curtailing the scope of MSPs to the protection of variable costs for a few commodities in selected regions and placing a greater emphasis on crop insurance and forward markets.

- Carrying out procurement operation on commercial lines by decentralizing and de-bureaucratizing the FCI and involving the states at the lower tiers of Panchayati Raj Institutions in the public distribution of food grains.
- Dovetailing price and trade policies in an effective manner.
- Accelerating the process of liberalization in agricultural marketing and removing bureaucratic hurdles.

Stress on Technology

It is the need of the hour, and as it is the prime mover of change as well, that both technology fatigue and technology gap should be avoided. The aim should be to enhance income per hectare on an environmentally sustainable basis. 'Lab to land' demonstration should include post harvest technology. For land less agricultural labour, the aim should be to convert them into skilled workers, there by adding economic value to their time and labour. The training should be in skills which can help in organizing market driven enterprises. The training methodology should be best on the principle of learning by doing. There should be a pro-nature, pro-poor and pro-women orientation to technology development and dissemination. Organic farming and low external input sustainable agriculture (LEISA) techniques should be promoted along with integrated pest management (IPM) techniques.

The role of women, both as farmers and farm labour is critical for the success of eco-farming practice. Hence, all programmes designed to faster access to technologies must be gender sensitive. 'Scientist-Panchayat' linkage is a must for the spread of the technology. Genome clubs may be organised in village schools and Krishi Vigyan Kendras (KVK) to spread genetic literacy, Energy is a key input. The energy sources needed by farm families, both electricity and diesel, should be available in a reliable manner and at affordable price. In addition, solar energy could be tapped where economical.

Water Management and Irrigation Imperatives

In the water sector; government spending in irrigation effectively promoted growth and poverty reduction, but the marginal returns of such spending has come down over time. Indeed, studies have shown that investments in rain fed areas have had high marginal returns for agricultural growth and poverty reduction. Major investment in harvesting rainwater through watershed, through public-private-partnerships, may help usher in a "multi-coloured revolution" (not just a "green" one) in agriculture. Lack of sufficient administrative and political will to devolve management power to the local water user associations' and inadequate infrastructure for building capacity inhibited the involvement of farmers in India.

Providing right incentives to farmers is crucial to promoting water saving. Increase in water use charges may not be feasible in the short to medium term without changes in the institutional set up. In India irrigation is affected by real politics as free electricity for pumping water is offered for political rent-seeking. The impact of reform like withdrawal permit system and volumetric charging can only be limited. Improved crop yields can also lead to a more efficient use of scarce water resources in agriculture. "More Crops per Drop of Water" should not remain just a slogan. All existing wells and ponds should be renovated. Demand Management through improved irrigation practices, including sprinkler and drip irrigation should receive priority attention. A water literacy movement should be launched and regulation should be developed for sustainable use of ground water. Sea water farming should be promoted in coastal areas through the cultivation of mangroves, salicornia, casuarina and appropriate halophytic plants. Hence, the choice of cropping systems should be based on irrigation water availability including rainfall pattern.

The key role of irrigation in the new technology in agriculture has been well recognized. It allows multiple cropping and support changes in cropping pattern. It is found that in most states households with access to irrigation have only about half the poverty incidence compared to house holds without irrigated land.

C.H.H. Rao (2003) observes tnat India has an irrigation potential of 58.5 million hectares from major and medium irrigation projects. The existing schemes exploit only 60 percent of this potential. The Bharat Nirman Programme proposes to create 10 million hectares additional assured irrigation. The Planning Commission, 2006 notes that achieving this goal would require accelerating the pace of 1.42 million hectares per year in recent years to 2.5 million hectares per year. According to ministry of irrigation capacity of water resources, 4.2 million hectares of irrigation capacity can be added by simply completing these projects. Planning Commission estimate that irrigated land transferred to water users association in India is only 7 percent; as compared to Indonesia (45 percent), Thiland (22 percent); and Philippines (66 percent).

Contract Farming

The contract farming model is relatively new in India. In this model, farmers are contracted to produce the commodity desired by a firm. The firm controls the production process without owning or operating the farms. While the farmers are assured procurement of the output at remunerative prices, India is witnessing a silent revolution in this form of mutually beneficial integration of farm, firm and consumer.

For example Nestle India Limited entered into the dairy business in 1961 by collecting 540 kg./day of milk from 180 farmers in four village and setting up a milk plant at Moge in Punjab. By 2002 the milk collection had grown to over 650 thousands kg/day from about 90,000 farmers. The company's success resulted from developing effective backward and forward linkages. Most of the milk comes from the small dairy producers. The company provides free veterinary aid and extension breeding services, information on fodder production techniques and so on for quality production. Thus the integration of production and marketing is critical for high value commodities, because they are perishable and their markets are restricted. To expand the scale of production, integrating production and marketing through cooperatives or contract farming seems to be a pre requisite.

Governance for Agricultural Reforms

Three types of governance problems can hamper the agricultural reforms. Lack of macro economic and political stability limits the development potential of the sector. Political economy problems lead to policy biases and also to under investment and misinvestment in agriculture that may cause failure in implementing the policy agenda, especially in agriculture base countries.

The anti-agriculture bias in marco economic policies has been reduced as a consequence of economic reforms in many countries. In addition agriculture is likely to benefit from general governance reforms that are now high on the agenda and include decentralization, result based public sector management, more rights to information and new accountability mechanism.

Evidences suggest that the political economy has been changing in favour of agricultural and rural development. Democratization and the rise of participatory policy making have increased the possibilities for small holders and the rural poor to raise their political voice. Countries are passing laws that promote rural equity.

From local to global, have to make special effort to seize these opportunities for realizing the agenda. To use the new political space created by democratization and decentralization and exercise political voice, small holders and the rural poor need to form more effective organization. Institutional innovations are required to better coordinate the agriculture agenda across different sectors.

Sound agricultural development strategies require stronger capacity far policy analysis and evaluation and a commitment to evidence-based policy making and – as past success show-using agriculture for development calls for vision and leadership.

The global agriculture for development agenda requires specialized institutions that have long term support and commitment such as the CGSAR and the standard setting bodies. It requires cross sectoral, issue-specific networks that can capture emerging opportunities and react quickly to emergencies and it requires new mechanism to ensure that the agenda is well coordinated and integrated into the overarching tasks of the 21st Century.

Priority to Agriculture Agenda

Local government institutions need to set priority, but what priority should they assign to agricultural reforms? Obviously, local political leadership matters. But the institutional design of local government institutions is important too. Special provisions can reduce elite capture and social exclusion. In India, the panchayati Raj reserves seats for women and for SCs and STs. A study of effects of reserving seats for women in two Indian states found that this participation increased investment in the type of infrastructure relevant to women.

Decentralization to local government does not necessarily increase public spending on agriculture. This shift in public spending is good news but local government needs the capacity to manage the agriculture specific agenda, as it becomes more important over time. For example, they often neglect agricultural extension, because it is less visible than physical infrastructure and thus associated with fewer electoral rewards. Enhancing the capacity of local administration to manage extension in consultation with the local producer organizations and with support from central agricultural departments can increase the relevance and quality of this service to farmers. Like local governments, communities typically concentrate first on meeting basic needs for health, education and infrastructure. Once they turn to income – generating activities, agricultural project including those that link small holders to high value markets become an important choice.

Making a Green Revolution through Vision and Leadership

Low investment in agriculture; imbalance in fertilizer use, low seeds replacement rate, a distorted incentive system and low post-harvest value addition continue to be a drag on the sector's performance. Share of agriculture in the country's GDP has declined from 48.7 in 1950 to 24.4 percent in 1996-97 and further 18.7 percent in 2007. Agriculture sector is the backbone of the country's development and lifeline for 65 percent of the population based in rural areas and approximately more than 58 percent of the population still dependent on agriculture for their lively hood. Besides this, to achieve an ambitious rate of growth for the country of as high as 9-10 percent in the eleventh five year plan, the country needs a strong pull up support to the agriculture sector which should grow at least at the rate of 4 percent per annum; all the more since in 2005-06 the growth in agriculture was merely 2.2 percent. As estimated by the national commission on population, the country's population is expected to touch 1.33 billion by 2020-21 and demand for food grains around 280 million tonnes. This means that food grain production has to grow by 2 percent a year over the next decade.

India's green revolution was possible only because political and administrative leaders addressed market failures and enabled large number of smallholders to intensify there production. It had the full political support of the prime minister, but it also required the vision and leadership of highly competent officials in the public administration. C. Subramaniam, Minister of agriculture from 1964-67; believed in the role of science and ability of smallholders to modernize agriculture. He pursuaded the skeptics in parliament and the planning commission of that role. And he spearheaded the reforms of institutions and policies to support agriculture, overcoming all kinds of administrative and regulatory obstacles. Likewise, vision and leadership are also required today to make intensive agriculture environmentally sustainable. M.S. Swaminathan, the scientific leader of India's green revolution, is now pioneering an "evergreen" revolution.

Effective regulatory agencies create an enabling investment climate for the private sector and farmer organization. Regulation has to strike an appropriate balance among different interest groups, avoiding both over regulation and under regulation, especially if there are risks and uncertainties—for example, with the new technologies. Regulatory agencies need reform to meet this challenge and avoid political and special interest capture. Investing in the capacity enforcing agricultural regulation is important too. Seed certification is an example. In Tamilnadu farmers suffered considerable income losses because they received spurious cotton seed.

Controlling Corruption in Agriculture

Corruption can blunt the agriculture for development agenda. Land administration is often one of the most corrupt government agencies. Large agricultural infrastructure projects, such as those for irrigation, are also prone to corruption. Companies may bribe regulators, as in biotechnology regulation in Indonesia and pesticide regulation in India. The more the state is involved in supplying inputs, such as fertilizer and credit, and in marketing agriculture product, the greater is the potential for corruption. That is why rolling back, the state can reduce corruption.

Both demand side and supply side, approaches can overcome corruption in agriculture. Public expenditure management reforms and procurement reforms are typical supply side approaches, which are often part of general public sector reform. A successful demand-side example is the monitoring of food prices in ration shops by women's groups in India. A study of strategies to reduce corruption in village road projects applied a randomized experimental design to compare, social audits, a demand side approach. The study suggests that grass root monitoring may reduce theft more when community members have substantial private stakes in the outcome. Another study found that government audits become more effective when they are publicized through local press or radio. New technologies, especially (e-government), can reduce the scope for corruption, as with computerizing land records in Karnataka. Despite such evidences, studies on strategies to deal with corruption in agriculture are rather scarce. More research would help to identify what works, where, and why especially if public investment in agriculture is to increase.

Conclusion

It is clear from the above discussion that the role of government by way of public policies, programmes, and investment is going to be extremely important. Success depends, as Prof.

C.H.H. Rao says, crucially on effective governance at the grass root level, as many of these programmes are going to be location specific.

Thus, once the above significant issues are addressed and agricultural functioning opened up to managerial efficiencies, India can afford to emerge as a new agricultural super power through substantial productivity gains. Then only the rural growth will be inclusive; technologically, environmentally and economically.

Policy Prescriptions

- Efficient use of resources through conservation of soil, water, energy and biodiversity.
- Focus on Demand Driven growth, catering to the need of domestic markets and maximizing benefits from exports of agricultural products. Demand side requires renewed focus to deal with price variability.
- Farmers should be encouraged to adopt mixed cropping and diversified into growing cereals, vegetables, flowers, tuber crops as well as animal husbandry and dairying.
- Government should fix minimum support prices of food grains in favour of farmers, provide insurance for all crops, free power supply, timely distribution of farm inputs, higher allocation of the revolving fund, subsidy to take up organic farming and launch awareness campaign on various schemes.
- Facility of short term workshops should be provided in villages which is helpful in the improvement of the skill and awareness of the farmers in general and women in particular.

REFERENCES

- Ackerman, John (2004), "Co-Governance for Accountability: Beyond 'exit' and 'voice'", *World Development* 32(3) : F47-63.
- Agarwal, Ani (2000): 'Drought? Try Capturing the rain', *The Asian Journal*, Vol. 7, No. 3.

- BBC News (2005), "Monsanto fined $1.5 m for Bribery." BBC news online, January, 7.
- Bhalla, G.S. and Gurmail Singh (2001), *Indian Agriculture; four decades of development*; Sage Publications, New Delhi.
- Chand, Ramesh (2000) Trade Liberalisation, Agricultural Prices, and Net Social Welfare in India, submitted at The Third Asian Conference of Agricultural Economists, Jaipur, October 18-20.
- Different issues of *Economic Survey* and *The Hindu Survey of Indian Agriculture*.
- Fan Shangen and Ashok Gulati (2006), 'The Dragon and the Elephant: Learning from Agricultural and Rural Reforms in China and India'. *Economic and Political Weekly*, June, 28.
- GOI (2008), "Agriculture", Chapter in the Eleventh Five year plan; Planning Commission, New Delhi.
- Gulati A. and S. Fan (end. 2007), *The Dragon and the Elephant: Agriculture and Rural Reforms in India and China*, Oxford University Press, New Delhi.
- *Handbook of Statistics on the Indian Economy* (2004), RBI; annual report, NABARD.
- Mishra, V.N. and M. Govind Rao (2003), 'Trade Policy, Agricultural Growth and Rural Poor', *Economic and Political Weekly*, Oct. 25.
- Olken, Benjamin (2007), 'Monitoring Corruption: Evidence from a Field Experiment in Indonesia', *Journal of Political economy*, 115(2): 200-249.
- Rao, C.H.H. (2003), 'Reform Agenda for Agriculture', *Economic and Political Weekly*, February 15-21.
- Rao, C.H.H. (1995), 'Liberalization of Agriculture in India: Some major issues', *Indian Journal of Agricultural Economics*, vol. 50, No. 3, pp. 450-472.
- Swaminathan, M.S. (2007), *Agriculture Can Not Wait*, Academic Foundation, New Delhi.
- Vyas, V.S. (2004), Report of the Advisory Committee on Flow of Credit to Agriculture and Related Activities from Banking Systems, Reserve Bank of India, Bombay, June.

2

Rejuvenating Indian Agriculture in a Globalized Regime: The Case for Small Farmers

Sib Ranjan Misra

Introduction

There is widespread concern in the country about the stagnation in agricultural production. This, together with the falling prices of agricultural produce and the rising prices of agricultural inputs, have seriously affected the economy of a large number of farmers. The well-being of millions of families dependent on agriculture for their livelihood is jeopardized. The spate of suicides of farmers in different parts of the country is a stark manifestation of these developments. A large number of people in the farm sector are witnessing serious erosion in their incomes and welfare. All this is happening at a time when the GDP growth in the country has been increasing at the rate of 8 to 9 per cent during the last few years, with a prospect of further acceleration in this trend. Another important point which deserves mention is that the change in economic regime instituted since 1991 has changed the pattern of growth in a way that has resulted in structural shifts in the nature of inter-sectoral linkages. A change in the pattern of growth, which allows for growing disproportionality between agricultural and industrial growth is a change in the pattern of demand and production, involving a reduction in the direct agricultural–input dependence of the non-agricultural sector. This is one of the most relevant elements of change in the environment

India,s opening up of agriculture to the world trade and further r increased emphasis on production for export s is likely to bring economic instability within the country with consequent instability in the earnings of the producers and their pattern of investment. High and frequent instability in prices not only negatively influence investment but brings peril to the small farmers. In Indian agriculture, more than two thirds of the farmers, being small and marginal in size, the question of their future is an important policy issue. They are affected negatively not only as producers of these commodities but as consumers also. Globalisation of trade of agriculture means that the country's agriculture will also be subjected to the global instability (Kumar 1995). There is a need to be aware of this problem and advance preparations are necessary to avoid harmful consequences.

There are studies which reflect that the countries which specialize in the export of primary commodities or those which like India intend to do so are bound to lose through the mechanism of the international trade. The evidence has an important policy implication which questions the wisdom of exporting primary commodities. The entire of international trade theory has been built on the assumption of perfect competition in the world market. There is a general neglect among the scholars on the issue of structure of trade market. The structure of the commodity market is an important determinant of distribution of gains between the producers, the consumers and the traders. Market imperfections affect the distribution of gains among these three categories of people. The opening up of trade of agriculture will expose the producers from the developing countries to the operations of the international giants (Gill 1996). Globalisation of trade will create increased international trading opportunities for those countries/regions which produce a large surplus of agricultural commodities. The possibility of these regions gaining from such opportunities depends on their export competitiveness.

A basic apprehension regarding the policy of new economic policy is regarding food security and the impact of agricultural trade on the price the poor for essential food items. It is often argued that there is an inadequate exportable surplus in agriculture in the short run and the agricultural supply response.

The attempt is made here to address the plight of the marginal section of the peasantry, the reasons for the decline in their incomes and the possible approaches to strengthen their income-earning capacity. It is sometime argued that the constituents of the large sections on Indian agriculture, because of their weak asset base, have limitations in responding to responding to economic stimuli on their own and therefore, need special attention.

For the purpose of our discussion, we shall treat the marginal farmers, i.e., those cultivating land below one hectare, as the marginalized section s of the peasantry. These, along with landless labourers and rural artisans, account for the bulk of the disadvantaged sections in rural society. It would clearly be submitted that the asset base of the households—rather than its location or social status—is the major determinant of its capacity to participate in the development process. In the rural sector of our country it is access to land that should determine whether a section should be identified as belonging to the marginalized sector.

Agrarian Structure in India

Two prominent features of the agrarian structure in the Indian economy can be identified which did not substantially change over the last few decades. These are : (a) an overwhelming proportion of the Indian population lives in the rural areas, and (b) there is no significant diversification of the Indian economy. According to 2001 census, 72.2 per cent of the population of the country lives in the rural areas. In 1951, this proportion was 82.2 per cent. So, it appears that over the period of five decades, the share of the rural population in the total population was declining at the rate around 2 per cent per decade. Over the last few decades, for the country as a whole, the composition of the population, in terms of urban and rural, has not changed in any remarkable way.

An equally significant feature is the overwhelming dependence on agriculture for livelihood in the rural areas.. according to the 2001census, out of the total number of rural workers in the country, 73.3 per cent were employed in agriculture. However, the composition of the agricultural workforce in terms of cultivators and agricultural workers is changing; so also is the size distribution of agricultural holdings.

The proportion of agricultural workers in the total agricultural workforce (cultivators plus agricultural workers) till 1991 had increased only at a slow pace. The situation has changed since then as the proportion of agricultural workers has increased significantly together with the increase in the marginal farmers. More and more marginal farmers with small plots of land are opting for agricultural labour as their main occupation. This is reflected in the fact that more than half of the agricultural labour households possessed some land. The increase in the agricultural workforce has mainly been due to the faster growth of marginal holding which could not provides adequate gainful employment to their operators. This process has accelerated in recent years. More and more agricultural houscholds are entering the category of marginal farmers. During the course of the quarter century, from 1970-71, to 1995-96, the number of marginal holdings as a proportion of the total holdings has increased from about half (50.62 per cent) to over 60 (61.58 per cent), while the area cultivated in these holdings has increased from 8.97 per cent to 17 per cent of the total cultivated area.

In this connection, it would be appropriate to maintain some relevant changes ythat have taken place in the agrarian structure. These may be enumerated as follows in short:

a) The landholding structure in India is sliding downwards, with progressively greater concentration in the marginal holdings group
b) The proportion of agricultural workers in the agricultural workforce has increased. however, the proportion of landless labourers in the total number of agricultural workers has not increased.
c) There has been a significant decline in the number of large holdings as well as the areas cultivated in them

d) The area reported under tenancy is relatively small though there is a large amount of conçealed tenancy and

e) All size groups of holdings participate as both lessors as well as lessees (Vyas 2008).

However, the most significant features of the above – mentioned features are the increase in the number and the area under marginal holdings. It is generally recognized that a large majority of cultivators in our country are marginal farmers. What is equally interesting to note is that a progressively increasing share of cultivated land is farmed by this group. Another point is that nearly half (48 per cent 0 of the total number of marginal farmers are located in three states—Uttar Pradesh (23 per cent), Bihar (16 per cent) and Andhra Pradesh (8 per cent). The following are the significant features of the agrarian structure in different states of the country. They are :

a) For the country as a whole, marginal farmers constitute the largest segment of agricultural holdings, with the major concentration in Uttar Pradesh, Bihar and Andhra Pradesh

b) In most of the states, and in the country, as a whole, the number of marginal farmers and the area cultivated by them is increasing

c) Practically in all the states, marginal holdings accounted for an overwhelming majority of the total holdings in each state (Vyas 2008).

It would be interesting to analyse the dynamics and reason for these changes over time. In fact, in view of the non-availability of panel data over large parts of the country, the study may be based on the periodic surveys or censuses. In practice, they will be a comparative picture at different points of time. (For all practical purposes, they may not reveal inter-group or intra-group dynamics.). We have to make a qualitative assessment by analyzing the likely impact of some of the different determining factors on the structural changes in landholdings and access to land by different groups. There are generally three reasons for this change.

Economy of the Marginal Farmers

We cannot ignore the well-being of the small farmers. It is important to understand the features of this segment.

One, there are some indications that farmers belonging to this group sustain themselves mainly on what they can produce from their land, together with two other important activities, viz., agricultural labour and animal husbandry. As far as their land resources are concerned, at the aggregate level, the area per holding has not changed over the last decade. In fact, there has been only a marginal increase from 0.39 to 0.40 hectares during the course of the decade (Rajivlochan 2005).

There are some indications to suggest that there is a floor below which cultivation is not generally practised. Therefore, the quality of land that they operate, the crops they produce and the productivity of their resources are important determinants of the income they earn. As regards, quality of land, it is the process that marginalisation of agricultural holdings arises due to distribution and partitioning of the small holdings, each successor will like to have land of comparable quality as his share. The rapid deterioration of the land surface prevails all over the country; the poor farmers have their share of degraded land. Secondly, with the rising share of purchased inputs in farming, the perceived advantages in terms of yields per hectare on the small holdings weakened considerably. In any event, changes in the dietary pattern, favouring a larger share of expenditures on non-foodgrain items will keep their income, real or imputed, highly subdued. So, if the present trends continue, the marginal farmers will face the prospect s of cultivating land of inferior quality and raising foodgrains and other low value crops, even if the yields of these crops on the marginal holdings can be raised, it is doubtful whether their economic status can be improved substantially.

Agricultural labour is an important source of income. The rising number of agricultural labourers, coupled with full employment of family labour, especially of women labourers in the family, has increased the labour pool. In sum, the elasticity of employment, with respect to output growth in agriculture, is approaching the near zero level. Agriculture has virtually ceased to employ more labour. Contraction of employment opportunities has adversely affected the income-earning prospects of marginal farmers. As regards agricultural wages, there has been an increase in the real wages of agricultural labourer in the 1990s, but the rate of growth has decelerated as compared to that prevalent in the 1980s. The increase in real wages was uneven, with the more progressive regions registering higher wages. Female labour did not benefit to that extent that male labour did. With an increase in the proportion of casual labour, uncertainty with regard to wage earnings increased. In any event, the marginal farmers tied to their small pieces of land could not avail themselves of peak season rise in wages. Another source of earnings for this group is animal husbandry and poultry. Emphasis on livestock and poultry is warranted for agricultural diversification to ensure higher income and employment for different reasons, the changing composition of the livestock and poultry stocks on marginal holdings has placed them in an disadvantageous position. Another important source of income for workers in the marginal holding group could be wage labour in non-farm occupations[1]. The wages in the non-farm section was higher as compared to farm wages for the country as a whole. However, during the post-reform period, the wages of the casual workers in the non farm sector registered a slower rate of growth as compared to the previous decade. In sum, it may be noted that: (a) sluggish growth in employment in the non-farm sector, which seems to have further slow economic down in the 1990s, (b) fast casualisation of the workforce in these sectors in the rural areas, and (c) among the non-farm activities, relatively higher growth in the tertiary sector, e.g., construction, trade, transport and communication was witnessed. All in all, it might be noted that employment opportunities for employment for marginal workers have not increased and the nature of employment is becoming progressively *ad hoc* and intermittent. Consequently, the plight of the largest section of the rural population, the marginal farmers, has worsened over time. The rural economy could not be rejuvenated unless special care is taken for this section of the population.

Let us not forget that employment in agriculture has almost been stagnating since the onset of economic reforms[2]. During the last decade, viz., 1994-2004-05, employment in agriculture grew at the rate of 0.9 per cent per annum. This is primarily linked with the slowdown in agricultural growth during the given period along with deceleration in agricultural growth. Wages for casual work in agriculture grew at a low growth rate of 1.9 per cent per annum during 1994-05, while the corresponding figure for casual work in non-agriculture was 3.2 per cent per annum. With limited scope for employment in agriculture and slow diversification in non-farm employment through the 1990s, both the unemployment and under-employment rates have been high which is also pegging the wages down.

Farmers belonging to this group sustain themselves mainly on what they can produce from their land. As far as their land resources are concerned, at the aggregate level, the area per holding has not changed over the last decade. In fact, there has been a marginal increase from 0.39 to 4.0 hectare s during the course of the decade (Vyas 2007).

The current favourite solution often offered by some policy makers is to depend on the privatizing various services like agriculture extension, health and education even though no system s have been put in place to check capitalist cupidity. The official checks on seeds, fertilizers and pesticides have already been parcelled out to private players

Even more dangerous is the focus on contract farming[3] to let big business into farming The sub-text to all such policies may be that the government does not have wish to re-tool the skills of the small farmer

Any practicable solution needs to take account of all the above and also to ensure due community participation and ownership so that expenditure is dictated by local needs and not by a few centralized schemes, packages or ideas. The following measures would take care of the most pressing needs of farmers today. In the first place, it is pertinent to provide knowledge inputs through extension workers. Secondly, it is to health inputs. The National Rural Health Mission provides a much needed emphasis in preventive health care, but does not address the issue of curative health. Curative health services by the government are so skeletal that the majority of expenditure on is today in the private sector. We also need to remember that health indebtedness is one of the major reasons for farmer,s suicide. The third measure is to make these functionaries directly accountable to and paid by the local panchayats, the government being merely a funding agency. Fourthly, it is essential to use information and communication technology tools to strengthen these knowledge and health services and to facilitate access to market information for farmers. And how to provide these information to the farmers should take into account specific local conditions instead of the details being dictated by some centralized norm s. Small farmers if provided the requisite knowledge inputs could well be the key to an economic upturn in the fortunes of farmers. Fifthly, it is to ensure a free competitive marketing system instead of the present system that is heavily weighted in favour of the merchants. To provide e-marketing and electronic auction halls which are connected to the national/international marketplace in each district for the sale of farm produce is another key requirement.. The use of market places would considerably improve prices for produce; they would also improve tradability, tagging systems which are so important for supply chain management. Again, it is to allow the creation of storage, grading and product handling facilities thereby (Rajivlochan 2008).

It is important to note that the present strategy which focuses on big business, the private sector and contract farming as a solution to the knowledge gap and setting up of big irrigation projects by government as a solution to the infrastructure gap sees the farmer as a foot soldier who can have no resources of initiative The alternative solution which suggests that all we really need to do is to empower the farmer by providing knowledge and health inputs and enable him to find his own solution.

Towards A Strategy for New Agriculture

The time is now ripe for planning a new agrarian system with vibrant small farmers. They may be the solution to the ongoing crisis in the farming sector in India (Rajivlochan 2008). Policies are, hence, required to be geared towards helping small farmers, perform agricultural operations and marketing their products with greater efficiency.

Hence, it appears that In view of the emerging agrarian structure of Indian agriculture in a globalised framework, certain strategy could be suggested to strengthen the economy of a vast majority of farmers and simultaneously to make Indian agriculture a dynamic sector.

The policy options may be, in sum, enumerated as follows:

a) Increasing the asset base of the small and marginal farmers. This calls for a radical land reform policies towards the small farmers. In this context, the small farmers should be encouraged and enabled to expand their holdings by purchasing or by leasing-in land to increase their operational area certain conditions are essential to achieve the free-lease markets. They are, in general, (a) proper record of rights, (b) proper enunciation of rights of the land-owner and the tenant, and (c) an effective machinery for adjudication and monitoring at the ground level. In other words, an active land market is required to be created which would, for all practical purposes, enable small farmers to enlarge their holdings

b) Improving productivity, especially value addition, on these farms—improving productivity is an obvious component for the strategy for enhancing the viability of the small holdings. There is a need for the diversification of their economy. Of course, the introduction of high value crops on these holdings is not that easy for different reasons like overarching compulsion of self-provisioning, high capital requirement and finally, high risk involved in raising high value crops; and

c) Increasing the scope for non-farm employment (Vyas 2007). Of course, these are not the appropriate effective alternative strategies and in most situations, they can be made complementary to each other. Also, these strategies will succeed to the extent that (a) supportive institutions for research, extension marketing and credit assist the emerging structure (b) farmers organize themselves to avail of better bargaining positions, and (c) there are effective measures to mitigate risks in production and marketing.

With several favourable factors, such as adequate financial resources, generated by a fast growing economy, a vast institutional network for research for research, extension, credit and marketing, the availability of a large number of trained people, improved infrastructure of roads and communication, and relevant experiences in our country and in other similarly placed countries of the region in effective farmer's organizations, it is possible to launch bold initiatives in favour of the millions of marginal farmers who have been left out of the mainstream of development to their as well as the country's disadvantage.

One, barring some exceptional circumstances, "hand-kerchief" holdings (may be of less than one acre) may not be necessarily viable. It is not; however, fair to say that large holdings do not have any intrinsic advantages in crop production. The agrarian structure characterized by small and medium –sized farms may carry out high-value, surplus –generating agriculture.

Two, it is not necessarily true to say that the only policy option is to enhance the further productivity of agricultural crops. What is further required is to strengthen infrastructureal facilities.and also to enhance agricultural research to achieve further major breakthrough in inventing new varieties of seed.

NOTES

1. We can learn lessons from Chinese experiences. In China, with the break up of the communes into small holdings, China witnessed a spurt in non-farm activities. The main reason for the growth of the non-farm activities in China was the fact that, along with the introduction of the "Household Responsibility system ", severe price distortions in agricultural produce were removed to a considerable extent. Both these developments provided the needed incentives to boost agricultural productivity, which was already quite high. With an increase in production and better prices, the cash

income of the farmers also increased significantly, leading to an upsurge in the demand for non-farm goods and services. Apart from many other reasons like higher investment in human development, effective technological support, the main reason was the strong demand-induced linkages forged between the agricultural and non-agricultural sectors (Vyas 2002).

2. Contract farming is not a new innovation in Indian agriculture. It was introduced decades ago by sugar factories in both private and co-operative sectors, and later by milk unions. It is sometime rightly argued that contract farming may be encouraged by the private sectors. However, fair terms have to be ensured for the contracting partners and at the same time, an effective adjudication mechanism should have to be evolved.

3. Wage employment in agriculture has actually fallen quite sharply. A large part of the increase in the self –employment is a distress-driven phenomenon., led by the inability to find adequately gainful paid employment. so the apparent increase in employment growth may be more an outcome of the search for survival strategies than a demand-led expansion of productive employment opportunities (Chandrasekhar 2007).

REFERENCES

Chandrasekhar, C.P. (2007): "The Progress of Reform and the Retrogression of Agriculture" in *Social Scientist*, New Delhi. January-February, Vol. 35, Nos. 1-2.

Gill, S. S. *et al* (1996): "Global market and Competitiveness of Indian Agriculture Some Issues" in *Economic and Political Weekly*, August 10, pp. 2167-86.

Kumar, T.K. *et al* (1995): "On Liberalizing Agricultural Trade" in *Economic and Political Weekly*, December 2, pp. 3069-78.

Rajivlochan, Meeta (2008): "Rejuvenating Agriculture with the Help of the Small Farmer" in *Economic and Political Weekly*, March 15, pp. 17-19.

Vyas, V. S. (2007): "Marginalized Sections of Indian Agriculture", in *The Indian Journal of Labour Economics*, January-March, Vol. 50, No. 1, pp. 1-13.

3

Globalisation and Agricultural Sector in India

R. Balasubramaniyan

Introduction

The aim of the global producers is to offer various products with good quality at low cost to achieve maximum efficiency. Globalisation in developing countries will improve the allocative efficiency of resources, reduce the capital output ratio and increase the inflow of the capital and updated technology into the country. But what constitutes globalisation?

The Term Globalization has Six Parameters, namely.

a. Reduction of trade barriers.

b. Allowing free flow of goods and services across national frontiers.

c. Permitting free flow of capital among nation states.

d. Delimiting the free flow of technology.

e. Creation of good environment in which free movement of labour is allowed among the countries of the world.

f. It envisages more trade, investment, employment and income growth among the nations to prosper economically and politically.

The Emergence of WTO

The International trade was not so smooth during 1940's, when there were many restrictions imposed by different countries with a view to protecting their domestic industry. After the end of the Second World War it was felt that the artificial restrictions imposed on international trade be removed and thus GATT was born. In 1948, some 23 countries, including India, formed General Agreement on Tariffs and Trade (GATT) as an international body with headquarters in Geneva, Switzerland to pursue the objective of free trade in order to encourage growth and development of all member countries. The main objective of GAT was to ensure healthy competition in commodity trade through the removal of trade barriers. It was after the formation of GATT that the average import tariffs in the world were reduced substantially at lower levels which enabled remarkable growth in world trade. Since the inception of GATT, eight rounds of negotiations on trade matters have been held.

The first round was held at Havana in 1947, the second at Annecy in France (1949), the third at Torquay in Britain (1950-51), the 4th, 5th and 6th were held in Geneva (1955-67) and the 7th Round in Tokyo (1973-79). The 8th round of Multi-lateral Trade Negotiations, popularly known as Uruguay round covered 7 years (1986-93) and took place at Punta del Este in Uruguay. There was a deadlock on certain critical areas such as agriculture, textiles, TRIPS and anti-dumping measures when agreement could not be reached. To break this deadlock, Arthur Dunkel, Director General of GATT brought a document and presented it before the member countries for possible settlement.

The WTO came into existence on 1-1-1995 with headquarters in Geneva, Switzerland. The Uruguay round negotiations on December 15, 1993 and the Marrakesh Declaration, Morocco on 15th April 1994 finally paved the way for emergence of WTO. It has 149 members including China. China joined the WTO in December 2001. The basic objectives of WTO is to ensure global free trade, expand production, remove tariffs barriers, optimal use of world's resources, etc. It acknowledges the need for special concern for LDC's. So far five conferences have been held. The first in Singapore (1996), second in Geneva (1998), third in Seattle (1999), fourth in Doha (2001) and fifth at Cancun, Mexico (2003), Hong Kong and Doha round (2008).

The Changing Equation

The world food situation is being redefined by new forces: income growth, climate change, high energy prices, globalization and urbanization. The influence of the private sector especially the leverage of food retailers is also rapidly increasing. Changes in food availability, rising commodity prices, and new producer-consumer linkages have crucial implications for the livelihoods of poor and food-insecure people. Many parts of the developing world have experienced high economic growth in recent years, for instance Asia, especially China and India where real GDP increased by 9% per annum between 2004 and 2006. Sub-Saharan Africa grew at about 6% in the same period. Even countries with high incidences of hunger reported strong growth rates. High income growth in low income countries readily translates into increased consumption of food.

Another major force altering the food equation is urbanisation and its resulting impact on spending and consumer preferences. However, three-quarters of the poor remain in rural areas. Higher incomes, urbanisation, and changing preferences are raising demand for high-value products in developing countries. The composition of food budgets is shifting from the consumption of grains and other staple crops to vegetables, fruits, meat, dairy, and fish. The demand for ready-to-cook and ready-to eat foods is also rising, particularly in urban areas.

The rest of the paper is organized as follows. Section II examines the objectives and methodology of the study. Section III presents the impact of WTO on agricultural sector. Section IV examines the relationship between globalization and agricultural trade and section V captures the summary and conclusion.

Objectives of the Study

1. To study the basic trends in globalization.
2. To examine the impact of globalization on agriculture.
3. To analyze the growth rate in agricultural sector.
4. To compare the growth rates of agricultural and non-agricultural sector.

Methodology

The study is based on secondary data. The agriculture data at the national level is primarily considered to gauge the pattern of growth, investment, landholdings and production. The basic data base is derived from the Ministry of Agriculture, Government of India, Season and Crop reports and certain Websites. The study attempts to read the 'hysteria' as well as success experience of agriculture at the State/Regional/Rural base levels. The study also compares India's Growth rate with Global Growth rate in GDP (%). The study makes an attempt to cover the impact of globalization on agriculture in India. To make the study more meaningful and appropriate, percentage-ratio/growth rate analysis is attempted in this study. The study covers a period between 2000-2008.

World Food Production

World cereal production in 2006 was 2.4%% less than in 2005 mostly as a result of reduced plantings and adverse weather in some major producing countries. On the positive side, coarse grain production in China increased by 12% and rice output in India increased by 9%. In 2007, world cereal production is expected to rise by almost 6% due to sharp increases in the production of maize. In 2006, global cereal stocks—especially wheat—were at their lowest levels since the early 1980s. Stocks in China, which constitute about 40% of total stocks, declined significantly from 2000 to 2004 and have not recovered since. In contrast the production of high value agricultural commodities such as vegetables, fruits, meat, and milk is growing fast in developing countries. Climate-change will have adverse impacts on food production with increased risk of droughts and floods due to rising temperatures. Consequently, dependency on food imports is projected to rise in many regions of the developing world. The riskier climate will increase the demand for innovative insurance mechanisms that include regions and communities of small farmers. This is an area for new institutional exploration. Technological change is not expected to increase yields to a rate that would keep up with growing food demand.

The Problem Focus

Decreasing wage goods of agricultural labourers, disguised unemployment and significantly higher basic food prices have largely dethroned the right to food, right to work and right to live with dignity in India. About 50 percent of women and children are affected by diseases and malnutrition. Around 47 percent of children are underweight and weak in physical appearance. The per capita availability of food is very low. The SC/ST households in rural India eat less than 1600 calories per day per person, which is visibly below the ICMR recommendation of 2400 calories per day, notwithstanding the fact that they spend 70 percent of their income on food. This tragic condition could have deteriorated further this year. When global food supply situation in food grains has become tight and global financial crisis has emerged.

Nutritional status should not be judged by mere food intake alone. Level of education, safe drinking water, hygiene factor, incidence and control of diseases- all of which have a direct impact on how efficiently food is utilized should be taken into account. The public distribution system (PDS) has lately been the subject of controversy for obvious reasons. Poor targeting and wrong identification of beneficiaries has led to high proportion of non-poor and non-eligible persons are consuming subsidized PDS products. In states like West Bengal, Kerala and Tamil Nadu, the coverage under PDS is not limited to the poor alone but for everyone irrespective of any income level. This poses a great danger that rich households are getting better deal than the poor households. The lack of accountability seems to be the major threat and Government takes full accountability in the implementation of PDS products. Hence, If any thing goes wrong, it is the responsibility of the state to correct it.

The Impact of WTO on Agriculture

The subject of 'Globalisation' has been in the spotlight recently for very obvious reasons. The parliamentary election campaign of 2004 with its 'India shining vs Aam adami' confrontation highlighted an apparently widespread perception that the benefits of economic growth were simply passing too many people by. The policy of inclusive growth is most visibly manifested in the theme of the XIth Five Year Plan [2007-2012]. The policy is towards faster and more inclusive growth, which clearly reflects the need to find a sustainable balance between growth and inclusion. Inclusiveness involves four dimensions namely, 1. opportunity, 2. capability, 3. access, and 4. security. Consistent with these dimensions, 'inclusive growth' is a process, in which, economic growth, measured by a sustained expansion in GDP. Robust economic growth in the first few years of the 21st century has helped reduce poverty worldwide. But new numbers show that the actual extent of deprivation in India and elsewhere is far greater than previously thought. This insight does not question the role of growth in improving livelihoods, but it spotlights the need for much greater inclusiveness in the growth process in the scale of poverty.

The new poverty estimates from the WORLD BANK incorporate the finding that living cost are actually higher than estimated before, reflected in a global poverty line of $1.25 a day. These calculations that suggest that as of 2005 there were 1.4 billion people worldwide living in extreme poverty. One-third of them would be in India, signifying the largest number of poor compared to other countries and even relative to the country's own past by these measures (Thomas, 2008). In order to increase inclusiveness in addition to agriculture and infrastructure, the two other critical areas we need to focus on are education and healthcare, as a result of liberalization, the government should do a lot in these areas. In agriculture, for example, a competitive market is important but the role of the State is also very important providing infrastructure, rural connectivity, rural electrification, investment in irrigation, watershed management and so on.

Table 1: Comparison of India's Growth with Global Growth in GDP (%)

Economy	*1980-1990*	*1990-2000*	*2000-07*
world	3.2	2.6	3.0
India	5.8	6.0	7.4
USA	3.0	3.4	3.6
China	10.1	10.3	9.8
Developing Countries	3.4	3.6	6.5
Developed Countries	3.1	2.4	2.3

Source: National Conference Volume, St. Joseph's College, Bangalore, 23-01-09, p. 25.

Table 1 presents the Comparison of India's growth with World growth in terms of GDP percentage. India has surpassed and broken the Bermuda Triangle of Hindu Growth Rate since 1990's. It has now emerged as one of the high growing economy and attained 9.2 per cent growth rate once in 2006-07. But when we compare it with China, the Dragon moving at a speed of Cheetah and we are moving at a speed of snails pace. Though the growth percentage places us ahead of USA and certain other countries, but still we shall have to go a long way to keep pace with China.

More creditable is the increasing gap between India's share of World GDP and of those countries which are currently behind it, as we move into the next three decades. For example, while India's share of the World GDP is projected to be 6.1 per cent in 2004, 8.2 per cent in 2015, 11.2 per cent in 2025 and 14.3 per cent in 2035, Japan's share is expected to be 6.7 per cent, 6.2 percent, 5.5 per cent and 4.8 per cent respectively. Germany's share may languish behind at 4.2 per cent, 3.5 per cent, 3.0 per cent and 2.6 per cent, and so on. Imagine, in 2035, Indian economy may be just about 11 per cent smaller than the U.S. economy while it would be three times as big as that of Japan, six times those of Germany and Russia, seven times those of France and U.K., and nine times as big as that of Italy (Chadha, 2008).

Table 2: Mean Growth in Per capita Income

Plan period	*Percapita NNP at current prices*	*Percapita NNP at constant prices (1999-00)*
I Plan	0.2	2.6
II Plan	6.5	1.7
III Plan	7.2	0.4
IV Plan	8.3	0.8
V Plan	7.9	2.6
VI Plan	12.8	3.1
VII Plan	11.4	3.3
VIII Plan	14.2	4.5
IX Plan	8.5	3.3
X Plan	10.8	6.1

Source: Economic Survey, 2007-08.

Table 2 provides the percapita net national product mean growth rate in current prices as well as in constant prices. Under current prices it has always shown the increasing trends except in V and IX plans, where the growth rate fell in relative terms over other plans. From a mere 0.2 per cent in I plan, it steadily increased to10.8 per cent in X Plan. On the other hand, the per capita income under constant prices provides us the manner in which it is growing. The annual growth rate has never touched peak level except in X Plan.

Table 3: Mean GDP Growth Rates of Agriculture and other Sectors at 1999-00 Prices in Percentage

Period	*Year*	*Total Economy*	*Agriculture & Allied sector*	*Crops & Livestock*	*Non-Agriculture*
Pre-Green Revolution	1951-1967	3.7	2.5	2.7	4.9
Green Revolution	1968-1981	3.5	2.4	2.7	4.4
Technology Era	1982-1991	5.4	3.5	3.7	6.4
Early Reforms	1992-1996	5.7	3.7	3.7	6.6
IX and X plans	1997-2007	6.6	2.5	2.5	7.9

Source: Sathiyavan *et al*, 2009, p. 159.

Table 3 shows the average growth rate of agriculture and other sectors at 1999-00 prices in percentage. Today, about 20 percent of the national income comes from agriculture but still it supports about 50 per cent of our population. Increased dependence on the Bt. Cotton by small and marginal farmers has led to much distress and farmers suicides in Vidharbha region of Maharashtra. The distance between the growth of agriculture and Non-agricultural sector has increased significantly since 1982 due to the shift towards services sector by both public and private sectors. The growth rate of agricultural sector is not only very low but also it resulted in demographic/social divide in rural regions.

Table 4: India's Foodgrains Production 1951-2008

(Million tonnes)

Period	*Production*
1950-51	50.82
1960-61	82.02
1970-71	108.42
1980-81	129.59
1990-91	176.39
2001-02	196.10
2004-05	198.40
2005-06	208.60
2006-07	217.30
2007-08	218.30

Source: Economic Survey, 2007-08.

Table 4 underscores the production of food grains in India for the period 1950-51-2007-08. The food grains production has increased significantly from 50.82 million in 1950-51 to 218 million tones in 2007-08. This success is possible only due to the positive impact of green revolution and to some extent globalization. This is further lends credence to the fact that new technology vis-à-vis new seeds, fertilizers, credit, etc., aimed at the progressive and dynamic farmers. States like Punjab, Haryana, Western UP, Coastal Andhra and Tamil

Nadu experienced buoyancy in fooodgrains production. Cash crops like sugarcane became important in several states where irrigation is available in peak season. But there are other areas posing great danger to agriculture causing considerable concern to the policy makers. Among the millets, ragi and jowar which the poor eat, await a green revolution. Moreover soil has been degraded in Punjab and elsewhere due to the exploitation of lands. This is clearly the flip side of the green revolution and it needs to be addressed.

The flow chart 1 has to be supplemented by the measurement of inclusive growth and how it is related to poverty reduction. Given that what cannot be measured cannot be managed, inclusive growth needs to be measured. Conceptually, measurement has to focus on average opportunities and distribution of opportunities (Ali and Son 2007a). Measurement of inclusive growth can be carried out for individual components, e.g., employment, access to education, access to health facilities, etc. The advantages of measuring the inclusiveness of growth by component is that the extent of progress can be determined individually before decomposing the change by major drivers, which are needed to design policy interventions.

Chart I

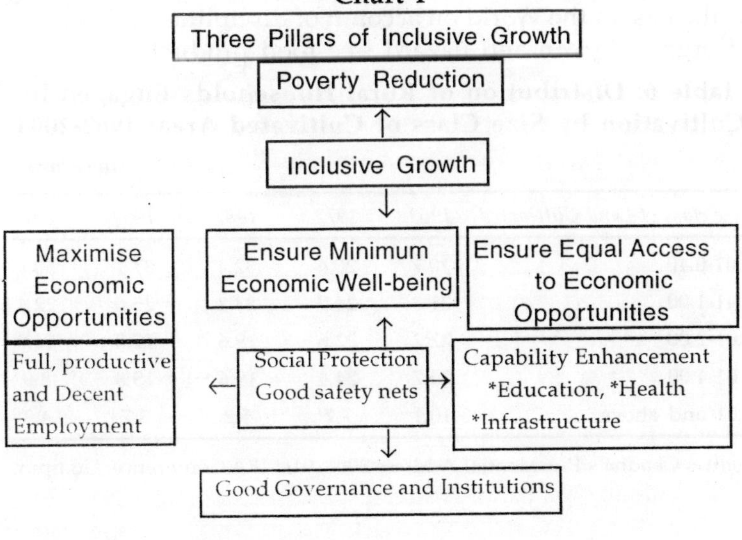

Table 5: Organic/Green Food in China 2007

China 2007	*Organic*	*Green*	*Hazard-free*	*Total*
Products	2647	14389	28600	45586
Enterprises	600	5315	24600	30513
Million hectares	3.11	10	21.07	34.18
% of cultivated ha	2.5	8.2	17.3	28.0
% eco-food in ha	9.1	29.3	61.6	100
Million tonnes	19.56	72	152*	243.56
Productivity tonnes/ha	6.3	7.2	7.2*	7.1*
Farm value in US $ billion	5.6-10.2	20.7	29.1-39.7	55.4-70.6

Source: SCIO, 2007. *Estimated.

Table 5 captures the quantum of organic/green food in China in 2007. It has produced more hazard-free agricultural products than any other country in the World. China is the number one country in the World as far as producing organic/green food is concerned. In terms of area under cultivation, it has recorded 3.11 million hectares under organic and 10 million hectares under green products respectively. The total farm value in terms of $ US accounted for 55.4-70.6 billion in 2007. This lends credence to the fact that China emerging as the best in the World on account of disciplined cultivation of organic/green and hazard free food products.

Table 6: Distribution of Rural Households Engaged in Cultivation by Size Class of Cultivated Area: 1962-2004

(In hectares)

Size class of Land Cultivated	*1962*	*1972*	*1982*	*1992*	*2004*
0.01-0.40	20.7	20.6	32.4	37.7	50.4
0.41-1.00	21.3	24.7	23.2	25.0	22.4
1.01-2.00	22.2	22.6	19.6	17.8	14.0
2.01-4.00	25.7	24.4	19.6	15.8	8.9
4.01 and above	10.1	7.7	5.2	3.7	4.3

Source: Chadha's Presidential Address 2008, 91st IEA Conference, Udaipur.

Table 6 captures the distribution of rural households engaged in cultivation during 1962-2004. It reveals that the proportion of land holdings measuring upto 0.40 hectares (1.00 acre) has been increasing steadily from 20.7 percent in 1962 to 50.4 percent in 2004. These are tiny farms providing an 'employment pillow' to family farm workers, naturally at low yield and poor income. Largely, the big army of the landless agricultural workers belongs to this segment. In the changing globalization, technology improvement and education of the farm people should be the agenda for future.

Table 7: Area, Production and Yield of Pulses

Region	*Area in million hectares*	*Production in million tonnes*	*Share in World Area (%)*	*Yield Kg/ hectare*
World	72.0	56.1	-	780
India	26.3	14.8	26.4	564
China	3.1	4.0	8.2	1499
Brazil	5.1	3.0	5.3	584

Note: Annual averages based on 1995-1997.

Source: Sathe and Agarwal, 2004.

Table 7 brings to the fore that area, production and yield of pulses in the World is highly insignificant due to area under cultivation of pulses is very low. Moreover, pulses is a rainfed crop. In India, pulses considered to be the poorman's rich protein. Pulses being the richest, cheapest and easiest source of best quality proteins and fats, and having a vast multiplicity of uses as food is sometimes called wonder crop. India's share in World area of pulses is 26.4 per cent and yield is just 564 Kg/ha. China is having a share of 8.2 per cent under area of cultivation of pulses but achieved a significant success in the yield of pulses by accounting for 1499 Kg/ha.

Globalisation and Agricultural Trade

A more open trade regime in agriculture would benefit developing countries in general. However, large advances in poverty reduction are not likely. In reaction to the lack of progress of the Doha Round, many countries are increasingly engaging in regional and bilateral trade agreements which may create more opportunities for cooperation among developing countries and for opening up their markets. Another development has been the improvement of the terms of trade for commodity exporters as a result of increases in global prices. The share of developing countries in global exports increased from 32% in 2000 to 37% in 2006, but there are large regional disparities.

Table 8: Average Annual Growth Rate of Exports for Five Asian Countries in (%)

Countries	*GDP 1970-1990*	*GDP 1971-2005*	*Export 1970-1990*	*Export 1991-2005*	*Import 1970-1990*	*Import 1991-2005*	*Investment 1970-1990*	*Investment 1991-2005*
India	4.3	6.21	7.24	11.91	6.03	13.15	4.70	8.26
Pakistan	5.78	4.25	6.18	7.20	3.32	5.33	5.49	2.20
Sri Lanka	4.29	4.71	3.90	6.80	3.73	8.10	8.19	6.40
Bangladesh	2.57	5.15	7.42	12.41	0.81	9.81	3.30	9.00
Nepal	3.75	4.10	5.43	7.13	7.04	7.16	5.56	5.20

Source: World Development Indicator, CD-ROM, 2007.

Table 8 provides the Average Annual Growth Rate of Exports for Five Asian Countries. It is evident that that most of the South Asian countries have improved their macro economic performance during the globalization period following trade reforms. Export performance of India, Bangladesh, Nepal and Sri Lanka are quite significant after the introduction of liberalization as compared to pre-liberalization period. Similarly, the investment pattern and growth rate have posted a positive development in South Asian countries during the same period. India has secured herself a place in the World Trade popular countries by introducing several global reforms.

Table 9: India's Exports of Floricultural Products to Major Countries in 2004-05

(Rs. Million)

Country	*Floricultural Exports*	*Country*	*Floricultural Exports*
USA	487.5	Spain	29.9
Holland	263.8	Canada	22.1
UK	251.2	Sweden	21.2
Germany	205.7	Portugal	18.3
Japan	123.1	South Africa	17.5
Italy	85.9	Singapore	17.0
France	53.1	Maldives	15.6
UAE	49.0	Switzerland	14.5
Belgium	49.0	New Zealand	14.3
Australia	41.5	Greece	14.1
Austria	41.4	Russia	12.9
China	39.4	Hong Kong	11.4
Poland	34.3	Saudi Arabia	10.8

Source: Kisan World, December, 2008, p. 15.

Table 9 presents the India's exports of floricultural products to major countries. It underscores that the flower export potentials of India has increased tremendously since the advent of globalization. India exports flowers to major countries in the World. The USA and Netherlands accounts for more than 50 per cent of our total exports. Demand from UK, Germany, Japan, Italy and France are also increasing. Newer markets in Asia like China, Singapore and Hong Kong are also opening for Indian flowers. West Asia is also a potential market for Indian roses. World trade in floriculture is estimated at $100 million. It has been growing at a rate of 15 per cent per annum. Of which, developed countries account for more than 90 per cent of the total trade in floriculture goods. Six Agro export zones and a large number of flower clusters under National Horticulture mission are expected to provide further boost to the international trade of floriculture products in the coming years.

Summary and Conclusion

The G-20 countries which include India, Brazil and South Africa have tried to tackle the issues concerning the global trade in farm products within the ambit of WTO. The G-20 was forced to accept the version of the Agreement on Agriculture (AOA) presented by the G-8 countries. The agreement sought to help opening up of the protected markets of India and China for agri-business for North America and the European Unions. The basic aim of the G-8 is to bring a trade fight within the group of developing countries in the global market for agricultural exports. The paradigm of the AOA as conceived in the WTO is not only alien to the kind of peasant farming that prevails in the G-20 countries but also creating a rift among developing economies. The propaganda and myth about trade liberalization was that it would lift India's poor from below poverty line come by providing market access to rich. The market access rules of WTO are however, not wiping out poverty, they are wiping out the poor (MPOS, November, 2008, pp. 4-5).

Article 4 on market access in the WTO Agreement on Agriculture robs the rural poor of livelihoods by enabling powerful corporations from rich countries to dump artificially cheap, subsidized products on poor countries, and preventing poor countries from protecting themselves from dumping that threatens the very survival of poor peasants and small producers.

Beckoning Remedy

1. *Contract Farming:* The contract farming or farm processing outsourcing (FPO) is the real solution for millions of farmers who are deprived of high cost technology in India. Under this agreement, the sponsor company gets the agricultural products from the farmers. In turn, the company provides an appropriate technology and easy credit to the farmers. The companies buy the agricultural products from the farmers at a predetermined price (Rate). The successful contract farming in India has been the Pepsico in

Punjab, UB Group (barely), LT Overseas (basmati rice), and Bharti group's fresh foods.

2. *Kisan SEZs:* The Indian Farmers Fertilizer Co-operatives (IFFCO) has created with great success a 'Kisan SEZ' at Nellore, Andhra Pradesh and presently running with huge profits. The IFFCO has set an example for the private players to follow.
3. *E-Agriculture and Retail Trade:* IT could be used for short term rain forecasting, soil mapping, water mapping and crop mapping in agricultural sector. To minimize exploitation of farmers by middlemen and protect them from daily price volatility retail supply chain could be used. Safal, India's oldest food and supply chain given customers products at prices lower than market rates and farmers prices higher than mandi prices since 20 years with great success. With big private players like Reliance Fresh, Bharti and future group also entering the retail race they are looking at a bigger role as parteners and advisors to farmers from crop planning stage to when crop is harvested and sold. Indeed in the Communist bastion Kerala Reliance has overcome the initial opposition by working with farmers directly and convincing them of the advantages of a tie up with their retail chain (Suma Sing, 2009).

REFERENCES

Balasubramaniyan R. (1989), "Water Resource Management: A Case Study", *Yojana,* 1-15 December, Vol. 33, No. 22.

Balasubramaniyan, R. (2004), "Estimation of Growth of Area, Production and yield of pulses in Tamil Nadu-A Discrete Analysis", *Quantanomics Journal*, RKMVC, Chennai, April-June, pp.12-16.

Balasubramaniyan, R. (2004), "Export of Flowers", *Kisan World*, Vol. 31, No. 7, July.

Balasubramaniyan, R. (2004), "Some Disconcerting Trends in Pulses Economy of India", *Third Concept Journal*, New Delhi, Vol. 18 [207], pp. 39-40.

Balasubramaniyan, R. (2004), "Instability in pulses production in Tamil Nadu-A Decomposition Analysis", *Quantanomics*, RKMVC, Chennai, July-Sept. pp.13-23.

Balasubramaniyan, R. (2004) "A Study of Economics of Pulses Production in India", *Kisan World*, Vol. 31, No.10.

Chadna, G.K. (2008), " India's March Towards a Knowledge Economy: Views of a Development Economist, Presidential Address, 91st IEA Conference, Udaipur, Rajasthan, December, 27.

Jeevitha, E. and Sridevi, K. (2008), " Floriculture and Exports," *Kisan World Journal*, December, pp. 13- 15.

Keshava, S.R. (2009), " India's Economic Growth in 60 years: Actual or Mirage," *Conference Volume*, St. Joseph's College, Bangalore, pp.23-36.

MPOS, (2008), " Global Trade in Farm Commodities," November, Vol. LIV, No. 2, pp. 2-8.

Pushpa M.S.,(2006), "Export Competitiveness of Pulses in India: A Case Study of Chickpea," *The Indian Economic Journal*, vol. 54 (3), Oct-Dec, pp. 65-83.

Ranjan Kumar Dash et al (2007), "Export-Led Growth in South Asia: A Panel Evidence," *The Indian Economic Journal*, vol.35 (3), Oct-Dec, pp. 132-146.

Sathyavan, D. and Rajivgandhi, J.(2009), "Agricultural Production in India: An Estimation of Technical Efficiency Using District Level Data," *Conference Volume*, St. Joseph's College, Bangalore, P.159-168.

Suma Sing, (2009), "Story of India's Agricultural Crisis in Globalization Era," *Conference Volume*, St. Joseph's College, Bangalore, pp. 171-175.

4

Structural Reforms in Indian Economy and It's Impact on Agricultural Future

Dr. P.C. Tiwari

Introduction

India after independence launched its massive five year plans and started heavy industries. Venkataraman (1997) observed that the regime of control and regulation that prevailed helped diversification of industries into new areas and also industrial dispersal to the back-ward and strategic areas. However, these regulations tended to stifle growth, promote artificial scarcities, foster inefficiency, stall modernization and induction of latest technology and create bureaucratic delays. Agarwal (1996) noted that Indian Economy today is confronted with some pertinent questions with regard to the policy instruments pursued for the realization of its national economic objectives. The middle of 1991 witnessed the beginning of a series of far reaching policy decisions to stabilize the economy and to initiate the process of structural adjustment. Under the circumstances the economic reforms of 1991 became necessary and inevitable.

These reforms are expected to maximize production, minimize cost, improve quality and create surplus which in turn, would increase income, eradicate poverty and improve the standard of life of the masses. These measures met with initial success on many fronts but our inability to control increasing debt burden and interest payment, to prune expenditure and the current deceleration in industrial growth and exports, etc have raised many questions over the future of the economy.

The critics of reforms point out that the process of unbridled globalization is bound to weaken the role of the endogenous factors. The planning process would have to trail behind the market processes and the external to the eighth plan. The planning process is basically made to respond passively to these influences. This would render planning even more of an empty box than has been the case so far, in the field of agriculture, liberalization i.e., creating conditions for more and more competitive, eliminating as much of imperfections in the market as possible, would mean greater and more access of the working peasantry or greater security of tenure with less extortionate and more liberal terms for the tenants. However, land reform is a forgotten episode. In a labour surplus economy, corporatisation of land or depeasantisation is not only an economic folly, it is a direct threat to the stability of the state.

Bandyopadhyay (1995) cautioned about export oriented agriculture. He observed that the experience of many countries in Latin America and Africa which followed structural adjustment programme induced export-oriented agriculture by displacing food has been a tale of unmitigated woe. Export oriented agriculture is vulnerable to world fluctuation of prices. Over the last decade and half there has been almost continuous decline in the prices of primary commodities over which developing countries have neither any control nor any influence. Under the circumstances they are forced to export more quantity to earn the same level of foreign exchange to meet the import bill. At a later stage they have to borrow more in the international market at harsher terms and conditionalities or allow their vulnerable population to starve. Patnaik and Chandrasekhar (1995) pointed out that the most palpable impact of structural adjustment has been on increase in rural poverty. Citing Tendulkar and Jai's (1995) computations, Patnaik and Chandrasekhar conclude that the increase in poverty is undeniable and the results are fairly robust. The supporters of the structural adjustment attribute this fact to causes other then the process of the adjustment. Patnaik and Chandrashekhar supported their argument by saying that by insisting on a reduction in the food subsidy, elimination of all input subsidies into agriculture and requiring prosperous farmers should not only get remunerative prices but international prices, structural adjustment necessarily ensures that the price of food in terms of the wage-unit, especially in the unorganized sector, goes-up. "A rise in rural poverty is an inevitable consequence of this phenomenon."

The prevailing development strategy through various barriers on trade discriminated against agriculture directly by the keeping the producer prices lower then what would have revailed under liberalized trade. The terms of trade were thus deliberately kept Unfarourable to agriculture in keeping with the prevailing wisdom to 'extract' surpluses From this sector for promoting industrialization. Beyond a point, however, both industry And agriculture suffered. It is true that the lower food prices by themselves favoured the poor, and they spend larger proportion of their income on food then the rich. Nayyar (1996) noted in this context that the issue price of foodgrains for the public distribution system were almost doubled over a shot period of four years in an effort to contain food subsidies. The resulting steep rise in the consumer price index for agricultural labourers in a period of Slow growth in output and employment eroded the real income of rural poor. The untargeted reduction in fertilizer subsidies led to a virtual stagnation in the consumption of fertilizer in the post-reform period (Govt. of India, 1995). There has been a decline in Real public investment in agriculture including irrigation which continued to decline A dampening effect on employment and wages in rural areas, especially in states where poverty widespread, as a evident from a significant decline in non-agricultural rural employment in the Immediate post-reforms period (Dev, 1995). Further Pathy (1996) put forward the argument that the available evidence suggests that the underdeveloped poorest regions and the oppressed classes and nationalistics tend to suffer most and experience absolute economic decline and deterioration in their economic levels and further unequal exchanges of their produces.

Parikh et. al. (1995) while supporting the reforms in favour of agricultural growth point out that the measures for the liberalization of trade and industry that have already been introduced are likely to have a beneficial impact on agriculture in the long run by turning the terms of trade din its favour, which may attract greater investments into this sector. However it may be noted that a more favourable price environment by itself may not be sufficient to evoke adequate supply responsde by attracting private investment unless public investment in infrastructure and human resource development is stepped up in the lees developed areas for ensuring a broad-based and employmentoriented growth.Hhanumantha rao (1996) observed that the development policy has to be more inclusive, concerned not merely with "structural adjustment" to market friendly, but also with "structural change" with a view to simultaneously making markets friendly to the poor, basically by strengthening their socio-economic position.

Structural Reforms and The Indian Agriculture

Agriculture is the primary occupation for earning livelihood to about three-fourth of regions population. Shifting cultivation is still practiced in about 2.7 million hectares of land. There is hardly any impact of reforms on settlement of jhumias to other gainful employment or bringing jhum land under settled cultivation. There is every likelihood to replace jhumming by improved forms of land management with least disturbance to the people. This would have impact on forest policy, decline in cash crops production particularly cotton and oil seeds, increase in production of horticultural produce and its trade in absence of adequate infrastructural facilities and export to the neighbouring countries. The settled land management require full support, by effective supply of inputs including seeds, fertilizer, tools, and implements, etc as well as by effective follow up programme which are lacking presently in the region.

The low level of consumption of fertilizer (ranging from 1.2 кg in U.P. to 19.5 kg. in M.P. except Hariyana 59kg per Hect), pesticides, insecticides, coupled with inadequate irrigation facilities (ranging from 11.1 per cent in M.P. to 18.8 per cent in Bihar excluding Jharkhand 27.9 percent and Hariyana 39.1 percent of total cropped area), the low proportion of cultivable land under HYV seeds, etc have resulted in low yield rate of food and non-food crops than the all India average of marketing facilities and lack of agricultural credit have kept agriculture as a subsistence sector and unremunerated to be taken up as a commercial venture. as a result, the region import a huge quantity of food grains, edible oil and other consumer items from other parts of the country. The thrust on exports leads to further shifts towards cash crops resulting in further loss of area under food crops resulting in increasing dependency on. Import of food grain. At present a huge quantity of food-grains is distributed through the public distribution system in the region. Therefore any decontrol of prices and drastic reduction leading to abolition of subsidies especially food subsidy will hit hard the rural poor and the tribals who may eventually reduce their food intake because of high prices and lack of high prices and lack of purchasing capacity of high cost food and led to deterioration in the consumption distribution.

New technologies, seeds, fertilisers, etc. are fast becoming expensive. The traditional and time tested methods do not provide the required competitive edge. Therefore, considering the discouraging experiences so far towards improving agricultural production, making it competitive seems to be an uphill task. Commercially profitable agriculture had remained a distant dream in the tribal areas. Agricultural innovations increased the cost of inputs and investment, making small holdings unviable. With large enterprises venturing in having large capital and advanced technology, rubber plantation, etc. small scale production units are not going to be viable and competitive. The tribal communities living on ecologically and economically vulnerable areas are more likely to be marginalized.

The region is most suited to alternate activities to promote horticulture, animal husbandry, floriculture, aquaculture, etc.

in all these areas new technologies have to be harnessed. There is a fear in the mind of people that the promotion of these activities in a big way, may allow corporate sector and multinational corporation to acquire vast tracts of land displacing them. the same is the case for large scale vegetable oil seeds production and plantation of tea, coffee, rubber, cashewnut etc. for which the region is suited most. Trade liberalisation will also displace landless, artisans fisher folk, and forest dwellers who would loose their traditional market and linkages with the agrosector as well as loss of food entitlement.

Every state government is trying hard to attract the multinational corporation and TNCs to exploit the available natural resources like water, minerals and agro -forest based ventures, etc. by providing more and more concessions, subsidies and tax concessions so that the long pending industrialization may begin in a big corporates. Pathy (1996) apprehended that the recent technological advancements, unrivalled economic and political strength of word capitalism, the rising powers of neo-colonialism and liberdalisation created favourable conditions for the invasion and extraction of natural resources from the ecologically fragile regions of the tribal people. Accordingly, the mammoth capital intensive development projects have become distressingly routine and mining activities introduced in a big way are always associated with the predatory activities of giant corporation and other project seeking agencies, connected with an undercurrent of authoritarian and ethnocentric values and political institutions.

With the depletion of forest cover more and more stringent measures are being adopted. The ban on extraction of forest resources by the hon'ble court has already put the dependents in deep trouble. The employment opportunities available in activities like afforestation, conversation and protection of forest, etc., are limited when compared to the landless tribals and rural poor who need such employment most. The recent imposition of the market liberalization process-with provision to lease out forest lands to private entrepreneurs, expanded social forestry and farm forestry to cater to forest based industries, etc.—will not only degrade the existing forest resources but also intensify marginalization of tribal poor.

Structural Economic Reforms & Rural Development

The rural people and the hill people do not possess high sophisticated skill and technical know-how. They are still endowed with primitive technologies. Rao (1996) has noted that the tribals are at a disadvantage to enter any king of markets, vez., labour market, product market and credit market. Even if they enter, they may not be in a position to receive fair returns. Rao has further noted that the disruption of traditional crafts and small scale industries is predictable as capital efficiency factor throwing out small scale unit. The entry of Joint ventures with multinational participation will be affecting small scale production because of capital intensive export-intensive enterprises. There will be more unemployment as traditional labour intensive small scale industries will be displaced by new technologies. They argument put forward here seems logical particularly in the north-east as whatsoever industries-medium, small end cottage exist in many parts of the region are based on labour intensive techniques of production and lack in adoption of new technologies. Therefore, adoption or advance technology may have adverse impact on the level of employment as pointed out by Parthasarthy (1996) that the effects of liberalization include in unemployment and rise in the number of those employed in the unorganized sector. Therefore, utmost care has to bestowed on maintaining and increasing employment opportunities commensurate with the growth of population. It is true that the free competition withtin the country will enable industries to sharpen their efficiency and upgrade technology. A time frame may be fixed thereafter national market may be progressively opened to external competition.

The ultimate aim of economic reforms is the welfare of the masses and if this objective is not achieved it will be of no consequence. Enhanced production without elimination of poverty, import of luxury goods without any food for the poor spell disaster. To counter the adverse effects of the reforms as advocated by the critics, efforts should be made to raise the productivity along with optimal use of natural resources using appropriate and relevant technology. Every care has to be taken to counter the adverse impact of patents and adverse impact of patents and rights on the regional wealth of flora and fauna, medicinal plants, their uses by the tribals and gene pool of living resources.

Environmental awareness need to be inculcated on a priority basic in view of the threat to natural resources and ecological degradation. The development of natural resources require greater attention in planning through survey and finding best ways of utilization of forest resources, development of industries derived from them and provision of related skills and market along with essential infrastructural facilities. At this juncture the dependency on public sector will be more to invest in infrastructure sector as it will be very difficult to involve private sector in true sense despite large concessions granted to them for promotion of irrigation, electricity generation, road construction and extension of communication facilities, etc. therefore, it is the responsibility of the respective state governments to build human resources and infrastructure for which necessary finances are to be mobilized by them from within the system and by putting their balance sheet in order by avoiding wasteful expenditures for more political gains and not in the interest of the economy.

The replacement of shifting cultivation by wet cultivation and promotion of horticulture and its products need attention to evolve a sustainable strategy of agricultural development taking into account the environmental preservation and micro-agro-climatic condition. Every effort should be made to protect the poor from the vagaries of market forces. The stress on human resource development in a desired manner will facilitate integration of local people's participation in new economic enterprises. It will also help the people to take up the challenges of market forces.

REFERENCES

1. Dev, S.M. (1995), "Economic Reforms and The rural poor", *Economic and Political Weekly*, Vol. 30, No. 33, August 19, pp. 2085-88.
2. Government of India, (1995), *Economic Survey* 1994-95, New Delhi, p. 127.
3. Nayyar, Rohini, (1996), "New Initiatives For Poverty Alleviation in Rural India," in C.H. Hanumantha Rao and

Hans Linnemann, eds., *Economic Reforms and Poverty Alleviation in India*, Sage Publications, New Delhi.
4. Agarwal, A.K. (1996), "Liberalisation and Its Impact On Indian Economy: Some Issue", A paper presented in 27th Regional Science Conference, Mussoorie, March 20-22.
5. Parikh, K., N.S.S. Narayana, Manoj Panda and A. Ganesh Kumar (1995), *Strategies for Agricultural Liberalisation, Consequences For Growth, Welfare and Distribution*, Indira Gandhi Institute of Development Research, Bombay (Mimeo).
6. Choudhury, Kr Ravindra (1996), "Agricultutal Economic Development in North-East: Chief Areas of Constraint and Remedies", *Journal of NEICSSR*, Vol. 20, No. 2, October, p. 51.
7. Parthasarthy, G. (1996), "Unorganised Sector and Structural Adjustment" *Economic and Political Weekly*, Vol. 31, No. 28, pp. 1859-67.
8. Hanumantha Rao, C.H. (1996), "Economic Reforms Agricultural Growth and Rural Poverty: Some Reflections on the Relevance of East and South-East Asian Experience for India", *The Indian Economic Journal*, Vol. 43, No. 4. April-June, pp. 1-11.
9. Bandyopandhyay, D. (1995), "Liveralistion and Rural Development", *Mainstream*, Annual number, December 9, pp. 39-42.
10. Kabra, K.N. (1996), "Indian Planning and Liberalisation", *Economic and Political Weekly*, Vol. 31, No. 40, October 5, pp. 2740-45.
11. Venkataraman, R. (1997), "Economic Reforms and National Imperatives", *Southern Economist*, Vol. 35, No. 17, January 1, pp. 7-10.
12. Tendulkar, Suresh D. and L.R. Jain (1995), "Economic Reforms and Poverty" *Economic and Political Weekly*, June 10.
13. Venkata Rao, P. (1996), "Liberalisation and Scheduled Tribes: Emerging Challengs", *The Indian Journal of Public Administration*, Vol. XLII, No. 3. July-September, p. 495.
14. Patnaik, Prabhat and C.P. Chandrasekhar (1995), "Indian Economy Under Structural Adjustment", *Economic and Political Weekly*, November 25.
15. Pathy, Jaganath, (1996), "The End of Millenium: Liberalisation and Accentuation of the Tribal Problematique", *The Journal of Public Administration*, Vol. XLII, No. 3, july-September, p. 485. X.

5

Trends in Land Use Pattern and Agricultural Production Before and After Economic Reforms in India

C. Dhandapani

Introduction

The prosperity of India is based on mainly on the development of agriculture since 65 to 70 percent of its population is engaged directly or indirectly in agriculture. Major export items are agricultural products which comprise nearly 7 percent of India's total exports. Its share in overall GDP fell from 30% in the early nineties, to below 17.5% in 2006. This is high compared to China and Brazil, at 12% and 5% respectively. The World Bank predicts that the shift towards the service sector will continue at the expense of agriculture, whose share could decline by 30% by 2030.

This sector is critical for expanding employment and generating broad-based growth and sustaining reduction of poverty among rural masses. Increase in agricultural productivity depends on the adoption of new farm practices such as high yielding variety of seeds, use of chemical fertilizers and pesticides, modern irrigation methods, farm machinery etc.

There has been a consistent decline in the growth of agricultural sector since the introduction of economic reforms in 1991 as compared to the 1980s. The growth rate of this sector was 4 percent in the last decade. The food grain production has been an abysmal -3 percent during the 1990s and -5 percent during 1999-2000 to 2007-2008. This is a serious issue on the nutritional status and food security of the country.

This paper contains four sections. Section I deals with the introduction, India's position in the world agriculture. Section II exhibits the changes in the land- use pattern of agricultural sector before and after economic reforms and area used for the cultivation of foodgrains. Section III analyses the trend in the production of food grains and non-food grains and compares the area, production and productivity of principal crops of Indian agriculture with other countries. Section IV discusses the index number of area, production and yield rate of food grains and non-food grains in India and elucidates the challenges of the agricultural sector in India.

India's Position in World Agriculture

India's agriculture position in the world in 2006 is exhibited in the below table. The percentage of India's land in the world is 2.4% which occupies seventh position in the world.Out of total world land 13,445 million hectares, India occupies 329 million hectares. The cultivable land of world is 1423 million hectares. India' cultivable land is 160 million hectares which accounts 11.2 percent of the total cultivable area of the world which occupies second position next to USA.

Table 1: India's Position in World Agriculture in 2006

Item	*India*	*World*	*Percentage Share*	*India's Position Rank*
		1. Area (Million Hectares)		
Total Area	329	13445	2.4	Seventh
Land Area	297	13015	2.3	Seventh
Arable Land	160	1423	11.2	Second

2. Population (Million)				
Total	1152	6593	17.5	Second
Agriculture	563	2606	21.6	Second
3. Crop Production (Million Tonnes)				
(A) : Total Cereals	239	2221	10.8	Third
Wheat	69	606	11.4	Second
Rice (Paddy)	137	635	21.6	Second
Total Pulses	14	60	23.3	First
(B) : Oilseeds				
Groundnut (in shell)	5	48	10.4	Third
Rapeseed	8	49	16.3	Third
4. Commercial Crops (Million Tonnes)				
(A) : Sugarcane	281	1392	20.2	Second
(B) : Tea	0.89	3.65	24.4	Second
(C) : Coffee (green)	0.27	7.84	3.4	Sixth
(D) : Jute & Jute like Fibres	2.04	3.11	65.6	First
(E) : Cotton(lint)	3.56	2484	14.3	Third
(F) : Tobacco Leaves	0.55	6.72	8.2	Third

People depend on agriculture in the world is 2606 million. In India people depend on Agriculture is 563 million which is in the second position next to China. This shows that a large number of people in India depend either directly or indirectly on agricultural sector. The world's total crop production in 2006 is 2221 million tonnes. India's share in that is 239 million tonnes which accounts 10.8 percent and ranks third next to China and USA. The world's wheat production in that year is 6.6 million tonnes. India's share is 69 million tonnes (11.4 %) which comes next to China.

World's paddy production during the year 2006 is 635 million tonnes. India's share is 137 million tonnes which accounts for 21.6 percent and occupies second position next to China. In the production of pulses India ranks first. Out of world's total production of 60 million tonnes, India's share is 14 million tonnes, i.e. 23.3 percent. In the oil seed production India ranks third position. World's groundnut production in 2006 is 48 million tonnes. In that India contributed 5 million tonnes, which accounts for 10.4 percent next to China and Indonesia.

In the production of commercial crops India,s share is much impressive. For example, 20.2 percent of world,s sugar cane is produced in India next to Brazil. World Tea production in 2006 is 3.65 million tonnes. India,s contribution is 0.89 million tonnes which is next to China. India occupies sixth position in the world,s coffee production. For several decades India stands first position in the production of Jute. Sixty-five point six percent of Jute is produced in India. In the world production of Cotton and Tobacco leaves, India occupies third position next to China and USA.

Land Use Pattern of Agricultural Sector in India

In India land use-pattern is more or less static in nature. During the year 1995-1996 the gross area sown is 187.47 million hectares. In that the gross irrigated area is only 71.35 million hectares. In the same year the Net area sowed is142.20 million hectares. In that the irrigated area was only 53.40 million hectares. Area under High Yielding Variety is only 72.11 million hectares.

Table 2: Land Use Pattern of Agriculture in India

(Area in million hectares)

Year	*Net Sown Area*	*Gross Sown Area*	*Net Irrigated Area*	*Gross Irrigated Area*
1995-96	142.20	187.47	53.40	71.35
1996-97	142.81	189.59	55.05	73.25
1997-98	142.08	190.57	54.99	73.00
1998-99	142.58	193.03	57.08	75.95
1999-00	140.96	189.44	57.11	78.81
2000-01	141.16	185.70	54.84	75.82
2001-02	141.42	189.75	56.30	78.07
2002-03	132.66	175.66	53.88	72.89
2003-04	140.95	190.37	56.00	77.11
2004-05	141.32	190.91	58.54	79.51
2005-06	141.58	190.89	58.43	79.53
2006-07	141.68	190.92	58.58	79.64

Source: Ministry of Agriculture, Government of India.

The pattern of land-use remained the same before and after the introduction of economic reforms with slight variations in India. In the year 2002-03, the gross area sown has fallen to 175.66 million hectares from 189.75 million hectares in 2001-2002. The net area sown also declined to 132.66 million hectares from 141.42 million hectares in the same years. Gross irrigated area and the net irrigated area showed a downward trend. As the latest data available for the land use pattern in India is 2004-05. During this year 2004-05, the gross area sown is 190.91 million hectares which includes the Gross irrigated area of 79.51 million hectares. The Net area sown for the year 2004-05 is 141.32 million hectares which consists of net irrigated area of 58.54 million hectares. The table briefs the land- use pattern for agricultural production which remained the same during the last decade.

Area Under Cultivation of Food Grains

The area under food grains cultivation is presented in the table 3. Out of the total cultivable land of 160 million hectares, 121.01 million hectares of land were used for the cultivation of food grains in the year1995-96 in India. In that cereals occupies 98.73 million hectares. Paddy was cultivated in 42.84 million hectares. Wheat area is under 25.01 million hectares. Pulses accounts for 22.28 million hectares. The land used for food grain production remained the same with small variations upto 2001-02.

After economic reforms especially during the year 2002-03 the area under cultivation of food grains had a sharp decline. It has come down to 113.87 million hectares from 122.77 million hectares in the previous year 2001-02. There is a sudden decline of the area under the cultivation of paddy from 44.90 million hectares in 2001-02 to 41.18 million hectares in 2002-03. The reason for this is the continuous failure of monsoons and the existence of drought conditions throughout the country. After that it has come to normal. In the year 2006-07 the area under cultivation of food grains remained 123.48 million hectares. For the cereals cultivation 100.37 million hectares of land were used in 2006-07. Out of that, paddy occupied 43.62 million hectares, wheat 28.04 million hectares and coarse cereals 28.71 million hectares. Pulses accounted for 23.11 million hectares.

Table 3: Area Under Cultivation – Food Grains

(Million hectares)

Year	*Cereals*				*Pulses*	*Total*
	Rice	*Wheat*	*Coarse Cereals*	*Total*		*Food grains*
1995-96	42.84	25.01	30.88	98.73	22.28	121.01
1996-97	43.43	25.89	31.81	101.13	22.45	123.58
1997-98	43.45	26.70	30.83	100.98	22.87	123.85
1998-99	44.80	27.52	29.34	101.66	23.50	125.16
1999-00	45.16	27.49	29.34	101.99	21.12	123.11
2000-01	44.71	25.73	30.26	100.70	20.35	121.05
2001-02	44.90	26.34	29.52	100.76	22.01	122.77
2002-03	41.18	25.20	26.99	93.37	20.50	113.87
2003-04	42.59	26.60	30.80	99.99	23.46	123.45
2004-05	41.91	26.38	29.03	97.32	22.76	120.08
2005-06	43.66	26.48	29.04	99.18	22.39	121.57
2006-07	43.62	28.04	28.71	100.37	23.11	123.48

Source: Ministry of Agriculture, Government of India.

From the table 3, it is clear that except 2002-03, the area under cultivation of food grains remained the same. The demand for food grains increased but the area under cultivation has not increased. Hence, there is a gap between the demand for and the supply of food grains. This could be increased by the modern methods of production, irrigation and application of fertilizers etc.

Agricultural Production—Food Grains

Food grain production is analyzed in this section between the years 2007-08. During the year 1995-96 the total food grain production was 180.42 million tonnes.

In that, rice, wheat, coarse cereals account for 168.11 million tonnes. Pulses account for 12.31 million tonnes. Among three cereals rice occupied top place of 76.98 million tonnes. Next to that, wheat production took 62.10 million tonnes. Coarse cereals production was 29.03 million tonnes.

Table 4: Agricultural Production—Foodgrains

(Million tonnes)

Year	*Cereals*				*Pulses*	*Total*
	Rice	*Wheat*	*Coarse Cereals*	*Total*		*Food grains*
1995-96	76.98	62.10	29.03	168.11	12.31	180.42
1996-97	81.73	69.35	34.11	185.19	14.24	199.43
1997-98	82.54	66.35	30.40	179.29	12.98	192.27
1998-99	86.08	71.29	31.33	188.70	14.91	203.61
1999-00	89.68	76.37	30.34	196.39	13.41	209.80
2000-01	84.98	69.68	31.08	185.74	11.07	196.81
2001-02	93.34	72.77	33.37	199.48	13.37	212.85
2002-03	71.82	65.76	26.07	163.65	11.13	174.78
2003-04	88.53	72.15	37.60	198.28	14.91	213.19
2004-05	83.13	68.64	33.46	185.23	13.13	198.36
2005-06	91.79	69.35	34.06	195.20	13.39	208.59
2006-07	93.35	75.81	33.92	203.08	14.20	217.28
2007-08	96.43	78.40	40.73	215.56	15.11	230.67

Source: Ministry of Agriculture, Government of India.

During the year 2002-03, the total food grains production has fallen to 174.78 million tonnes from 212.85 million tonnes in the previous year 2001-02. The production of paddy had a sharp decline from 93.34 million tonnes to 71.82 million tonnes. In the very next year 2003-04, the food grains production started increasing to 213.19 million tonnes in India. Again, the total food grains production has come down to 198.36 million tonnes in the year 2004-05. After that it started increasing.

During the year 2007-08, the total food grains production in India was 230.67 million tonnes. In that, production of food crops showed an increasing trend. The rice production increased to 96.43 million tonnes from 93.35 million tonnes in the previous year 2006-07. The wheat production also showed an increasing trend from 75.81 million tonnes from the previous year 2006-07 to 78.4 million tonnes in 2007-08. The pulses production also increased from 14.20 million tonnes to 15.11 million tonnes in the year 2007-08. But during the consequent years 2008-09 and 2009-10, the production of food grains decreased due to failure of monsoon and drought conditions.

Area, Production and Yield of Principal Crops in Various Countries

The table reveals the picture of major crops production in various countries in 2006. As a whole, 1, 54,344 thousand hectares of land are used for paddy cultivation in the world. The average yield per hectare is 4112 kgs. In the table, it is clear that Egypt ranks first in the production and productivity of paddy. The land used for paddy cultivation is only 613 thousand hectares. The yield per hectare is 10,598 kgs. Next to Egypt, in USA, the total land used for the cultivation of paddy is 1142 thousand hectares and the yield per hectare is 7694 kgs. Whereas, in India the land used for paddy cultivation is 43,700 thousand hectares and the yield per hectare is only 3124 kgs which is comparatively lower than any other developed country in the world.

Table 5: Area, Production and Yield of Principal Crops in Various Countries in 2006

Country	*Area ('000 Hectares)*	*Production ('000 Tonnes)*	*Yield (Kg./Hectare)*
	<u>*1. Paddy*</u>		
World	154324	634606	4112
Egypt	613	6500	10598
U.S.A.	1142	8787	7694
Japan	1688	10695	6336
India	43700	136510	3124
	<u>*2. Wheat*</u>		
World	216100	605946	2804
U.S.A.	20280	57298	2825
France	5247	35367	6740

Egypt	1287	8308	6455
U.K.	1833	14735	8039
India	26480	69350	2619
	3. Groundnut		
World	22232	47768	2149
China	4722	14722	3118
Indonesia	707	14700	20804
Argentina	164	496	3031
India	5800	4980	859
	4. Sugarcane		
World	20399	1392365	68257
Egypt	135	16317	120887
Australia	415	38169	91973
China	1220	100684	82528
Colombia	426	39849	93601
India	4200	281170	66945

Source: www.faostat.fao.org

In the production of Wheat, 2, 16,100 thousand hectares of land were used all over the world and the average yield per hectare is 2804 kgs. The productivity is more in UK. In UK 8039 kgs of wheat is produced per hectare of land. The size of land used for wheat cultivation is 1833 thousand hectares. But in India, the land used for the cultivation of wheat is 26,480 thousand hectares. The yield per hectare is only 2619 kgs. This shows lower productivity of both land and labour.

Even among commercial crops, the productivity in India is much lower while compared with other countries. For instance, in Indonesia, only 707 thousand hectares of land is used for the cultivation of groundnut but the yield per hectare is 20,804 kgs. Whereas, in India the area used for the cultivation of groundnut is 5800 thousand hectares but the yield is only 859 kgs per hectare. This is due to failure of monsoon and less utilization of modern techniques.

One of the major commercial crop is sugarcane. In Egypt only 135 thousand hectares of land is used for the cultivation of sugarcane. The yield per hectare is 1, 20,887 kgs. Australia occupies the second position. The average yield is 91,973 kgs. But in India, the yield is comparatively low.i.e.66, 945 kgs per hectare and the size of land used for the cultivation of sugarcane is 4200 thousand hectares. This shows under utilization of High Yielding Verities of seeds, irrigation methods and lack of application of modern machineries.

Index numbers of Area, Production and Yield of Food grains, Non-Food grains and All Crops in India

The index numbers for Area, Production and yield for food grains, Non-food grains and all crops in India have been analyzed by keeping 100 as index value for the base year 1993-94.

Table 6: Index Numbers of Area, Production and Yield of Foodgrains, Non-Foodgrains and All Crops in India

Year	*Food grains*			*Non-food grains*			*All Crops*		
	Area	*Production*	*Yield*	*Area*	*Production*	*Yield*	*Area*	*Production*	*Yield*
1995-96	125.4	131.4	104.8	118.3	122.0	103.2	123.0	126.8	103.1
1996-97	128.4	145.1	113.0	120.2	130.3	108.4	125.6	137.8	109.7
1997-98	128.7	140.9	109.5	118.8	176.8	101.5	125.3	120.6	104.4
1998-99	130.0	150.0	115.4	120.1	131.9	109.9	126.6	141.1	111.4
1999-00	127.8	152.9	119.6	117.5	123.8	105.4	124.3	138.5	111.4
2000-01	125.7	141.9	112.9	114.3	118.2	103.4	121.8	130.2	106.9
2001-02	127.5	155.3	121.8	114.9	124.6	108.5	122.7	140.1	114.3
2002-03	118.2	132.2	111.8	102.4	110.8	108.2	113.1	121.6	107.6
2003-04	128.2	155.1	121.0	111.2	130.8	117.7	122.6	143.1	116.7
2004-05	124.7	144.2	115.6	122.0	134.1	109.9	123.5	139.2	112.7
2005-06	126.3	152.5	120.8	124.5	130.0	104.4	125.4	146.7	117.0
2006-07	128.2	158.0	123.2	123.1	150.4	122.2	126.3	163.8	129.7

Source: Ministry of Agriculture, Government of India.

The Table 6 reveals the area under all crops have increased slightly from 123.0 in 1995-96 to 126.3 in 2006-07. Only in the year 2001-02, it has fallen to 113.1 from 122.7 in 2001-02. The index for the agricultural production of all crops showed a tremendous increase. In 1995-96, the index value for the production was 126.8 and that increased to 163.8 in 2006-07 except in the year 2002-03 which has come down to 121.6.

The index value for the yield of all crops in India also increased from 103.1 in 1995-96 to 129.7 in 2006-07. Among the food grains all area, production and yield have shown a positive trend. The index value for the yield of food grains in 1995-96 was 104.8 and it increased slowly to 123.2 in 2006-07. The food grains production also increased from 131.4 to 158.0 during the same years. But the index value for the area under cultivation of food grains the remained same with slight increase. That is, in 1995-96 it was 125.4 and it has increased only to 128.2 in 2006-07. The same condition prevailed for area under cultivation of non-food grains also. In 1995-96 the area under non-food grains was 118.3 and increased to 123.1 but the index value for the production showed a continuous increase. In 1995-96, the index value for the production of non-food grains was 122.0 and increased to 150.4. In the same manner the yield per hectare of non-food grains also increased from 103.2 in 1995-96 to 122.2 in 2006-07.

From the table it is clear that area under cultivation of both food grains and non-food grains remained the same but the production increased.This is because yield per hectare increased due to innovative techniques and application of modern methods of production. So the productivity of land in the last decade increased but after that the production and productivity of agriculture in India decreased due to consecutive failure of monsoon and existence of drought in the country. Hence, the demand for food grains increased whereas the supply of it could not be increased. As a result, the price of food grains escalated which affected the common man.

Challenges of the Agricultural Sector in India

On the supply side, the yield of most crops has not increased significantly and in some cases fluctuated downwards. The scope for increase in the net sown area is limited and farm size has been shrinking. In the case of certain crops like sugarcane, the average yield and production over the years varied.

There is a need for the continuous focus on improving productivity and step-up the growth of allied activities and non-farm activities. The irrigation sector requires a renewed thrust both in terms of investment and modern management.

The gap between producer prices and consumer prices must be reduced by removing the online trade in the agricultural sector. The development of marketing infrastructure and storage and warehousing are the need of the hour.

More credit and financial facilities to the farmers with low interest rates by keeping their risk - bearing ability must be worked out. An area that requires focused attention is the issue of sustainability of agriculture with due emphasis on environmental concerns, soil erosion, water logging, and reduction in groundwater

In total, the challenges faced by the agriculture and the allied sector are numerous. The possibilities for new investment, the use of new technologies that could generate value to the farming society and incomes to the rural masses are emphasized.

REFERENCES

Andharia, J.A. (2008): 'Agricultural Production and Problems of Agriculture in India', *Southern Economist*, Vol. 47, No. 11, Oct., Bangalore.

Maithreyi Krishnaraj (2006):"Food Security, Agrarian Crisis and Rural Livelihoods –Implications for Women", *Economic and Political Weekly*, Vol: XLI, No: 52Dec.30, 2006-Jan5, 2007, a Sameeksha Trust Publication, Mumbai.

Sasi, K.N and Rani Ratna Prabha, J. (2008): "Agricultural Credit in India Pre and Post-reform Period", *Southern Economist*, Vol. 47, No. 12, Oct, Bangalore.

Ramesh Chand, S.S. Raju, L.M. Pandey (2007): 'Growth Crisis in Agriculture – Severity and Options at National and State Level", *Economic and Political Weekly*, Vol. XLII, No. 26, June 30-July 6, 2007, A Sameeksha Trust Publication, Mumbai.

National Accounts Statistics 2008 (New Series), Central Statistical Organization, Ministry of Statistics and Programme Implementation, New Delhi.

Gupta S.P. (2002) Report of the Committee on India Vision 2020, Planning Commission, Government of India, New Delhi.

Agriculture in the Eleventh Five-Year Plan, Planning Commission, New Delhi.

Economic Survey of India 2008-09, Government of India, New Delhi.

Ministry of Agriculture, Government of India, New Delhi.

RBI Bulletin, Various Years, Reserve Bank of India, Mumbai.

6

Agrarian Crisis and Farmers' Suicides in India in the Era of Globalisation

N. Suresh Babu

Indian agriculture is currently passing through a period of severe crisis. An important feature of the present agrarian crisis is the sharp deceleration in the agricultural growth rate and stagnation in agricultural production. The slow down is accompanied by a significant reduction in the share of agriculture in national product, but without much reduction in the share of workers depending on it for their livelihood. The most disturbing feature is the stagnation in the production of food grains, which has resulted in a decline in the per capita production of food grains. The deceleration in yields has been witnessed in practically all crops and in a majority region. In fact, there was virtual stagnation in the yields of 'commercial crops, during the 1990s with sugarcane registering less than 1 per cent growth in yield per year, and cotton witnessing negative growth.

The spate of suicides since 1997-98 is considered a tragic manifestation of the deteriorating condition of the farmers. It is argued that Indian farmers are committing suicide due to successive crop failures exacerbated by factors like the increased cost of inputs, spurious seeds and fertilizers, inadequate irrigation, the burden of loan on farmers, unremunerative prices for produce. For thousands of years farmers have to depend on the earth to sustain their families. Now, in the twenty-first century, their livelihood, prosperity, and the well being of their families for generations to come are being threatened by globalization. The National Agricultural Policy of the ministry of agriculture, government of India (2000) said: "Agriculture has become a relatively unrewarding profession due to generally unfavourable price regime and low value addition, causing abandoning of farming and increasing migration from rural areas. The situation is likely to be exacerbated further in the wake of integration of agricultural trade in the global system, unless immediate corrective measures are taken". In view of this, an attempt has been made in the present study to understand the impact of WTO on farmers, suicides and agrarian crisis in India.

The important literature review, objectives and methodology of the study is presented in Section II; Section III looks at the Indian agricultural structure and agrarian crisis. Section IV examines the farmers, suicides and agrarian distress in India during the pre WTO period and the post WTO period and concludes by outlining some general strategies as a way to tackle agrarian crisis in a suitable manner in Section V.

Literature Review

A case study of wheat and rice export of Punjab and Haryana proved that till 1994, these commodities are not internationally competitive (Bigrami, 2002). If any improvement is realized in some commodities in some years that too is very insignificant. The WTO Agreement on Agriculture (AoA) so far caused mal consequences on the agrarian economies of the Third World (Kurien, 2006). Unlike other states in the country, trade liberalization adversely affected the agricultural sector in Kerarla because more than 80 per cent of the agricultural commodities produced in the state are dependent on domestic or international market situation (GoK, 2003). Jeromi (2007) in his study in Kerala found that trade liberalization and also due to a host of other factors like deficient rain fall, excessive concentration of export-oriented perennial crops, decline in production and productivity, fall in prices, etc, the agricultural sector has been facing a crisis which led to a rise in farmers, indebtedness and suicides. Mitra and Sangeeta (2007) traced cotton farmers, suicides to the stagnation of the Indian cotton farmer against the backdrop of an international setting, which was dynamic. Liberalisation in agricultural trade policies of the government had a major impact on the cotton economy. In 1994 with the opening up of the economy, cotton lint exports were placed under an open general licence (OGL), i.e., they were freely importable. This made India,s cotton economy susceptible to price shocks from the world market. The new seed policy announced in 1998 has nothing positive to offer to farmers of India but offers a promise of monopoly to private seed industries, which has already pushed thousands of Indian farmers to suicide through dependency and debt caused by unreliable, high dependency and non-renewable seeds (Shiva, 2006). Economic globalization is leading to a concentration of the seed industry, the increased use of pesticides, and finally increased debt. In the regions where industrial agriculture has been introduced through globalization, higher costs are making it virtually impossible for small farmers to survive (Shiva, 2000). The most significant impact that trade liberalisation had on Indian agriculture was the sharp fall in domestic prices of many commodities after the mid-1990s. Due to the absence of quota controls as in the pre-WTO period and the ineffectiveness of low tariffs, the surge in the imports of various crops contributed in different degrees to the decline in their domestic prices (Bhalla, 2004). The case of fall in cotton and oilseed prices is a good example in this regard.

Objectives

The objectives of the study are as follows:

1. To discuss the agrarian scenario in India
2. To examine the growth rates of agricultural sector and various group of commodities during the pre WTO period and post WTO period.
3. To analyse the impact of WTO on prices of farm produce.

4. To study the impact of WTO on farmers, committing suicide and
5. To suggest policy measures.

Methodology of the Study

The present study is exclusively based on the secondary data collected from different published sources such as Economic Survey of India, WTO International Trade Statistics, and Agricultural Statistics at Giance etc. The objectives of the study have been verified using secondary data.

Agrarian Scenario in India

The share of agriculture in GDP has come down from 55 per cent in 1950-51 to 17 per cent in 2008-09. Notwithstanding the fact that the share of this sector in GDP is declining over the years, its role remains critical as it accounts for about 52 per cent of the employment in the country (CSO, 2008). With an average growth of over 4.9 per cent over the years (2005-06 to 2007-08), the growth originating from agriculture and allied activities declined to 1.6 per cent. India,s agricultural area is vast with total arable and permanent crop land of 170 million hectares in 2003-2005. The average size of holding in the late nineties was about 1.4 hectares and continues to decline, as farms are usually divided on inheritance. Out of India,s 116 million farmers, around 60 per cent have less than 1 hectare and together they farm 17 per cent of the land. The share of medium to large farms (above 4 hectares) is very small at just over 7 per cent of all holdings, but these farms account for around 40 per cent of the land. The implication is that many of the very small farms are subsistence holdings, with low investment and little productivity growth. It clearly speaks of the backwardness of Indian agriculture.

With a few irrigation facilities, Indian farmers have little choice but to depend on rains for their livelihoods. Sixty per cent of India,s land is not irrigated. The area and productivity of major crops like wheat and rice have stagnated over the last ten years. In India, agricultural products constitute a sizeable component of external trade even today. This is true despite the fact that there have been steady declines in the share of agricultural products in the total exports in recent years. The agricultural export as percentage of total exports was 12.2 per cent in 2007-2008. Declining growth rates in production, stagnant prices and high cost of production have hit the agricultural sector as a whole. This entire scenario in Indian agriculture raises the question that does WTO agreements really offers a help to farming community.

Agrarian Distress

In India although some features of the crisis started manifesting themselves in certain parts of India during the late 1980s, the crisis has assumed a serious dimension since the middle of the 1990s. One of the tragic manifestations of the crisis is the large number of suicides committed by the farmers in some parts of India.An important feature of the present agrarian crisis is the sharp deceleration in the agricultural growth rate and stagnation in agricultural production. The slow down is accompanied by a significant reduction in the share of agriculture in national product, but without much reduction in the share of workers depending on it for their livelihood. The most disturbing feature is the stagnation in the production of food grains, which has resulted in a decline in the per capita production of food grains. The per capita annual production of cereals has declined from 192 kg in 1991-95 to 174 kg in 2004-07 and pulses from 15 kg to 12 kg. The deceleration in yields has been witnessed in practically all crops and in a majority region. In fact, there was virtual stagnation in the yields of 'commercial crops, during the 1990s with sugarcane registering less than 1 per cent growth in yield per year, and cotton witnessing negative growth.

The falling public investment in agriculture has been a cause for concern because it is crucial for the development of infrastructure like irrigation, electricity, agriculture research, roads, markets and communications. The share of agriculture in total capital formation has shown a continuous decline except in 2001-02. It has declined from 8.6 per cent in 1999-2000 to 5.8 per cent in 2006-07 which is a cause of concern. It indicates that agricultural sector in India has been neglected over the period of time even though the majority of people in depend on agricultural sector.The support systems to farming have weakened and institutions have become unresponsive. In the absence of any breakthrough in cost reducing technologies, the rising input prices have made cultivation un-remunerative. The result is the manifestation of agrarian crisis, often, in the extreme form of distress that results in suicides by some farmers. Though there are a number of factors behind the present agrarian crisis, it is the globalisation that draws attention.

The most important aspect of the agrarian crisis is that agriculture has become unremunerative and is increasingly becoming unviable for the bulk of the peasantry. After improving steadily from 1980 to 1997, the terms of trade turned against agriculture between 1999 and 2004 and reduced profitability of farming quite sharply. Declining growth rates in production, stagnant prices and high cost of production have hit the agricultural sector as a whole.

WTO, AGRARIAN CRISIS AND FARMERS' SUICIDES

Declining Growth Rates of Agriculture

In recent years, the slowdown in agricultural growth has become a major cause of concern. India,s agricultural growth rate slowed down to less than 2 per cent per year, compared to about 3.5 per cent per annum in the preceding decade. In the states, such as Madhya Pradesh, Orissa, and Rajasthan, growth in the last decade was below 1 per cent per year. Growth rates in GDP of economy and agricultural and allied sectors are displayed in Table 1. It is revealed that in overall growth rates, the process of deceleration in the growth of agriculture had started in the post WTO period. This is evident that growth rate of agricultural sector during the pre WTO period (1990-91 to 1995-96) was 3.2 per cent. It declined to 1.8 per cent in the post WTO period. It is also observed that the growth rate of agriculture and allied sector has shown wide fluctuations over the period of time. The growth rate of agriculture and allied sector was 5.8 per cent in 2001-02. It turned to negative growth of -7.2 per cent in 2002-03 and this growth rate rose to 10.0 per cent in 2003-04. The growth rate of agriculture sector declined to 4.0 per cent during 2006-07 from 5.8 per cent during 2005-06. The growth in agriculture and allied activities decelerated from 4.9 per cent in 2007-08 to 1.6 per cent in 2008- 09.At the same time, the share of agriculture and allied activities in GDP at constant prices has declined from 21.7 per cent in 2003-04 to 18.5 per cent in 2006-07 and further it declined to 17 per cent in 2008-09. It clearly exhibits that the process of deceleration in the growth of agriculture had started in the post WTO period.

Table 1: Growth Rates in GDP of Economy and Agricultural and Allied Sectors

Year	*Growth rate of GDP*	*Growth rate of Agriculture and allied sectors*
1990-91 to 1995-96	5.6	3.2
1996-97 to 2001-02	5.5	1.8
2000-01	4.4	-0.1
2001-02	6.5	5.8
2002-03	3.8	-7.2
2003-04	8.5	10.0
2004-05	7.5	0.0
2005-06	9.5	5.8
2006-07	9.7	4.0
2007-08	9.0	4.9
2008-09	6.7	1.6

Source: Economic Survey, Various Issues.

Figure 1: Trends in Growth Rates of GDP and Agriculture and Allied Sector

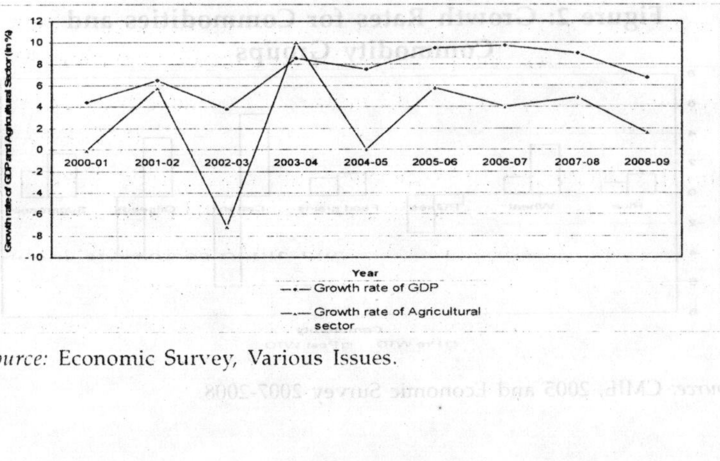

Source: Economic Survey, Various Issues.

In order to understand precisely the implications of WTO, growth rates for commodities and commodity groups during pre WTO period and post WTO period are analysed. This is shown in Table 2.

Table 2: Growth in Yield for Major Crops During Pre WTO Period and Post WTO Period (in Per Cent)

Commodities/Groups	*1989-90 to 2006-07*	*Pre WTO (1990-91 to 1995-96)*	*Post WTO (1996-97 to 2001-02)*
Rice	0.75	1.27	0.75
Wheat	1.41	3.27	1.12
Pulses	-0.76	-0.66	-2.51
Food grains	1.23	1.51	1.17
Cotton	-4.56	5.53	-6.06
Oilseeds	-1.38	3.91	-3.94
Sugarcane	-0.53	2.92	1.74

Source: CMIE, 2005 and Economic Survey, 2007-2008.

It is observed that there is decline in the growth rates of all commodities. It is shocking to note that in the post WTO period, the growth rate of pulses, oil seeds and cotton was negative. Though other factors such as rain fall, fertility of the soil, technology etc; affect the growth rates of agriculture and performance of commodities, one of the important reasons for decline in growth rates of agriculture and commodities is WTO agreement on agriculture.

Figure 2: Growth Rates for Commodities and Commodity Groups

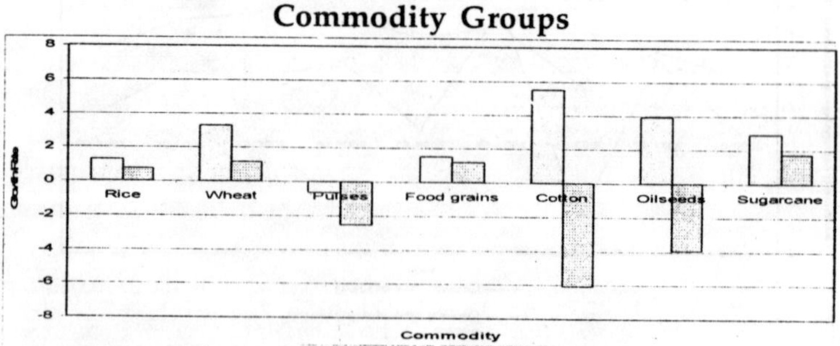

Source: CMIE, 2005 and Economic Survey 2007-2008.

International Comparisons of Yield

One of the major challenges following the dismantling of quantitative restrictions on imports, as per the WTO Agreement on Agriculture for the Indian farmers is to raise the level of productivity and quality standards to internationally competitive levels. While analyzing the data it becomes clear that productivity of several agricultural commodities in India is less than the world average. Table 3 shows the international comparisons of yield for selected commodities in 2004-05.

Table 3: International Comparisons of Yield of Selected Commodities–2004-05

(Metric tonnes/ hectare)

Commodities	*India*	*World Average*
Paddy	2.9	. 3.96
Wheat	2.71	2.87
Maize	1.18	3.38
Cotton	4.64	7.33
Major oil seeds	0.84	1.86

Source: Economic Survey 2006-07.

Prices of Farm Produce

An important reason for recent farm distress was that farm prices fell even as farm production decelerated. Liberalization in agricultural trade policies of the government has a major impact on agricultural sector in India. With the signing of the WTO agreements, Quantitative import restrictions in agricultural sector have been relaxed. Import tariff on most commodities has been brought down. Export policies are being progressively liberalized. These developments expose farmers in India to the vagarious of not only the domestic markets but also to the price fluctuation at the international level. As a result of free trade policies of the WTO, farmers in India are facing the dramatic fall in prices of farm produce. Export prices of primary agricultural commodities in post-WTO period are portrayed in Table 4. It is revealed that there is sharp decline in the export price of principal agricultural commodities. It is evident that the export price of cotton has decreased by 44 per cent over a period of 11 years. It is to be noted that the majority of the farmers who took their lives are cotton growers. During the WTO period the decline in the export prices of cereals, wheat, rice, and sugarcane are in the percentage of 15, 14, 10 and 19 respectively. The decline in international prices of agricultural commodities is contrary to the projection that implementation of WTO AoA would result in reduction in subsidies and thus increase in cost of production and prices.

Table 4: Export Prices of Primary Agricultural Commodities

Commodities	*1995*	*1996*	*1997*	*1998*	*1999*	*2000*	*2001*	*2002*	*2003*	*2004*	*2005*
Food	100	108	99	88	78	79	81	82	86	98	98
Cereals	100	119	93	79	69	67	70	80	81	87	85
Wheat	100	117	90	71	63	64	72	84	83	89	86
Maize	100	133	95	82	73	71	73	81	85	91	80
Rice	100	105	94	95	78	64	54	60	62	77	90
Barley	100	115	93	82	73	74	90	105	101	95	91
Sugar	100	92	87	73	58	66	67	57	62	68	81
Cotton	100	82	81	67	54	60	49	47	65	63	56
Beverages	100	85	112	97	76	65	54	63	67	69	83
Fish	100	86	78	78	75	76	61	62	63	70	85
Shirmp	100	97	109	105	108	113	113	77	73	66	63

Source: WTO International Trade Statistics (2006).

Note: Indices are period averages based on dollar prices.

Seed Policy and Indebtedness

Though there are a number of factors behind the present agrarian crisis, it is the growing indebtedness that compels attention. Studies in various states identified an unbearable debt burden as the main reason for farmers, suicides (Pramod Kumar and Sharma 1998; Iyer and Manick 2000). The agrarian crisis and farmers, distress are closely linked to the neoliberal policy regime implemented in the country in the recent past. The New Seed Policy announced in 1998 allowed large private sector entry in India across a range of crop and relaxed restrictions on seed imports. In 1998, India was forced to open its seed sector to global agri-business such as Monsato, Cargill and Syngenta. As a result of this adjustment traditional farms saved seeds have been replaced with genetically engineered seeds which are non-renewable, thus requiring repurchase for each growing seasons. A free resource available on farms became a commodity which farmers were forced to buy every year. This leads to indebtedness. Globalisation therefore is aimed at destroying the very foundations of the farming system thereby paving the way for a corporate takeover of Many MNCs. MNCs made local farmers dependent on the company and thus eroded the autonomy and self-reliance of Indian farmers. Hence, it is clear that the WTO regime promotes technology-driven high-cost farming and encourages monopoly of corporate houses in the sector. This mainly serves to promote the interests of agri-business multinationals at the expense of small and marginal farmers of the developing countries.

WTO and Farmers' Suicides

According to a report by the National Crime Records Bureau, as many as 16,196 farmers killed themselves in 2008, constituting 13 per cent of the total number of suicides in the country. Farmers, suicides were reported across the country in 2008 represent a slight drop from 16,632 in 2007. The recent NCRB report say that, "1, 99,132 Indian farmers committed suicide in twelve years from 1997 to 2008. These particulars are shown in Table.5.

Table 5: Farmers' Suicides in India

Year	*Maharashtra*	*Andhra Pradesh*	*Karnataka*	*Madhya Pradesh & Chhatisgarh*	*Other States*	*All India*
1997	1917	1097	1832	2390	6386	13,622
	(14.1)	(8.1)	(13.4)	(17.5)	(46.9)	(100.0)
1998	2409	1813	1883	2278	7632	16,015
	(15.0)	(11.4)	(11.8)	(14.3)	(47.5)	(100.0)

1999	2423	1974	2379	2654	6652	16,082
	(15.1)	(12.3)	(14.8)	(16.5)	(41.3)	(100.0)
2000	3022	1525	2630	2660	6766	16,603
	(18.2)	(9.2)	(15.8)	(16.0)	(40.8)	(100.0)
2001	3536	1509	2505	2824	6041	16,415
	(21.5)	(9.2)	(15.3)	(17.2)	(36.8)	(100.0)
2002	3695	1896	2340	2578	7462	17,971
	(20.6)	(10.6)	(13.0)	(14.3)	(41.5)	(100.0)
2003	3836	1800	2678	2511	6339	17,164
	(22.3)	(10.4)	(15.7)	(14.7)	(36.9)	(100.0)
2004	4147	2666	1963	3033	6432	18,241
	(22.7)	(14.6)	(10.8)	(16.7)	(35.2)	(100.0)
2005	3926	2490	1883	2660	6172	17,131
	(23.0)	(14.5)	(11.0)	(15.5)	(36.0)	(100.0)
2006	4453	2607	1720	2858	5422	17,060
	(26.1)	(15.3)	(10.1)	(16.7)	(31.8)	(100.0)
2007	4238	1797	2135	2856	5606	16,632
	(25.5)	(10.8)	(12.8)	(17.2)	(33.7)	(100.0)
2008	3802	2105	1737	3152	5400	16,196
	(23.5)	(13.0)	(10.7)	(19.5)	(33.3)	(100.0)
Total	41404	23279	25685	32454	76310	1,99,132
	(20.8)	(11.7)	(12.9)	(16.9)	(38.3)	(100.0)

Source: Various issues of the accidental deaths and suicides in India, National Crime Records Bureau, Ministry of Home Affairs, Government of India.

Note: Figures within parentheses show row percentage.

It is observed that the incidence of suicide has been on the rise in Andhra Pradesh. It saw a 138 per cent increase in the farm suicides during 1997-2006. It witnessed an increase of 308 suicides in 2008 against its 2007 total. Maharashtra reported 55 per cent increase in the farm suicides in the 1997-2007 periods. It saw a decline of 436 suicides in 2008 against its 2007 total. In Karnataka the suicides are less compared to other worst affected states. For Madhya Pradesh and Chhatisgarh there is a wide fluctuation in number of farmers committing suicides between 1997 and 2008. But it is to be noted that they experienced an increase of 296 suicides in

2008 over the previous year. In India, the maximum numbers of suicides have taken place in 2004. It shows that financial relief packages and economic policies of the Central and state governments has not helped to stop farmers committing suicides.

Farmers' Suicides in Big Five States

With regard to farmers, suicides the worst affected states are Maharashtra, Andhra Pradesh, Karnanataka, and Madhya Pradesh and Chhatisgarh. These particulars are given in Table 6.

Table 6: Farmers' Suicides in Big Five States in India

Year	*Total of Big Five States*	*All India*
1997	7236(53.1)	13,622
1998	8383(52.5)	16,015
1999	9430(58.7)	16,082
2000	9837(59.2)	16,603
2001	10374(63.2)	16,415
2002	10509(58.5)	17,971
2003	10825(63.1)	17,164
2004	11809(64.8)	18,241
2005	10959(64.0)	17,131
2006	11638(68.2)	17,060
2007	11026(66.3)	16,632
2008	10796(66.7)	16,196
Total	122822(61.7)	1,99,132

Source: Various issues of the accidental deaths and suicides in India, National Crime Records Bureau, Ministry of Home Affairs, Government of India.
Note: Figures within parentheses show percentage of total farm suicides.

It is revealed that the share of Big five states or 'suicide belt, in 2008 remained very high at 10,796 or 66.7 per cent of the total farm suicides in the country. The share of Big five states in total farm suicides has increased from 53.1 per cent in 1997 to 61.7 per cent in 2008, Within Big five states, Maharashtra registered higher numbers in twelve years from 1997 to 2008. However, it is to be noted that the share of Maharashtra in total farm suicides has declined from 25.5 per cent in 2007 to 23.5 per cent in 2008. Professor K. Nagaraj says of the NCRB data: "There is hardly any decline in suicide belt, though individual states may show variations across 12 years. If this the state for 2008, the year of the Rs.70,000 crore loan waiver and multiple farm packages, then 2009, drought year, could show very disturbing figures. The underlying agrarian problems seem as acute as ever." (The Hindu, January 22, 2010). It clearly indicates that farmers are committing suicide during the post-WTO period, because, the farmer is losing social, economic identity as a producer. A farmer is now a consumer of costly seeds and costly chemicals sold by powerful global corporations. The logic of freeing agricultural product markets required as parts of commitments made to the WTO has affected Indian farmers adversely. One of the reasons for this due to many of the farmers who felt they had no choice but to shift to the intensive attractively marketed GM seeds now face debts caused by unaffordable, spurious inputs such as futile seeds, pesticides and fertilizers. Government policies relating to exports and imports had hit the farm sector hard. Reducing import duties on agricultural commodities had resulted in the arrival of multinational in the country. Indian farmers are not in a position to withstand the competition and are forced to resorts to extreme actions.

Conclusions and Suggestions

This study concludes that globalization is partly responsible for the present agrarian crisis and farmers, suicides. WTO Agreement on Agriculture has not benefited Indian farmers and Indian economy. The growth rate analysis reveals that there is a sharp decline in growth rate in agricultural sector and growth rates of yield for commodities such as pulses, oil seeds and cotton was negative during the post WTO period. There is a sharp decline in the export prices of principal agricultural commodities and for several commodities productivity is less than the world average. The farmers are committing suicide and losing social, economic identity as a producer during the posι WTO period. The WTO regime mainly serves to promote the interests of agri-business multinationals at the expense of small and marginal farmers of the developing countries. Therefore, in the present study the following suggestions are given to protect the interest of farming community particularly marginal and small farmers.

1. Public investment in agriculture and allied activities should be increased.
2. Institutional credit at low rate of interest should be easily made available to the farmers.
3. Both Central and many State Governments offer financial relief packages only to the families who are unable to pay their bank loans. This scheme should include farmers who have taken loans from money lenders because loans taken from private money lenders are the most difficult for farmers to pay back.
4. All loans taken by small and marginal farmers should be restructured by offering easy repayment installments for a period of ten years.
5. State Governments should take severe action against private money lenders who charge exorbitant interest rates.
6. A crop insurance scheme must be carefully implemented so that farmers who are affected by crop failure will be relieved of the subsequent financial burden.
7. The government should evolve a model to ensure supply of quality seeds and other inputs and markets to produce.
8. Appropriate economic policies related to agriculture should be framed to safeguard the interest of marginal and small farmers from the injustice of free trade based on high subsidies and dumping.

REFERENCES

Bhalla, G.S. (2004): *State of the Indian Farmer: Globalization and Indian Agriculture* Vol. 19, Academic Foundation, New Delhi.

Bhanumurthy, N.R. and Sapna Sinha (2004): 'Industrial Recovery: Can It Be Sustained', *Economic and Political Weekly*, Vol. 39, No. 5, January–February.

Bilgrami, S.A.R. (2002), 'Indian Agricultural Export Performance and the Emerging World Trading System: Prospects and Challenges' in B.M.Jahari *India's Development after Independence*, Gyan Publishing Housing, New Delhi.

CSO (2007): 'National Accounts Statistics and Back Issues', Central Statistical Organisation, Ministry of Statistics and Programme Implementation, Government of India, New Delhi.

Government of India (2000): 'National Agricultural Policy', Ministry of Agriculture, Department of Agriculture and Cooperation, New Delhi.

Government of India (2007): 'Agricultural Statistics at a Glance', Directorate of Economics and Statistics, Ministry of Agriculture, New Delhi.

Government of Kerala (2003): Report of the Commission on WTO Concerns in Agriculture, 'Building a Sustainable Agricultural Trade Security System for Kerala'.

Iyer, Gopal K. and Mehar Singh Manick (2000): *Indebtedness, Impoverishment and Suicides in Rural Punjab*, Indian Publishers and Distributors, Delhi.

Jeromi, P. D. (2007): 'Farmers' Indebtedness and Suicides: Impact of Agricultural Trade Liberalisation in Kerala', *Economic and Political Weekly*, Vol. XL 11, No. 31, August 4.

Kumar, Pramod and S.L Sharma (1998): *Suicides in Rural Punjab*, Institute for Development and Communication, Chandigarh.

Kurian, Mathew, (2006): 'WTO Agreements and Agriculture: A Third World Perspective', *Mainstream*, Vol. XLV, No.1, Dec, 22-28.

Mitra, Siddhartha Sangeeta Shroff (2007): 'Farmers' Suicides in Maharashtra', *Economic and Political Weekly*, Vol. XL 11, No. 49, December 8.

Shiva, Vandana (2000):"Globalization and poverty." Resurgence, Issue 202: September-October. URL: http://www.resurgence.org/resurgence/issues/shiva202.htm (Accessed: June 12, 2007).

Shiva, Vandana (2006): 'Seeds of Suicide: The Ecological and Human Costs of Seed Monopolies and Globalization of Agriculture', *Navadanya*, New Delhi.

7

Globalization, Crop Diversification and Agricultural Development

S.N. Tripathy

Introduction

The process of Economic Reforms or the New Economic Policy (NEP-1991) initiated changes in the areas of trade policies, monetary & financial policies, fiscal & budgetary policies, and pricing & institutional reforms. The salient features of NEP-1991 were: (i) liberalization (internal and external), (ii) extending privatization, (iii) redirecting scarce Public Sector Resources to Areas where the private sector is unlikely to enter, (iv) globalization of economy, and (v) market friendly state. Research reports revealed that this macro-economic adjustment programme was remarkable for its relatively painless transition compared with similar programmes elsewhere and a large part of the credit for absorption of these shocks is due to the steady increase in agricultural production. The GATT Agreement signed in 1995 has fundamentally changed the global trade scenario in agricultural sector.

Diversification of Crops and Food Processing Industry

Green revolution has transformed India from a land of deficiency to a land of surplus. India is currently the world's second largest producer of food, and has the potential of being the significant producer of food, with developing food and agricultural sector. Growing economy, surplus food and changing lifestyle has shifted the consumption pattern, from cereals to more varied and nutritious diet of fruit and vegetables, milk, fish, meat and poultry products. Though the outcome of such changing situation was the diversification of crops to meet the changing demand of the people, this gradual development has also led to the opening of increased number of food processing industry in India. The food processing sector in the country with its vast potential has emerged as one of the major drivers of economic growth. Interestingly, the fact is while the country,s GDP growth rate had increased from 3.5% in 2002-03 to 9% in 2006-07; the food processing sector has grown from 7% to 13.1% during the same period. However, market experts were of the opinion that in future, the food products is to contribute substantially towards India,s GDP growth. India,s food processing sector primarily covers fruit and vegetables; meat and poultry; dairy products, alcoholic beverages, fisheries, plantation, grain processing and other consumer product groups like confectionery, chocolates and cocoa products, Soya-based products, mineral water, high protein foods etc. India presently accounts for less than 1.5% of international food trade, which indicates that both investors and exporters are having the prospects of gains more from the Indian food processing industry. It was estimated that the food processing industry requires about Rs 29,000 crore in investment over the next five years to create necessary infrastructure, state-of-the-art-technology and expand production facilities to match the international quality and standards. To promote the sector, the Indian government had taken several steps such as de-licensing of the sector, several duty and tax relief, financial assistance for infrastructure building and setting up of food processing units. It is anticipated that in future bulk investments and modern food processing technologies are going to turn the fortune for Indian food processing industry.

The sub-sectors such as soft-drink bottling, confectionery manufacture, fishing, aquaculture, grain-milling and grain-based products, meat and poultry processing, alcoholic beverages, milk processing, tomato paste, fast-food, ready-to-eat breakfast cereals, food additives, flavours etc has become the driving force behind the Indian food processing industry.

India ranks first in the world in production of cereals and milk. Ours is the second largest fruit and vegetable producer and is among the top five producers of rice, wheat, groundnuts, tea, coffee, tobacco, spices, sugar, and oilseeds. With an industry size of US$70bn, the food processing industry in India ranks fifth in terms of production, consumption, export and expected growth. The industry contributed 6.3% to India,s GDP in 2003 and had a share of 6% in total industrial production. The industry employs 1.6mn workers directly and accounts for 13% of the country's exports and 6% of total industrial investment. The overall food processing industry has achieved a growth rate of 8% in FY05 with an estimated figure of Rs. 3, 584 bn. However, the unorganized, small players account for more than 70% of the industry,s output in volume terms and 50% in value terms. The food processing industry has been largely unorganized, 75% of the processing units belong to the unorganized category. The organized category though small, is growing. India's share in the global processed food trade was a minuscule 1.5%. Majority of the food units have been engaged in primary processing. Production base of secondary and tertiary processed foods has been low, resulting in low value addition. Value addition to foods by processing is a mere 8% of total production currently and is expected to increase to 35% by the end of 2025. An estimated 25% of fruits and vegetables valued at about Rs. 250bn-300bn are used to be wasted annually due to poor post harvesting technology and inadequate storage and transportation. The level of processing of fruits and vegetables is a mere 2% and is expected to increase to 10% in 2010 and to 35% in 2025, according to the Ministry of Food Processing, India. Processed food exports for the period April to September 2004 was Rs 85.83bn, while India,s total agriculture and food exports in FY05 was Rs 400bn (provisional). Post-liberalization of food sector (1991) the government has taken various steps to encourage the industry like removal of price controls, de-reservation from small scale and decrease in import controls.

Globalization has today become a fact that the entrepreneurs have to live with. The world of multinationals and disappearing boundaries of nations has become irreversible sooths of the Indian business scenario. India's economic borders are more international at present. While a window of opportunities has opened up for entrepreneurs, smaller firms are likely to come under severe resource pressure, lest they adhere to benchmarks, like, better products, lower cost, quality, competitive prices, technology and reduced response time. The Small Scale Sector plays a vital role in the economy but the present scenario demands that to burgeon they will have to master the new rules of governing competition.

The focus of farm planning must shift from an approach geared just towards increasing productivity to a livelihoods approach, with special attention on small and marginal farmers. Almost two-thirds of workers in villages are farmers. Of these, an overwhelmingly large percentage are small and marginal farmers—those with land holdings of less than 2ha. These small holdings require a separate strategy to deal with the issues they face. The National Commission for Enterprises in the Unorganized Sector, or NCEUS, has recently submitted a blueprint for a special programme for marginal and small farmers. Small and marginal farmers make up at least 80% of all farmer households but own a little less than 50% of the total arable area. Land fragmentation over the years has ensured that their numbers have increased significantly. At the same time, their contribution in total crop production has also increased and is now a little more than half of the total output. The latest data from the situation assessment survey of farmers of the National Sample Survey Organization has reconfirmed the traditional productivity advantage enjoyed by small and marginal farmers over medium and large farmer.

It is important to note here that a significant percentage of small and marginal farmers cultivate food grains and their contribution to food security is crucial. Despite their significant role in the agrarian economy, they continue to remain disadvantaged in terms of accessing technology, inputs, credits and government subsidies. It is well known that a large part of subsidies is cornered by medium and large farmers. Even in the private sphere, market imperfections are a big stumbling block to small and marginal farmers who lack the necessary skills, information and asset base to take advantage of market conditions.

Information asymmetry and high transaction costs in the private market always work as disadvantages to small and marginal farmers. It is well known that the farm sector is in the midst of a severe crisis since 1997. The situation worsened both due to domestic neglect of the sector as well as the international context after the World Trade Organization,s regime, where domestic farmers are unable to compete with protectionist regimes and large subsidies doled out by the developed countries.

As the NCEUS report highlights, the nature of small farming has seen substantial changes over the years. The survey also makes clear that small and marginal farmers do not earn enough from farming despite higher productivity per unit of land. Given their small asset base, public investment and government support and subsidy is crucial to their survival. This is particularly true in the case of access to credit, security of tenure and access to latest technology; inputs and irrigation at subsidized rates. The small asset base and meager profits from farming have also meant more and more small and marginal farmers are not looking at farming as their primary activity. Some of these issues have been highlighted in numerous committees of the government. But there has not been commensurate action to address these problems.

Crop Diversification

The farming community has reacted to the changing consumption patterns of consumers by diversifying its production portfolio towards high-value food commodities. Experiences from many developing countries have exposed about the changing production portfolio at the farm level due to altering dietary patterns. Besides rising income levels, the expanding urbanization, increasing infrastructural development and liberalization of trade policies have been identified as factors that activated the process of agricultural diversification out from the arena of staple food production. Despite a 'silent revolution, in the high-value food segment, performance of the agricultural sector was not as remarkable as that of the overall economy of the country.

The changing scenario of agriculture has forced the farming community and policy makers in agriculture, to investigate for a more remunerative and viable production portfolio. The diversification of agriculture towards non-food grain and high value commodities has been the right answer for it, because these commodities have potential of income augmentation, employment generation, poverty alleviation and export promotion. It is, therefore, important to diagnose the production-consumption linkages in the context of agricultural diversification. It will require identification of the driving forces that can alter production portfolios and consumption baskets. It is also imperative to understand how the production portfolio is evolving itself in response to changes in the consumption pattern, in a scenario where smallholders dominate agriculture and a majority of them live in the rural areas.

Agricultural diversification in India is gradually picking up momentum in favor of high-value food commodities primarily to augment income rather than the traditional concept of risk management. The nature of diversification differs across regions due to existence of wide heterogeneity in agro-climatic and socio-economic environments. It was considered interesting to delineate the key regions and sub-sectors of agriculture where diversification was catching up fast.

Crop diversification aims at providing a wide range of choice in the production of a variety of crops in a given area so as to expand production related activities on various crops and also to minimize risk. Crop diversification in India has been usually viewed as a shift from traditionally grown less remunerative crops to more remunerative crops. The crop shift (diversification) also takes place due to governmental policies and thrust on some crops over a given time, for instance creation of the Technology Mission on Oilseeds (TMO) to offer thrust on oilseeds production as a national need for the country's requirement for less dependency on imports. Market infrastructure development and certain other price related supports also induce crop shift. Often low volume high-value crops like spices also aid in crop diversification. Higher profitability and also the resilience/stability in production also induce crop diversification, for instance sugar cane replacing rice and wheat. Crop diversification and also the growing of large number of crops are practiced in rain fed lands to diminish the risk factor of crop failures due to drought or less rains. Crop substitution and shift are also taking place in the areas with distinct soil problems. For example, the growing of rice in high water table areas replacing oilseeds, pulses and cotton; promotion of soybean in place of medium and deep black soils etc.

Changes in consumption patterns has been leading to increased demand for "high value" products such as vegetable oils & meat in developing countries and fresh fruits & vegetables and organic products in developed countries. At the same time, food scares and health concerns have challenged the confidence in food quality. As such, consumers expect retailers to ensure food safety measures through their purchasing practices. Therefore, competition among retailers increasingly involves food safety aspects. Consumers are also demanding more transparency, traceability and guarantee in the food chain. Meeting these requirements is a significant challenge for entering global value chains of food products.

The organization of commodity chains has also changed extensively. A few decades ago, the dominance of large companies in world commodity economy was mostly in terms of their marketing initiatives in international markets. In recent years, increasingly, these companies are also influencing what is to be produced. Thus, at the international level, there is a continuing concentration of trade and vertical integration of large firms. At the level of commodity-exporting developing countries, trading networks (both for domestic and export markets) are being appropriated by foreign firms. In the retail markets of developed countries, the most important change has been the growth of supermarkets, which has led to the near eradication of independent traders and increased the significance of brand name. Under these evolving production and marketing systems and considering the large number of small farmers in agricultural production, the constraints that characterize Indian exports fall in three broad areas: (i) access to information; (ii) access to finance; and (iii) access to marketing and trade networks. This is under the assumption that agricultural trade liberalization will progress subsequent to the ongoing negotiations.

"The process of diversification in cropping pattern from food grains to non-food grains which began during 1980-83 to 1990, continued in 1900-93 to 2003-06 albeit at a slower rate and the share of food grains in GCA declined from 67.3% in 1990-93 to 63.7% by 2003-06. The economic reforms initiated during the early 1990s were expected to hasten the process of crop diversification from low value food grains to high value non-food grain crops. However, during the post-reform period, the yield growth rates of most of the important crops including wheat and rice, oilseeds, sugar cane decelerated considerably compared with the pre-reform period 1980-83 to 1990-93. Consequently, during the post-reform period, the pace of cropping pattern changes towards higher value crops slowed down as compared with the pre-reform period 1980-83 to 1990-93. During 1990-93 to 2003-06, like during 1980-83 to 1990-93, the shift has occurred mainly from the area under coarse cereals and from some other crops like pulses. However, unlike the earlier period 1980-83 to 1990-93, when oil seeds were the main gainers, during 1990-93 to 2003-06, although share of oilseeds has also increased marginally, it is the remaining crops which are the biggest beneficiaries. Some other crops like cotton and sugar cane have also marginally increased their share in area during this period. But the share of pulses has declined" (Bhalla and Singh, 2009, pp. 40-41).

India has also the potential to develop niche markets especially in fresh fruits and vegetables. The approach could be either in developing producer-driven commodity chains or buyer-driven chains. However, the challenge is that of the effective governance of food chains. Especially, in cases where the food retailers in developed countries are sourcing from developing countries, it is important to close the gap between producer capabilities and the requirements of the export markets. Secondly, considering that food products have distinct marketing channels, it is important to monitor the coordination between the producer and retailer, particularly when the product quality is not standardized.

The above approaches for revamping the food export systems, has clear implications for Foreign Direct Investment (FDI) both in developing production systems and retailing. In this regard, it is important to define the permissible role of FDI in developing these networks. Although the various programmes/schemes for production enhancement, infrastructure development and export promotion have highlighted the underlying issues, the possible role of FDI in these areas has not been clearly defined.

Further, creation of infrastructure, watershed development, increased availability of subsidized inputs and greater thrust on research, extension and risk management is required to compete with imports. Better integration across rural markets is necessary for price signals from abroad to be fully successful in generating comparative advantages. A danger posed by weak integration across rural markets is that the price depressing effects of potential imports can be quicker and affect more regions and farmers.

Therefore, India,s initial negotiating proposals should seek to protect the interest of Indian agriculture especially on its concerns for food and livelihood security, demanding more flexibility for protection from surge in imports and by yielding minimal market access. These negotiating proposals with matching efforts of protection, support and market-friendly domestic policy regime will take Indian farming to higher levels of growth and prosperity.

Nature of Agricultural Diversification

Crops, livestock, fisheries and forestry constitute the core sectors of agriculture. The crop sector is the principal income-generating source in agriculture followed by the livestock sector. A strong synergy exists between these two sectors, both being complementary to each other. The fisheries sector has a distinction in the coastal areas, and forestry dominates in the hilly regions.

The share of crop sector in the agricultural gross domestic product declined marginally during the 1980s (from about 76.25% in TE 1981-82 to 73.65% in TE 1990-91) but recovered slowly during the 1990s (rising to 74.60% in TE 1998-99). The two obvious reasons for this phenomenon are: (i) normal monsoons during most of the years in 1990s, and (ii) greater emphasis on horticultural crops, leading to their higher production. Another exposure was a quantum jump in the share of livestock sector during the 1980s; from about 18 percent in TE 1981-82 to 23 percent in TE 1990-91. Later in 1990s, the value of livestock (at constant prices) though nearly doubled; its share in agriculture remained almost stagnant at 23 percent. It was because the value of bigger sector of crops increased relatively more than that of the livestock sector and hence masked the latter,s performance. The same was true of the fisheries sector. The value of fisheries sector swelled by about 50 percent during the 1990s, but its share in agricultural gross domestic product declined marginally to about 1.02 percent in TE 1998-99 from 1.35 percent in TE 1990-91. It was despite the fact that fisheries production has increased at an annual rate of 5.35 percent during the decade of 1990s. In general, the regional patterns unfolded a shift from crops to livestock during the 1980s and 1990s. The exceptions were eastern and northeastern regions, where the shares of both crop and livestock sectors increased in the total value of agricultural output at the cost of fisheries and forestry. In the southern region also, the shares of fisheries and forestry in the total output during the 1980s and 1990s declined. The livestock sector across different regions expanded as a result of higher demand for products, like milk, meat and eggs. The 'cooperative model, and the 'contract farming, concept linking cultivation, processing and retail distribution seemed to have attained a reasonable degree of achievement, contributing to increased livestock production.

Diversification within Crop Sector

The crop sector has been described a steady diversification in India with replacement of food grain crops with nonfood grain crops. The share of non-food grain crops in terms of area went up from 30 percent in TE 1981-82 to 35 percent in TE 1998-99, and in value terms it had a significant rise, from about 52 to 60 percent. Several non-food grain crops such as oilseeds, fruits, vegetables, spices and sugarcane have substituted mainly coarse cereals in the farmers, pursuit for higher income. Regional patterns in crop diversification in India were quite stark. The southern region depicts maximum diversification followed by the western region. It is noteworthy that these were the regions, which had accomplished higher agricultural growth during the 1990s over the preceding decade. These regions moved rapidly towards more non-cereal crops, which perhaps contributed to the acceleration of agricultural growth. These regions were relatively less developed in irrigation and largely relied on rainfall. Since pulses and oilseeds require less water, they had found niches in these regions. Like pulses and oilseeds, these regions witnessed substantial increase in area under fruits and vegetables also. The government-supported programs had promoted the cultivation of fruits and vegetables. Among others, watershed program had facilitated conservation of rainwater and gave higher priority to the cultivation of fruits and vegetables. Among cereal crops, maize was picking up fast in the southern region and to some extent in the western region also, largely as poultry feed. Among the crops gaining in these regions, oilseeds were under serious threat in the wake of import liberalization of edible oils, as the cost of imported oils, especially palmolean, was much lower than their domestic price. To sustain oilseed production, technical efficiencies in their production and processing will have to be innovated with better management and technology options.

The northern region in India has more specialized in rice and wheat crops. The favorable government pricing policies, assured procurement, high-yielding technologies, and irrigation development have encouraged farmers to allocate more area in favor of these crops. Rice and wheat have replaced coarse cereals and pulses in this region and it is diversifying only marginally towards non-cereal commodities. With the availability of short-duration black gram, green gram and pigeon pea, pulses had started regaining area in this region. Other important crops of the region were sugarcane, vegetables and fruits. There are reports, however, that extensive cultivation of rice and sugarcane was causing negative externalities related to soil and water resources. The soil fertility with respect to macro- and micronutrients was declining, and the water resources were depleting. These negative externalities have adversely affected the total factor productivity of rice-wheat based cropping system in this region. It has potential for cultivating a variety of fruits and vegetables, but its exploitation depends on developing appropriate infrastructure with suitable linkages between production and consumption.

The eastern region of India is considered as the most backward in terms of per capita income, agricultural growth and infrastructure development. The yield levels are low because of the uncertain production environment and poor adoption of improved varieties and technologies. Overall, the region was food-based concentrating largely on rice, with little diversification. The humid atmosphere and high rainfall make cultivation of rice more favorable in this region. In the limited non-rice areas, however, there was high diversity. It is an important vegetable growing area with about 44 percent share in the total vegetable area in the country in TE 1998-99. The cultivation of fruits was also increasing gradually. It has emerged as an oilseeds producing region too with cultivation of crops like rapeseed-mustard, groundnut, sesame and soybean.

During the post-green revolution period, fruits and vegetables performed impressively in all the regions of India. It was due to the greater thrust to these commodities. To encourage the horticulture sector through coordinating production and processing of fruits and vegetables, National Horticultural Board was constituted in 1984 on the lines of

The performance of agriculture was quite diverse across different regions. It was much better in the western region with an annual compound growth rate of 3.8 percent during

1990s. In agriculture-dominated northern region, the performance of agriculture was dismal, with an annual growth rate of 2 percent during the 1990s as against 3.2 percent during 1980s. The results of decomposition analysis on the sources of agricultural growth in different regions revealed that 'yield increase, was the predominant source of agricultural growth in all the regions during the 1980s, while during the 1990s, these varied across regions. As for example, it was prices in the eastern and northern regions, and crop diversification in the southern and western regions. A brief account of growth sources in different regions is given below:

Northern Region

Rice, wheat, sugarcane and fruits & vegetables were the principal commodities which has contributed about 77 percent to the gross value of crop output in TE 1999-2000. Rice and wheat were the main crops that had brought the 'Green Revolution, in this region. During the 1980s, the real prices of major commodities declined in the region but were well compensated for by (i) phenomenal rise in the yield levels of important crops, and (ii) crop diversification in favor of rice, wheat, sugarcane and fruits & vegetables (Table 5). The situation changed dramatically during the 1990s, when increase in the real prices of rice, wheat and sugarcane dominated in the value of agricultural output. Expansion in area and crop diversification towards rice and wheat continued during 1990s but the pace slowed down. However, area expansion and crop diversification picked-up speed for fruits & vegetables. The future growth opportunities in this region would rely on another technological breakthrough to augment yield of important crops and promote agricultural diversification towards more remunerative food commodities for processing and value-addition.

Eastern Region

Rice and fruits & vegetables were the major commodity groups, which accounted for roughly 69 percent share in the gross value of agricultural output during the 1980s and 71 percent during the 1990s. The region witnessed a decline in the net and gross cropped area during the 1990s as compared to 1980s. The decline in agricultural growth due to fall in cropped area was compensated for by: (i) rise in prices, (ii) higher crop yields, and (iii) crop substitution towards more remunerative commodities. Besides rice and fruits & vegetables, this region experienced expansion in areas under oilseeds, pulses and wheat through crop substitution. This region characterized as 'low-yielding and slow-growth, areas needs introduction of improved technologies or diversification towards such commodities as could tap the potential of available resources such as labor and water.

Western Region

Crop diversification was the leading source of agricultural growth during both the decades of 1980s and 1990s followed by rise in prices and yield in this region. However, the contribution of yield to agricultural growth was less during the 1990s than 1980s, while the trend was just the reverse for prices. Among commodities, pulses, oilseeds and fruits & vegetables made a significant contribution (76 percent) to agricultural growth during 1980s. During 1990s, production portfolio included wheat, pulses, oilseeds, cotton and fruits & vegetables, with contribution of about 80 percent growth in the crop sector. The contribution of fruits & vegetables, wheat and cotton increased during the 1990s, while that of pulses and oilseeds decreased. Interestingly, crop diversification and prices were mainly responsible for the growth in wheat and fruits & vegetables, while these were crop diversification and higher yields in the case of cotton. The region had witnessed a transformation as a result of investment in the watershed programs and incentives on adopting water-saving technologies. These initiatives in the region led to crop diversification and higher crop yields, which ultimately contributed to agricultural growth.

Southern Region

This region viewed crop diversification as the major source of agricultural growth and its pace was much faster during the 1990s than 1980s. Rice, oilseeds, fruits & vegetables and spices substituted coarse cereals during the 1980s, with a contribution of roughly 80 percent to the agricultural growth. During the 1990s, their contribution improved to 88 percent, substituting oilseeds and cotton. Coarse cereals, particularly maize also boomed in the region for the poultry sector. Increase in the yield of major crops also emerged as an important source of agricultural growth in the region, as a major part of it was characterized as rain fed and technologically laggard. However, greater emphasis on the watershed development in the southern and western regions had augmented water availability, leading to adoption of improved technologies, and consequently higher yields of crops.

Drivers of Agricultural Diversification

Numerous forces influence the nature and momentum of agricultural diversification from staple to high-value food commodities. The earlier evidence suggests that this process of diversification was triggered by the rapid technological change in agricultural production, improved rural infrastructure, and changing consumers, preferences. These are broadly classified as demand and supply forces. The demand side forces that have been hypothesized to pressure the agricultural diversification include per capita income and urbanization. On the supply side, this diversification is largely influenced by infrastructure (markets and roads), technology (relative profitability and risks in different commodities), resource endowments (water and labor) and socio-economic variables (pressure on land and literacy rate). In this section, we have identified the key drivers of agricultural diversification.

Private sector has not been strongly participating in the process of agricultural diversification. The important constraints discussed by the private sector representatives are stated below:

High-value food commodities require an infrastructure that is quite different from that of cereals and pulses. Most of the high-value food commodities are perishable in nature, which require refrigerated transportation and cold storages at every stage of value addition. These are, however, woefully lacking and hence, there are substantial post-harvest losses.

To sum-up the regional patterns of agricultural growth, it can be concluded that the southern and western regions have conspicuously followed the growth path of crop diversification towards high-value commodities during the reform period. Consequently, the agricultural growth has been much higher in these two regions than in the eastern and northern regions, which have witnessed only price-led growth. Also, the southern and western regions are rapidly switching over to the high-value commodities. The annual compound growth rates of area and gross value of high-value commodities in these regions are much higher than in the eastern and northern regions, and difference has been more during 1990s than 1980s. The share of high-value commodities in the gross cropped area and value of agricultural output has risen consistently in the southern and western regions during the period 1980-2000. Therefore, these regions need concerted efforts in strengthening the supply chain of high-value commodities. Policies to promote agro-processing industries could reap the benefit of value-addition in these commodities. These regions require incentives for investments in the agro-processing sector and strengthening of innovative institutional arrangements. In their absence, the pace of crop diversification may be affected adversely. In contrast to the southern and western regions, the agricultural growth in the eastern and northern regions has relied more on increase in prices of agricultural commodities. Efforts, therefore, be directed towards gradually switching-over to commodities yielding higher returns. This could be achieved by using advanced technologies. The eastern region though has a sizable area under high-value commodities, is not able to exploit the potential benefits because of its lower yield levels and poor road and market infrastructure. The northern region critically needs to diversify away from rice-wheat system to high-value and resource-conserving commodities for motivating growth in agriculture.

Policy Implications

The pace of agricultural diversification has not been found

as fast as that of demand for high-value food commodities. The projections for 2025 are that demand for these commodities will grow at a much faster rate than for cereals and/or foodgrains under the existing and high-growth scenario. As for example, under the assumption of the existing income growth scenario, the per capita demand will increase by 43 percent for vegetables and 45 percent for fruits. These figures are much higher under the assumed high-growth scenario. On the contrary, the per capita demand for food grains is projected to fall by about 2.5 percent. Considering the growth in population also, the increase in demand for various commodities under the existing income growth scenario is projected as follows: food grains, 28 percent; vegetables, 90 percent and fruits, 92 percent. Besides, the rise in the consumption of high-value commodities will contribute significantly to agricultural GDP. To accelerate agricultural growth and meet the rising demand for these commodities under the land-constraint scenario, there is a need to design a comprehensive strategy comprising innovative technology, policy support, infrastructural development and appropriate institutional arrangements, including reforms in the financial sector.

Technology

The share of non-food grain commodities in the total value of agriculture has already crossed the fifty percent level, but it is not getting the required attention and resources. It needs to be corrected by reprioritizing R&D portfolio for agriculture. There is a strong case for allocating relatively higher research priorities to horticulture sector based on their rising demand and higher contribution to the agricultural growth in the country. Improved technologies can be targeted for high-value food commodities to increase their productivity, minimize post-harvest losses, enhance shelf-life and improve commodity traits as per consumers, preferences (like shape, color, size, nutrition, etc.). The conventional research complemented with biotechnology is anticipated to pay high dividends from investments in R&D on high-value commodities. The research in these commodities has already shown its positive impact by evolving novel food commodities in non-traditional areas even in unconventional seasons. Higher resource allocations are required to promote agricultural diversification in the non-traditional areas and conduct R&D on their production, marketing and processing including their technical sustainability and economic viability.

A new set of policy framework is necessary to promote high-value commodities. Institutions like price support and assured procurement by the government may not be feasible for these commodities. A strong policy thrust is warranted to attract the private sector, promote agro-processing through special incentives and tax concessions, de-reserve important food commodities from the processing list of Small-Scale Industries, and strengthen financial and insurance management. The government needs to enhance resource allocations to marketing, storage and processing of high-value commodities.

India seems to have constrained its own potential by restrictive laws towards the development of high-value chain in this segment of agriculture. Giving preference to cooperatives or public sector firms in the past has restricted the entry of big players of private sector into the field of food management and food processing. This has to be rectified to unleash a revolution in the areas of value-addition to food commodities. The legal impediments restricting the entry of big private players to marketing, storage and processing facilities of agricultural commodities need to be modified. Several acts like Essential Commodities Act, Agricultural Produce Marketing Act, the Cold Storage Act, the Small-Scale Industry Reservation, etc., will have to be either abolished or modified with regard to agriculture. It was ironic to observe that it took 10 long years to de-license the dairy and sugar industries, and many others in agro-processing, including processing of groundnut and mustard oilseeds, reserved for Small-Scale Industries are still waiting.

Retail chain stores with FDIs have not been permitted as yet (as per the latest task force on FDIs) by the Government of India. The bureaucratic procedures are so cumbersome in the country that they discourage the entry of private sector and even mar the spirit of some positive policy directions.

Large investments in the retail chain sector, processing and storage of agricultural commodities could be encouraged, if legal environment is made transparent, friendly and attractive providing a level playing field to the private sector vis-à-vis cooperatives and public sector. These call for immediate corrective measures. The government should evolve a mechanism for a regular monitoring of the impact of changes in policies and institutions, particularly with regard to smallholders and underprivileged.

Infrastructural Development

Unlike cereals, the high-value food commodities require a different set of infrastructure. These being perishable in nature should reach the consumer or processed in a short period to minimize losses. In India, the existing infrastructure for agro-processing is inadequate but demand for the processed food has been increasing. Establishment of cold chains in large numbers, good road network, and a reliable and quality power supply are some of the pre-requisites for increasing production of high-value commodities and minimizing their post-harvest losses. Even the production of these commodities needs to be modernized to increase their productivity. Adoption of hi-tech agriculture and modernization of green houses require huge investments, and therefore the role of financial institutions is becoming important in meeting the changing needs. Investments in the basic infrastructure, especially roads and power, where private sector is reluctant to enter, will have to be made more attractive. The government programs on highways and rural roads are laudable, but power sector reforms depict a painful story of failure. Major institutional and price reforms are required in the power sector to plug leakages, raise efficiency, and generate surpluses to plough back into investments. The participation of private sector in generation, transmission and distribution of power will have to be expedited.

A broad scenario of the major cropping patterns in India can be presented by taking the major crops into consideration. To begin with, the south-westerly monsoon crops (kharif), bajra, maize, ragi, groundnut and cotton. Among the post-monsoon crops (rabi), wheat, sorghum (rabi) and gram can also be considered to be the base crops for describing the cropping patterns. With such an approach, the crop occupying the highest percentage of the sown area of the region is taken as the base crop and all other possible alternative crops which are sown in the region either as substitutes of the base crop in the same season or as the crops which fit in the rotation in the subsequent season, are considered in the pattern. Also these crops have been identified as associating themselves with a particular type of agro climate, and certain other minor crops with similar requirements are grouped in one category. For example, wheat, barley and oats, are taken as one category. Similarly, the minor millets are grouped with sorghum or bajra. Certain other crops, such as the plantation crops and other industrial crops are discussed separately.

Institutional Arrangements

A strong linkage amongst production, marketing and processing is a primary requirement for the promotion of high value commodities. The markets for these food commodities are thin, fragmented and lack basic facilities. Suitable institutional arrangements in the form of contract farming or cooperatives can integrate production with markets. Literature showed that innovative institutional arrangements can effectively link production and markets and improve the marketing efficiency. The innovative institutions are involving smallholders also in production and marketing of high-value commodities. A 'silent revolution, of innovative institutions is becoming visible and is sharing the benefits of emerging opportunities with the smallholders. Such arrangements augmented the income of smallholders and generated employment opportunities for them in the rural areas. The other advantage of new institutional arrangements is in research and extension services. Many institutions provide free extension and support services to the producers, as a part of the contract. The public extension system has been under criticism for its inefficiency in delivery of services and as a rising burden on the public exchequer and the government is looking out for alternative cost-effective models. Institutions such as contract farming and cooperatives can be considered such models to facilitate the process of privatization of public extension services at no cost to the public exchequer. Similarly, many private firms have established their own R&D system to undertake agricultural research, which was limited so far. The aim is to achieve the desired attributes of raw materials and acquire competitive edge. These developments in agribusiness could improve the interface between private and public sector research, and is a welcome augury. Many contracting firms arrange for credit and insurance (in terms of risk sharing) also for producers. In the poor economies where markets for high-value food products are underdeveloped and imperfect, such schemes have the potential to ease capital constraint on the public exchequer and provide protection against risks and uncertainties.

Reforms in Financial Sector

The role of financial institutions is critical in stepping-up investments in the key areas to promote high-value commodities and their processing. High-value food commodities need more working capital, and face higher risks in both production and marketing. Though some private sector banks are participating through innovative institutional arrangements in promoting these commodities, the overall credit scenario in Indian agriculture sector presents a grim picture. The commercial banks are saddled with excess liquidity while farmers have to rely on informal sources of finance for almost 45 percent of their requirements and that too at interest rates much higher (normally two to three times) than charged by the commercial banks. Schemes like 'Kisan Credit Cards, are welcome steps and could increase the credit flow to agriculture manifold by facilitating credit through processors, input dealers, etc. Such schemes will revolutionize the agricultural financing if the government provides due policy support. To harness the emerging opportunities in the high-value food segment, it is essential to create a congenial environment by strengthening vertical coordination between farmers, processors and retailers (farm-firm-fork linkages). It is essential to involve the smallholders in such a transformation of agricultural systems and protect their interest through policy changes and/or institutional arrangements. Though the smallholders are efficient producers, they need reduction in their transaction costs and minimization of risks for riding the wave of globalization and becoming competitive internationally. India has to graduate from producing low-value raw commodities to high-value and processed commodities by adding value and developing brand equity through participation of smallholders and contributions from the private sector.

Bhalla and Singh, (2009) has rightly observed that "Agricultural growth during 1990-93 to 2003-06 reflects the impact of economic reforms on agricultural performance. The most important feature of this period is that agricultural growth decelerated sharply at the all-India level and in all regions. At the all-India level, the output growth decelerated to 1.74% pa during 1990-93 to 2003-06 compared with a growth rate of 3.37% pa during 1980-83 to 1990-93. At the regional level, during the same period, the growth rate of agricultural output decelerated from 3.55% to 1.58% pa in the north-western region, from 3.61% to 1.00% pa in the eastern region, from 3.27% to 3.15% pa in the central region and from 3.41% to only 0.48% pa in the southern region. All states except Gujarat, and to some extent, Maharashtra registered a sharp decline in their output growth rates in the post-reform period. Gujarat was an exception because this state registered a very high output growth rate of 5.33% pa during the post-reform period compared with a growth rate of only 0.90% pa during the immediate pre-reform period. This remarkable performance was primarily because of the very rapid spread of BT cotton in the state during the last triennium. The main reason for the deceleration of growth during the post-reform period was a visible deceleration in investment in irrigation and other rural infrastructure".

It should be borne in mind that agricultural Sector is the mainstay of the rural Indian economy around which socio-economic privileges and deprivations revolve. Any change in its structure is likely to have a corresponding impact on the existing pattern of social equity. Sustainable agricultural production depends on the judicious use of natural resources (soil, water, livestock, plant genetic, fisheries, forest, climate, rainfall, and topography) in an acceptable technology management under the prevailing socio-economic infrastructure. Various research studies and policy papers highlight that the Indian Agricultural sector faces resource constraints, infrastructure constraints, institutional constraints, technology constraints, and policy induced limitations. To achieve sustainable agricultural development, it is essential to combine natural resources, capital resources, institutional resources, and human resources (i.e. to optimally utilize the agricultural resources). As an enabling technology, Information Technology (IT) plays an important role in the rapid economic growth and social transformation in developing countries.

With the basic thrust on higher growth in food grain production and other agricultural commodities, increase in productivity and efficient use of resources in agriculture has received special emphasize all through the process of the development, since independence. Sustainable agricultural production depends on the judicious use of natural resources (soil, water, livestock, plant genetic, fisheries, forest, climate, rainfall, and topography) in an acceptable technology management under the prevailing socio-economic infrastructure. Food and Agriculture Organization (FAO) has formulated the following definition for sustainable development in the context of agriculture, forestry and fisheries:

"Sustainable development is the management and conservation of the natural resource base and the orientation of technological and institutional change in such a manner as to ensure the attainment and continued satisfaction of human needs for the present and future generations. Such sustainable development (in the agriculture, forestry and fisheries sectors) conserves land, water, plant and animal genetic resources, is environmentally non-degrading, technically appropriate, economically viable and socially acceptable".

Promoting agricultural diversification towards high-value commodities, doing value-addition through their processing and creating appropriate markets for them can be used as effective measures to alleviate rural poverty, generate rural employment and conserve natural resources in the niche areas.

REFERENCE

Bhalla, G.S. and Gurmail Singh (2009), "Economic Liberalisation and Indian Agriculture: A State-wise Analysis", *Economic & Political Weekly*, December 26, No 52.

8

Reforms in Agriculture Sector and Food Security in India

M.P. Singh & Vimal Shankar Singh

Food is essential for the survival of human beings. In the Gita, Lord Krishna has stated that creatures of entire universe are created by food grains and food grains are produced from agriculture with rainfall.[1] It means agriculturists are akin to God. Further, Bhishma Pitamah states – agriculturists as 'Annadata, (who provides food) and agriculture as 'Ratnagarbha, (who bears ratnas, here as food grains)[2].

The survival of mankind depends on food, which is reflected in food security. Food security is defined as the physical and economic access for all people at all times to enough food for an active, healthy life with no risk of losing such access and as such is directly connected with livelihood in the developing countries. Amitava Mukherjee is of the view that a nation or a community or a household is considered to be food-secured or free from hunger provided food is available all times, i.e., there is enough food in the system, available food in the system should also be culturally accepted, people have enough purchasing power to buy culturally accepted food and have physical access to food, i.e., there must be a place where people can buy food. Food should also have nutritional value for a healthy-life, people should access to portable water for proper absorption of food by the body. Mukherjee emphasizes that in case of any of these conditions or some combinations thereof are violated food security is doubtful and hunger sets in.[3]

In this paper, an attempt has been made to examine the effects of reform measures launched in agriculture in India on food security and suggest remedial measures to make effective food security.

Reform Measures

Before Independence India was facing the acute shortage of food, hunger and malnutrition. Standard of the living of the common masses was very low and they were the victim of food insecurity. This situation of food insecurity continued even after the Independence. Consequently, the Government formulated food policy and proceeded to green revolution. The objectives of the food policy were to avoid famines and open under nutrition, to provide remunerative prices to the farmers, to encourage farmers to use modern inputs and technology, to stabilize prices, to provide price support to the farmers, where rapid fall in food grains prices was occurring, to maintain food prices through administrative measures, to supply food rains to poor masses at below market prices and to build and maintain the buffer stock of the food grains, etc. Government of India also adopted a national nutritional policy in 1993 for food security. Public distribution system (PDS) was introduced as a safety met to the poor to ensure that food grains reach to the common people at subsidized prices. Similarly, in order to encourage farmers to produce more and protect them from the falling prices of the products, minimum support price was introduced by the Government of India.

Recent Measures

In order to raise food production and productivity, Government of India has initiated and strengthened a number of measures, such as, support prices for food items, improvement in irrigation facilities; encouragement to capital formation in agriculture sector, credit support to agriculture, i.e., Kisan Credit Card, revamping of cooperative credit structure; agriculture insurance, weather based crop insurance, rehabilitation package for distressed farmers, reforms in agricultural marketing and some new initiatives like National Food Security Mission, Rastriya Krishi Vikas Yojana, National Policy for farmers and so on.

An Evaluation of Agricultural Reforms

Technological changes introduced by the Government of India and implemented by farmers, brought the country from hunger to hunger free. This is a spectacular achievement in agricultural sector. In 1950-51 the total production of food grains was 50 million tonnes, which increased to 82 million tonnes in 1960-61 and it had increasing trend up to 1999-2000, being 209.8 million tonnes. Thereafter, it indicated a fluctuating trend. Since 2001-2002 the production of food grains showed stagnation at around 210 to 216 million tonnes.

Similar trend in observed in case of productivity of food grains. For instance, it was 710 Kg. per hectare in 1960-61 which increased to 1734 Kg. per hectare in 2001-02. No doubt it is the result of our agricultural reform measures. But, thereafter it showed fluctuating trends and it increased from 1734 Kg per hectare in 2001-02 to mere 1750 Kg per hectare in 2006-07, revealing stagnation.

The stagnation in agricultural production and productivity can be attributed to the factors, such as, deterioration in technological progress, gross irrigated area, area under food and vegetables, total cropped area, net sown area, cropping intensity, terms of trade, NPK use, etc., which can be well expressed with the help of the Table 1.

The Table indicates that except credit supply, the other factors responsible for agricultural output growth have shown deterioration. For instance, the sue of technology showing potential of new varieties of paddy, rapeseed, mustard, groundnut, wheat and maize has declined from 3.3 per cent per year during 1980-81 to 1990-91 to 0.0 per cent per year during 1996-97 to 2005-06. Likewise, public sector net fixed capital stock also went down from 3.9 per cent per year to

1.4 per cent per year during the same corresponding years. Consumption of electricity in agriculture became negative (-0.5 per cent) during 1996-97 to 2005-06 from 14.1 per cent during 1980-81 to 1990-91. Growth rate of terms of trade shows the similar trend from 0.2 per cent per year during 1980-81 to 1990-91 to -1.7 percent year during 1996-97 to 2005-06. Total cropped area and net shown area also went down from 0.4 per cent to -0.1 per cent and from -0.1 per cent to -0.2 per cent respectively during the same corresponding periods. Growth rates in cropping intensity and gross irrigated area also declined. Rapid decline is observed in use of NPK from 8.2 per cent to 2.3 per cent during the corresponding years. On the other hand growth rate in credit supply has increased substantially from 3.7 per cent per year during 1980-81 to 1990-91 to 14.4 per cent per year during 1996-97 to 2003-04. On the whole, the growth trend shows rapid decline with the exception of credit supply and it is causing serious deficit to food security.

Table 1: Decennial Growth Trend in Area, Inputs Use, Credit and Capital Stock in Agriculture During 1980-81 to 2003-04 (Percent/Year)

Period	*1980-81 to 1990-91*	*1990-91 to 1996-97*	*1996-97 to 2005-06*
Technology[a]	3.3	2.8	0.0
Public sector net fixed capital stock	3.9	1.9	1.4b
Gross irrigated area	2.3	2.6	0.5[b]
Electricity consumed in agriculture	14.1	9.4	-0.5[c]
Area under fruits and vegetables	5.6	5.6	2.7[c]
Private sector net fixed capital stock	0.6	2.2	1.2[b]
Terms of trade	0.2	1.0	-1.7[b]
Total net fixed capital stock	2.0	2.1	1.3[b]
NPK use	8.2	2.5	2.3
Credit supply	3.7	7.5	14.4[b]
Total cropper area	0.4	0.4	-0.1
Net sown area	-0.1	0.0	-0.2
Cropping intensity	0.5	0.4	0.1

a Yield potential of new varieties of paddy, rapeseed/mustard, groundnut, wheat, maize

b Up to 2003-04, c Up to 2004-05

Source: Economic Survey, 2007-08, page No.160.

In order to meet the food shortage, Government of India has to import food items like cereals and cereal preparations, amounting to Rs.181 crores in 1960-61, which increased to Rs. 213 crores in 1970-71 and declined to Rs.182 crores in 1990-91. It was still amounting to Rs.159 crores even in 2005-06. This may increase in future keeping in view the growth of population and if production and productivity are not increased. It will aggravated the picture of food insecurity, which would be a great challenge before mankind.

Although food security largely depends on production and productivity of food items but other factors like distribution, balanced diet, purchasing power, food policies and poverty, etc., are also important.

Another concern of food security is related to the public distribution system. Though the PDS has benefited both the poor and non-poor, but failed to achieve the desired level. The supply of subsidized food grains through PDS has not come out as improvement in household level food security. Self-sufficiency of food grains at national level and availability of food grains at affordable cost at local level have not gone into household level food security for the poor. It shows ineffectiveness of PDS system, due to faulty and corrupt distribution system. This problem is to be considered seriously.

Likewise, poverty is another cause and effect of food insecurity in India. It is reflected in terms of low purchasing power. In India, in 2007 there were about 20 per cent people living below poverty line. If we take $2 PPP a day as the world standard of indicating poverty, there is high incidence of poverty (about 80 per cent) in India.

As far as undernourishment of the people is concerned, the share of undernourished people in total population is still very high. Another problem relating to food security in India is lack of balanced diet to the masses. Balanced diet provides nutrition. Nutrition is obtained from cereals, pulses, fruits, vegetables, milk and milk products, sugar, fats and oils, flesh, etc. Further, balanced diet is influenced by a number of factors, such as, economic, geographical and traditional factors, food habits and attitudes, education, preferences, prestige and religion, etc.

Women,s and men,s food consumption can be seen from the Table 2. The Table 2 shows that 53 per cent men and women consume pulses and beans daily and around 9.6 per cent occasionally, while 68.1 gram pulses per day are required for balanced diet, which is not obtained by them. Likewise, milk or curd, which is another important nutrient providing item, is consumed by about 43 per cent of the people and about 9 per cent of population never consumes milk or curd, while for balanced diet 189.4 gms. per day are required. Similarly, about 13 per cent people of the country consume fruits daily and 3 per cent never consume it, while 39.6 gm are required per day per person for balanced diet. Men are less likely than women to completely abstain from eating chicken, meat, fishy or egg. On the whole, 33 per cent of women and 24 per cent of men are vegetarians. In India, people are taking cereals, vegetables, milk and milk products more than the required magnitude for a balance diet due to less availability of pulses and other food items.

Table 2: Women's and Men's Food Consumption Percent Distribution of Women Age 15-49 and Men Age 15-49 by Frequency of Consumption of Specific Foods, India, 2005-06

Type of food	*Frequency Of Consumption*						
	Daily	*Weekly*	*Occasionally*	*Never*	*Total*	*Number*	*Requirements in gm. for a balanced diet of women & men*
			WOMEN				
Cereals							266.0
Milk or Curd	39.8	15.6	33.2	11.4	100.0	124,385	189.4
Pulses or beans	52.7	36.8	9.6	0.9	100.0	124,385	68.1
Dark green leafy vegetables	64.2	28.7	6.8	0.3	100.0	124,385	116.4
Fruits	12.7	27.2	56.6	3.5	100.0	124,385	39.6

Eggs	3.5	28.8	32.9	34.8	100.0	124,385	-
Fish	6.3	21.9	34.3	37.5	100.0	124,385	-
Chicken or meat	0.9	21.8	42.4	35.1	100.0	124,386	37.6
Fish or chicken/ meat	6.8	28.5	32.0	32.6	100.0	124,385	
			MEN				
Milk or Curd	36.7	20.5	25.8	7.0	100.0	69,751	
Pulses or beans	52.1	38.6	8.4	0.9	100.0	69,751	
Dark green, leafy vegetables	59.1	34.5	6.0	0.4	100.0	69,751	
Fruits	13.1	34.4	50.0	2.6	100.0	69,751	
Eggs	5.2	36.1	35.3	23.3	100.0	69,751	
Fish	6.2	25.1	38.2	30.5	100.0	69,751	
Chicken or meat	1.2	27.1	46.0	25.6	100.0	69,751	
Fish or chicken/ meat	6.9	34.1	35.1	23.9	100.0	69,751	

Source: National Family Health Survey -3, India and Food and Nutrition Board, Department of Food, Government of India.

Unbalanced diet creates several deficiencies in men and women like low height, weight and anemia. The nutritional status of women, according to NFHS -3 shows that 11.4 per cent of women are having height below 145 cm. and 35.6 per cent of women are having below normal Body Mass Index (from 18.5 to 24.9) aging 15-49 years. As against this 34.2, per cent of men are below the normal BMI of the same age group. Consumption of unbalanced diet in India is causing any anemia in women (55.3 per cent) and in men (24.2 per cent) in the age group of 15-49 (NFHS-3, pp. 304-312).

Conclusion and Policy Prescription

In fact, In India, production and productivity have almost

stagnated due to decline in total cropped area, cropping intensity, NPK and electricity consumption, public and private sectors, net fixed capital stock, gross irrigated area, deterioration in terms of trade, etc. Demand for nutritious food is increasing with the increase in the purchasing power of middle and high income groups. This demand is met by eating more cereals, milk and milk products and vegetables and pressure is mounting on these food articles. With the decline in poverty and increase in population, demand for food and micro nutrients will further increase resulting in to inflation which will deteriorate the already low standard of living of poor masses. This necessitates second green revolution with the help of research and development. Side by side, emphasis should be given to use the flowing water by linking of rivers rather than drawing of water from the ground. The latter reduces the water level and makes the land infertile.

PDS should be strengthened and improved by streamlining the administrative machinery. Inflation in food articles can be tackled by creating food chain with neighbouring countries and whole hearted effort should be made to arrest climatic change by afforestation and limiting the emissions of green house gases. The greatest effort should be made to reduce population growth.

REFERENCES

1. GITA, Adhyay-3 and Shloka -14.
2. Bhishma Pitamah was an Ancient Thinker. He was in Mahabharata period. Quoted from Ghildiyal Achutananda Prachin Bhartiya Arthik Vicharak, p.157. Publisher Vivek Ghildiyal Bandhu, Sigra, Varanasi, 1972.
3. Amitava Mukherjee, 'Micro-Level Hunger in Contemporary India: Perspectives of the Hungry', *The Indian Economic Journal*, April-June 2001-02, Vol. 49, Number 4, p.2.
4. W.T.O. Committee on Agriculture, Special Session on Negotiations on WTO Agreement on Agriculture, Proposal by India in Areas of Food Security, Jan. 15, 2001, pp.1-5.
5. Hans Lofgren & Alan Richards. Food Security, Poverty and Economic Policy in the Middle East & North Africa. T.M.D. International Food Policy Research Institute, Washington D.C.,

20006, U.S.A. Feb.2003, MMD Discussion Number 111, pp.1-2.

6. M.S. Swaminathan. 'Food and Environment-Walking the Tightrope', Forum of Free Enterprise, Mumbai, 20 Jan., 2001, p.5.
7. FAO, 2000.
8. *Economic & Political Weekly*, July 10, 2004, p. 3122.
9. M.P. Singh & Vimal Shankar Singh, 'The Economy of U.P.: Population, Food and Nutrition', *Economy of Uttar Pradesh: Emerging Challenges*, edited by Dr. Madhuri Srivastava, Department of Economics, B.H.U., I.E.A., 87th Annual Conference, Dec. 21-23, 2004, pp. 122-130.
10. Amitava Mukherjee, *Op.Cit.* pp. 1823.
11. Planning Commission, Ninth Five Year Plan (1997-2002), Vol.2, p.529.
12. *Ibid*, 529.
13. FAO, 2002.
14. Sachin Chaturvedi, 'Regional Cooperation for Poverty Alleviation and Food Security in South Asia' RIS, Dec.2004, p.10.
15. G. Kalloo, Convocation Address, 17th Convocation Address, Institute of Agricultural Sciences, As a part of 87th Convocation of the B.H.U., Varanasi, dated 12.3.2005, pp.4-11.
16. M.S. Swaminathan, *op.cit.*, p. 19.

9

Food Security—Agricultural Development in India

R. Kumar

Introduction

The World Food Day celebrated every year on 16 October gives an impetus to food security, but the major challenges are to be surpassed for human welfare. Food security means an access by all people, at all times to enough food for an active, healthy life. It is a basic right of every one to adequate diet. At present, food security in India is insecure and may probably collapse in future, because food is not available with the recommended quantity of nutrients and the number of malnourished/under nourished persons is increasing everyday. Climate change and agriculture are interrelated and climate change over the next century may have significant effects on crop production and food availability.

Food security involves physical availability of food to the entire population in the country. People have enough purchasing power so that they can acquire the food they need. To help the poor sections, the Government of India introduced the Targeted Public Distribution system and adopted dual price mechanism. But due to political pressure, the Government adopted universal PDS. The result was that the non-poor also began to benefit and the poor are not able to enjoy the benefit of PDS.

Dantwala (1976) stated that agricultural performance in the pre-independence period was far from satisfactory. This was clearly stated in George Blyn's study of agriculture between 1891 and 1947. However, he also noted that in 1976 in spite of the tremendous increase in population after independence, this backward agriculture has been able to provide, with marginal imports a per capita availability of about 450 grams per day. But He warned that by the end of the century, India's population will be about 1,000 million. The availability of food will be become insufficient Deshpande (2004), Growth in productivity does not induce area allocation as a rule, but there are instances where area under crops has increased keeping in view productivity growth. Second, the emphasis on foodgrains has been going down over the decades and more sharply during the later part of the five decades. Consequently, the area allocations towards commercial crops are increasing.

More recently, Swaminathan (2001) says because of our policy of ensuring minimum support price to basic food crops through the food corporation of India as well as state food corporations, the production of wheat and rice increased steadily on the flip side he says we now have as many children, women and men suffering from poverty induced hunger as the entire population.

Vyas (2006) notes that additions to the output have been realized by increases in yield per hectare rather than by an expansion of cultivated area, latter has remained more or less stable. It can be well appreciated that to obtain increase in production by intensive agriculture is more difficult than raising additional output with the expansion of cultivable area.

Ninth Five Year Plan (1997-2002) emphasizing this very point states: "One of the first effort of the country was to build up a food security system to ensure that the threat of famine no longer stalks the country. The fact that the country has not witnessed famine and acute starvation on a massive scale in the last five decades is the most eloquent testimony for the success of these efforts.

Climate change may affect food systems in several ways ranging from direct effects on crop production (e.g. changes in rainfall leading to drought or flooding, or Warmer or cooler temperatures leading to changes in the length of growing season), to change in markets, food prices and supply chain infrastructure. The relative importance of climate change for food security differs between regions. For example, in South Africa climate is among the most frequently cited drivers of food insecurity because it acts both as an underlying on going issue and as a short – lines shock. The low ability to cope with shocks and to mitigate long-term stresses means that coping strategies that might be available in other regions are unavailable or inappropriate.

The impact of climate change on agriculture is therefore likely to lead to a loss of stability in productivity and an over all decline in food production. Unless urgent action is taken, climate change will undoubtedly worsen global food security and dramatically increase the number of people facing hunger and malnutrition. Current estimates indicate that climate change could put 63 million more people at risk of hunger by 2020. Such efforts must necessarily focus on the 500 million small holder farmers' world wide that currently support around 2 billion people, or one third of the world's population. Increasing their productivity is essential not only to secure the food and nutrition needs of these farmers, but also of the millions of people who depend on them.

Looking Future

Food security is determined by food availability, food access and is interlinked with livelihood. To meet the UN millennium development goal of reducing the number of hungry people to half by 2015, there is a need to bridge the huge gap between attainable yield and average yields harvested by the farmers especially in developing countries under fragile environment.

Slow agricultural growth is a concern for policy makers as two-thirds of India's population depend on rural employment for a living. Current agricultural practices are neither economically nor environmentally sustainable and India's yields for many agricultural commodities are low. Poorly maintained irrigation system and almost universal lack of good extension service are main factors responsible. Farmer's markets is hampered by poor roads, rudimentary market infrastructure, and about 360 million people, 40 percent of India's population, live in chronic poverty consuming less than 80 percent of minimum energy requirements. Integrated farming system agro processing and renewable energy, are essential both to meet food production targets for increasing food and nutritional security.

The concept of food security does not encompass merely in the boundary of food production alone but also cover livelihood security, poverty alleviation and economic capacity of the people so that they can buy food. Food security also covers access to portable water; health care for all sections particularly children, females and non-working aged people. Food security ensures availability of food for everybody at every time with adequate quantity, quality and variety of cereals with economic accessibility. Food security covers health care through assurance of employment. The green revolution in India has increased food grains production to large extent through yield enhancing technology, support services and infrastructure.

Need of Food Security

The need for food security arises primarily due to the fluctuations in food production and non-availability of sufficient food from domestic sources. Large proportion of the world's underfed population starves not because of general food shortage but because of the insufficient access to food shortage, the insufficient access to food supplies and insufficient income to purchase good. Amartya Sen, in his scholarly work on the great Bengal famine, has attributed the death of millions to the inadequacy, or rather non existence of an official policy, to cope with the food supply crisis.

Poverty is the lack of purchasing power, therefore, becomes the crucial consideration in attainment of food security. As most of the poor people in developing countries including India dwell in the countryside the policies relating to rural development in its comprehensive from encompassing development of agriculture, health, nutrition, education, literacy, etc, would alone lead to enduring solution to the problem of food insecurity, poverty, unemployment and social tension in the region.

World Food Security

The world is facing many challenges; prominent among these are sustainable development, environmental degradation, climate change and food security for growing population. On a global level, food security for all requires that the supply of food be adequate to meet the total demand for food. While this is a necessary condition for the achievement of food security, it is by no means sufficient. It is estimated achievement of food security, it is by no means sufficient. Although currently enough food is supplied globally, it is estimated that in 1990-92 some 893 million people in the developing countries had inadequate access to food, fundamentally because they lacked the ability to purchase, that is, they lacked the means to exert effective demand. This figure reflects a substantial degree of progress since the beginning of the 1970s; the number has declined in absolute terms from about 917 million and in relative terms from 35 percent of the population of developing countries to 21 percent, mainly as a result of progress in East Asia and parts of South Asia, such as India and Pakistan. The situation is most serious in Africa where the number of chronically undernourished people in the sub-Saharan countries doubled more over the period according to FAO estimates.

The world's population is expected to grow from 6 billion people in 2000 to 7.5 billion people in 2020. Studies suggest that global agricultural production could be maintained relative to expected baseline levels over the next 100 years with moderate climate change. However, regional effects experience reduced output even if they take measures to adapt. Availability of land for farming is on the decline, and water for agriculture and other uses is increasingly scarce. Many other countries turned increasingly to imports to feed their people, either because domestic production was too low or income rose far faster than population escalating demand for future food and feed grains. Although developing countries will account for most of the increase in global demand for cereals, growth in their demand is not as rapid as it was earlier. Diversifying diet and slower population growth in developing countries, growth in cereal demand of developing world is projected to decline from 2.3 percent a year in 1974-97 to 1.3 percent in 1997-2020. The world demand for meat and poultry is predicted to rise by more than 55 and 40 percent respectively between 1997 and 2020.

Food Security in India

Improving the food security is an issue of considerable importance for the developing countries like India where millions of people suffer from hunger and malnutrition. Food availability and stability were considered good measures of food security till the seventies and the achievement of self-sufficiency was according high priority in the food policies of developing courtiers, like India. Achieving food security has been the overriding goal of agricultural policy in India. Though India was successful in achieving self-sufficiency by increasing its food production and also improved its capacity to cope with year-to-year fluctuations in food production, it could not solve the problem of chronic household food insecurity.

The concept of food security has undergone considerable changes in recent years. India is one of the few countries which have experimented with a broad spectrum of programmers for improving food security. It has already made substantial progress in terms of overcoming transient food insecurity by giving priority to self-sufficiency in food grains and through procurement and public distribution of food grains, employment programmers, etc. However, despite a significant reduction in the incidence of poverty chronic food insecurity persists in a large proportion of India's population. India has solved the problem of food security which is reflected in mounting buffer stocks, but there are millions of food insecure and undernourished people in India. The limitation is not food supply, but its distribution. The single most important implication of India's rapid population growth during the second half of the twentieth century was the threat it posed to national food security.

In view of the upsurge in food grain production recorded in the India to increase the investment in agriculture through Rashtriya Krishi Vikas Yojana with an investment at about Rs. 25,000 Cores and increasing the reach of technologies to relativity less favored districts through national food security commission with an investment of about Rs. 5,000 Cores in the 11-plan, the projected demands are likely to be achieved as a short term measures. However to maintain the productivity levels of most productive regions in sustainable manner and to avoid the over exploitation of natural resources and to maintain the growth in food grain production, alternate food grain basket need to be created as several highly productive regions in the country which change preformed exceedingly well in the past are a experiencing soil fatigue and heavy pressure on natural resources.

India has adopted two sorts of measures for food security one is the measure adopted after independence and another is recent measures. By and large, the measures introduced by the Government of India are formulation of food policy, national nutritional policy, PDS minimum support price, improvement in irrigation facilities credit support to agriculture including revamping of cooperative credit structure, weather based cropped insurance, establishment of national food security mission, Rashtriya Krishi Vikas Yojana and formulation of national policy for farmers and so on.

Public Distribution System in India

All State Governments run public Distribution System (PDS) with the help of Government of India. Beside central government store grains for poverty alleviation and employment generation through food for work programme especially during famine, drought, flood and other natural calamities. In the Targeted Public Distribution System (TPDS) there is a provision to supply 35 kg of food grains every month to the poor households on subsidized prices. Similarly, under the Antyodayal Annapurna Yojana, there is a provision to provide 35 kg of food grains on the very cheap rate (Rs. 2 per kg rice and Rs. 2 per kg wheat) to the families living below poverty line (BPL). The provision of mid-day meals for school going children and the beneficiaries of National Old Age Pension (NDAP) provide relief to the poor parents and aged people. Government also provide nutritious dose to the pregnant women in rural and urban aware through Anganwadi centers, which run under the integrated Child Development Scheme. Sampoorna Grameen Rozgar Yojana (SGRY) also provides food security to the people along with employment opportunity.

Procurement of Foodgrain

The Food Corporation of India in association with the state procuring agencies procures the foodgrain and distributes them to the family Ration card holder through the fair price shops in the different states. Table 1 below presents the procurement of rice and wheat by the Government of India from 1995-1996 to 2004-2005.

Table 1: Procurement of Rice and Wheat (Million Tonnes)

Year	*Rice*		*Wheat*	
	Qty	*Percentage*	*Qty*	*Percentage*
1995-1996	10.07	-26.55	12.33	3.88
1996-1997	12.97	29.80	8.16	-33.82
1997-1998	15.59	20.20	9.30	13.97
1998-1999	12.60	19.18	12.65	36.02
1999-2000	18.23	44.68	14.14	11.78
2000-2001	22.13	16.73	16.35	15.63
2002-2003	16.42	-25.80	17.05	-7.66
2003-2004	22.83	39.04	15.80	-17.06
2004-2005	14.34	-59.20	16.80	6.33

Source: Department of Food Public Distribution System. As on January 14, 2005.

Consumption Requirement and Production Prospects

The consumption requirement alone for food grains for 1200 million population likely to happen in 2011, on normative requirement at 182.50 kg/cu/per year, comprising 167.90 kg cereals and 14.6 kg pulses, are recommended by National Institute of Nutrition (NIN), Hyderabad, works out to 204.74 million tones which be about 234 million tones, assuming seed, feed and wastage, as 12.5 percent of the gross output. The planning commission also estimated the food grain requirement to the tone of 236 million tones by 2011-12.

Table 2: The Production of Food Grains

Year	*Rice*	*Wheat*	*Coarse Cereals*	*Pulses*	*Total food grains*
1950-51	20.58	6.46	15.38	8.41	50.82
1966-67	30.44	11.39	24.05	8.35	74.23
1976-77	41.92	29.01	28.88	11.36	111.17
1986-87	60.56	44.32	26.83	11.71	143.42
1993-97	81.74	69.35	34.10	14.24	199.44
2006-07	93.35	75.81	33.92	14.20	217.28
2007-08	96.43	78.40	40.73	15.11	230.67

Source: Economic Survey of Various years.

The production of food grains increased from 50.82 million tones in 1950–51 the highest ever of 230.67 million tones in 2007-08. This is remarkable achievement and about in million tones higher over the production of 2006-07. This is also the highest production gains over an immediate previous year's production since with very marginal increase in the (0.8 million) the highest every yearly increased of about 39 million tones was recorded in 2003-04 but with additional 10 million the more arrange over 2002-03, the year which was marked by severe drought in most parts of the country. Over the years, the food grains production has increased over 4.5 times, rice over 4 times, wheat about 12 times and pulses over 2 times.

Demand for Food

The food management is to strike a balance between the

supply of and the demand for various food items which would provide stability to the economy. It is also extremely important to know the pattern of demand of various food items that would prevail in the future. The table presents the data relating to current production and demand projection of various commodities. It is seen from the table that in case of commodities like wheat, all cereals and meat-fish, we have already surpassed the projected demand for the year 2010. However, it has to be noticed that we have a long way to go to meet the targets for the year 2020. Each increment to the finishing level of production may be costly given the lower intensity of irrigation and declining capital formation in agriculture.

Table: 3 Projections of Food Demand and the Supply for India

(in Million tonnes)

Sl. No.	*Food item*	*Current production 2006 - 2007*	*Demand Projection 2010*	*Demand Projection 2020*
1.	Rice	92.7	97.99	118.93
2.	Wheat	74.9	72.07	92.93
3.	All Cereals	201.9	181.12	221.11
4.	Pulses	14.2	14.58	19.53
5.	Food grains	216.1	195.69	240.64
6.	Milk & milk products	100	7.67	10.94
7.	Edible Oils	5.96	7.25	10.8
8.	Meat and fish	10.16	17.23	25.07
9.	Sugar	28.32	75.21	
10.	Fruit and Vegetables	186.9		

Source: Economic survey (2007-2008) Government of India.

Declining Per Capita Food Grain Availability in India

The per capita availability of food grains has fallen substantially during the last decade of reforms, and the maximum decline has taken place during the last five years. The population and food grain production growth per capita availability of food grain is presented growth, per capita availability of food grains. Although there is wide variability from one year to the next, broad trends can still be picked up from the figure showing multi-decade data. The early years of bounty from the green revolution period were followed by more gradual increase leading up to a peak of 186.2kg/person/year at national level in 1990-91. Since then, food security has steadily declined, throughout what is popularly referred to as the years of liberalization and 'reforms' as per 2001/ per capita availability of food grain is seen in the late 1970 s and early 1980 s, which was at lower stage of about 152 kg, at national level it is due to the fact that during the last decade, the food grain production grew at the rate of 1.60 percent annum at national level. Low growth rate during 1970–71 to 1980-81 was due to the low production base (due to drought). During overall period (1960-61 to 2000-01), the food grain production increased at the rate of 2.59 percent per annum at national level.

Table 4: Population and Foodgrain Production Growth in India

Year	*Population*	*Decadal population growth rate (%)*	*Cereals production (million tonnes)*	*Per capita food grain (%)*	*Growth rate of food grain production*
1961	43.92	21.51	69.32	171.10	-
1971	54.82	24.80	96.60	171.10	2.51
1981	68.52	25.00	111.96	166.00	2.24
1991	86.63	23.85	162.13	186.20	2.89
2001	102.70	21.35	185.20	151.90	1.60

It can be seen from the above table that India has made rapid progress in the production of food grains during last four decades. The annual growth rate of food production including non-cereal food increased from 2.51 the 1960s to 2.64 percent in the 1961s to 2.24 percent in the subsequent decade and further to 2.89 percent during the 1980s. Between 1960 and 1980 food production barely kept pace with the population but in the 1980 per capita food production increased at a satisfactory rate of 1.6 percent per annum. India achieved self sufficiency in the availability of food grains by the mid-seventies. The trend rate of food grains production improved from 2.5 percent during the 1960 s to 2.9 percent in the 1980s. It is particularly note worthy that India could build enough buffer stock to cope with year-to-year variations in food grain production.

Conclusion

India's population are steadily rising, production of food grains rose equally. Non-availability of cereals has gone up except in same years. But the government had to import large quantity of cereals from other countries to increase the net availability of cereals in the economy PDS should, therefore be reformed and made more efficient. The scheme of decentralized procurement of food grains should be encouraged and more states should be brought under its fold. All restriction on inter state movement of food grains should be removed. Public investments in agriculture have been declining for quite some years. In the context of international trade, there is an added urgency to reverse this trend and increase investment in Research, integrated market development, storage and warehousing facilities, road development etc. Public expenditure on research and technology infrastructure creation and rural development will raise our AMS without reduction commitments.

Conservation of grain varieties is important to invent newer ones that can adopt to environmental changes which is a necessity for food security. The degree of sustainability varies from state to state. States with a strong natural resource base may rank high in sustainability but may not be in a position to produce enough food. India needs another green revolution to bring food security to its billion plus population which will help to remove distress of farming community and to make agriculture globally competitive. Productivity needs to be enhanced in foodgrains, oilseeds, dairying and poultry and vegetables. Investments in technology, rural sector and agriculture has to be intensified which promise food security and poverty alleviation. Instead of concentrating only on rice and wheat, those food crops with potentials for exploitation must be focused. Agricultural infrastructure at local level should have to be revived and maintained properly for another sustainable green revolution.

REFERENCES

1. V. M. Rao (2008) : "Through Cloudy Glasses: Viewing Food Insecurity form the Top", *Economic and Political Weekly*, No. 20.
2. Verma, Renu (2007) : Agriculture: How to Make it Sustainable 'Economic Affairs' Vol. 52 (2) 2007.
3. Islam, S. (2007) : "Need of a New Revolution in Agriculture", *Agriculture Situation in India*, Vol. LXIV (5) New Delhi.
4. N. Deepa &Vanitha (2007) : "Food Security Old Issues, New Challenges and Emerging Opportunity", *Indian Economic Panorama*, Vol. 16(4).
5. Swaminathan, M.S. (2001) : "Food Security and Sustainable Development", *Current Science*, 81.
6. Dantwala, M.L., (1976) : "Agricultural Policy in India Since Independence", *Indian Journal of Agricultural Economics*, Vol. 31 (4).
7. Vyas, V.S., (2006) : India's Agrarian Structure, *Economic Policies and Sustainable Development*, New Delhi.
8. S.S. Kalamkar (2008) : "Food Security in India in Global Perspective", *Agricultural Situation in India*, Vol. LXV (5), August.
9. Awasthi (2007) : Food Security and Fertilizer - A Global Perspective, IFFCO - New Delhi.
10. Rajkumar & Gnanavelan : "WTO and Food security in India", 92nd IEA, Annual Conference Volume, School of Management, KIIT University, Bhubaneswar, Orissa, 27-29 Dec. 2009.
11. Government of India: Ninth Five Year Plan (1997–2002).

10

WTO and Indian Agriculture: The Implications for Food Security

K. Ramesh

Introduction

The World Trade Organisation (WTO) is the only international organisation dealing with the global rules of trade between nations. It basically ensures a free, smooth and predictable flow of trade. The trading system that is created by the WTO was developed through a series of trade negotiations held under various rounds of General Agreement on Trade and Tariff (GATT). The final round—the Uruguay Round (1986-94) - led to the creation of the WTO, which came into being in 1995. The basic objectives of this paper are to analyse the impact of freeing agricultural trade on the export and import of the agricultural commodities and thus on the area and production of major agricultural crops in the last decade and finally to analyse the fluctuations in the per capita net availability of food grains in the post-WTO period. Next section briefly reviews some of the relevant studies and section-3 explains the methodology and data sources. Section-4 analyses India's agricultural trade. Section-5 deals with the changes in the area and production of major crops in the last 28 years, followed by the analysis on food security in section-6 and the final section presents the conclusion.

Review of Literature

Many studies have attempted to trace the impact of WTO on the Indian agricultural sector and especially on food security. The study by Azad (1996) on the tribal households of Andra Pradesh showed that the market-oriented production though resulted in some improvement in overall food consumption, for about half of the households food security in fact deteriorated. The main impact was the weakened women's control over household food supply. Because, the market-oriented production resulted in non-food crop cultivation (contract farming) and therefore, the money income went to the hands of men in the households.

Bapna (1997) showed that in fast developing east-Asian countries food security improved but at the same time, several sections of people's food security was adversely affected. Particularly, the small and marginal palm tree growers in Malaysia were eased out due to large scale technological change following liberalisation.

Nayyar and Sen (1994) and Gill and Brar (1996) indicated that volatility in global farm prices will increase when countries like India get integrated with the world. Because, as India is the largest producer of many agricultural commodities, even a small volume of export will dampen the global price level. Gulati and Narayanan (2003) examined the global rice trade and concluded similarly saying that world agricultural markets are very thin and any sizable export by even one country will increase the international price volatility.

Bhattacharya and Pal (1999) concluded that export restrictions kept the domestic price level and thus reduced farm incentives and so, liberalisation will pave the way for increased supply of agricultural commodities. But, Desai and Namboodiri (1999) argued that increasing the supply of agricultural commodities would not be easy since, the price elasticity of agricultural supply is low. There is no any conclusive evidence on either side as far as the effect of WTO on food security is concerned.

Methodology and Data Sources

The impact of WTO on food security is analysed with the help of secondary data on India's agricultural trade, area and production of major food and non-food crops, procurement and off-take of major cereals and net availability of food grains. Time-series data on all these variables are taken since 1984-85 (except trade data which are from 1990-91). The data are classified into pre-WTO period (up to 1994-95) as Period-1 and post-WTO period (since 1995-96) as Period-2 and the whole period as Period-3. For all these periods, Compound Growth Rate (CGR), mean and Co-efficient of Variation (CV) have been calculated. Data are taken from various issues of Economic Survey and Agricultural Statistics at a Glance published by the Government of India.

Liberalisation and Agricultural Trade in India

In pursuant to the changing nature of global agricultural trade under WTO, the government announced a National Agricultural Policy in July 2000, which included measures aimed at 'structural, institutional, agronomics and tax reforms'. The Central Government took a lead in replacing the restrictive legislations such as Rice Milling Industries (Regulation) Act, 1958; Ginning and Pressing Factories Act, 1925; and Licensing, Price Control and Requisitioning under Cold Storage Order, 1965 etc. (Government of India, Ministry of Finance, 2001: p.170). Moreover, the government also introduced measures to liberalise agricultural trade in conformity with the WTO norms. These included removal of QRs, lowering of tariff rates, abolishing of licensing apart from other procedural simplifications.

Agricultural Exports

The impact of all these changes in the agricultural sector could be seen in the changes taken place in its trade. Table 1 presents the trade data on the export of agricultural commodities since 1990-91.

Table 1: India's Exports of Major Agricultural Commodities

(Percentage share in Total Agricultural Exports)*

Sl. No.	Commodity	Period-1 (1991-95) CGR	Mean	CV	Period-2 (1996-08) CGR	Mean	CV	Period-3 (1991-08) CGR	Mean	CV
1.	Rice (Non-Basmati)	120	1.9	63	-40	9.2	63	150	6.4	91
2.	Wheat	42	0.4	175	23	1.9	105	68	1.4	129
3.	Foodgrains	6.4	10.4	15	-1.2	18.2	28	14.6	15.2	37
4.	Tea	-11.7	12	38	-17.5	6.4	25	-5.6	8.6	46
5.	Coffee	18.1	5.0	34	-76	5.4	31	-2.4	5.3	30
6.	Tobacco	-11.4	4.0	32	5.3	3.2	25	-2.4	3.5	30
7.	Spices	3.6	4.4	7	2.9	5.5	20	1.8	5.1	20
8.	Cashew	5.7	8.4	8	Nil	6.6	23	-1.4	7.3	21
9.	Oil Meals	6.15	14.3	24	-8.0	9.1	41	4.7	11.1	39
10.	Fruits & Vegetables	-1.1	3.6	14	2.8	3.2	9	-0.6	3.3	12
11.	Processed Fruits	18.0	1.3	31	5.1	1.7	10	10.8	1.6	38
12.	Meat Preparation	6.1	2.7	11	4.0	3.6	19	6.0	3.3	21
13.	Marine Products	13.4	20.1	20	2.6	19.0	11	1.9	19.4	15
14.	Floricul. Products	20	0.4	175	8.3	0.4	25	30.7	0.4	1
15.	Total Agri. Exp.#	24.0	17.4	5.7	7.8	16.6	16.5	30.7	16.9	13.1

Note: * Based on Rupee Value of Exports. # Based on percentage share in Total Exports. CV in percentage.

Source: Calculated from the data taken from Agricultural Statistics At a Glance, various years.

The analysis shows that the CGR of rice export has come down dramatically in period-2 from period-1 though, the CGR of the whole period (period-3) has been higher than period-1. While the CGR has declined in period-2, the mean share of rice in total agricultural exports has increased quite considerably from 1.9 per cent in period-1 to 9.2 per cent in period-2 and the overall percentage too was quite high at 6.4 per cent. The CV during the two periods (1 and 2) also shows that the export of rice has been quite stable. The export trend of wheat, the other major cereal, is also similar. While the CGR has decreased in period-2, the mean share has gone up with lesser variability. The same trend is repeated in case of food grains which includes rice and wheat apart from others. Its mean share has gone up to 18.2 per cent in period-2 from 10.4 per cent in period-1. During the post-WTO regime, it is also clear that, export of fruits, vegetables, spices and floricultural products has gone up. These imply that the freeing of agricultural trade has led to increased export of major food grains on the one hand and on the other the CGRs of the share of horticultural and floricultural products have gone up.

Agricultural Imports

The arrival of WTO has also altered import of agricultural commodities. The changes in imports since 1990-91 are presented here.

Table 2: India's Imports of Major Agricultural Commodities

(Percentage share in Total Agricultural Imports)*

Sl.	Commodity	Period-1 (1991-95)			Period-2 (1996-08)			Period-3 (1991-08)		
No.		CGR	Mean	CV	CGR	Mean	CV	CGR	Mean	CV
1.	Rice	-19.0	1.8	72	Neg.	0.04	175	Neg.	0.7	164
2.	Wheat	-20.0	6.4	164	-12	3.8	116	-7.6	4.8	146
3.	Cereals Preparation	-16.1	6.1	57	-5.2	0.7	57	-7.0	2.8	122
4.	Pulses	-15.0	20.5	58	3.7	10.5	58	-4.7	14.4	67
5.	Milk & Cream	-13.3	0.7	83	-3.0	0.2	166	-10.0	0.4	130
6.	Cashew Nuts	1.1	15.0	29	-6.0	8.0	38	-2.6	10.6	45
7.	Nuts & Fruits	-8.1	7.4	23	-4.5	5.3	24	-4.6	6.1	29
8.	Sugar	940	7.8	220	-12.0	3.0	109	-6.0	4.9	214

9.	Oil Seeds	-16.0	1.0	144	-12.3	0.1	200	-7.5	0.5	222
10.	Vegetable Oil	-12.1	13.4	63	4.1	44.6	16	7.0	32.6	54
11.	Spices	225	0.8	177	22	2.1	33	280	1.6	75
12.	Total Agri. Import#	78.5	4.04	38.9	23.8	6.1	20.6	101.4	5.3	31.6

Note: * Based on Rupee Value of Imports. # based on percentage share in Total Imports.

Neg – Negligible. CV in percentage.

Source: Calculated from the data taken from Agricultural Statistics at a Glance, various years.

Table-2 shows that during the post-WTO period, the CGRs of only pulses, vegetable oil and spices have turned positive and the mean share of the last two have gone up sizably in this period. In case of spices, the mean share has increased from 0.8 per cent in period-1 to 2.1 per cent in period-2, while that of vegetable oil from 13.4 per cent to 44.6 per cent. The import of vegetable oil has increased quite considerably during period-2 which has pulled down the CV from 63 per cent in period-1 to 16 per cent in period-2. While the CGR of pulses has gone up from -15.0 per cent in period 1 to 3.7 per cent in period 2, though its mean share in total agricultural imports has come down from 20.5 per cent to 10.5 per cent. Other notable items of import were cashew nuts and other nuts and fruits. Though their mean share has come down, still it remains quite noticeable. Thus, trade liberalisation in the agricultural sector has led to sharp increase in the import of vegetable oils which now form about half of the total agricultural import. While this is encouraged in the name of efficient resource-use in some quarters, (Bhalla, 1995 and Gulati and Sharma, 1997) no doubt, it has affected the domestic processing industry.

GROWTH AND STABILITY OF MAJOR CROPS

Changes in Area under Major Crops

Liberalisation policy alters not only trade, but also cropping pattern. To trace those changes in the post-WTO period, cropping pattern data since 1980-81 are analysed here. Table-

3 explains the changes in the area under major food and non-food crops.

Table 3: CGR, Mean and CV of Area under Major Crops

Crops	*Period-1 (1981-95)*			*Period-2 (1996-08)*			*Period-3 (1981-08)*		
	CGR	*Mean*	*CV*	*CGR*	*Mean*	*CV*	*CGR*	*Mean*	*CV*
Rice	0.4	41.3	3.3	-0.1	43.5	3.6	0.	42.1	4.2
Wheat	1.0	23.7	4.2	0.7	26.2	3.7	0.8	24.6	6.3
Jowar	-1.8	14.8	11.5	-1.8	10.2	7.7	-1.7	13.1	20.4
Bajra	-0.8	10.7	8.4	1.3	9.4	8.5	-0.4	10.2	10.5
Maize	0.1	5.9	1.7	2.7	6.4	6.2	0.9	6.1	6.2
Coarse Cereals	-1.5	37.8	9.0	-0.04	31.0	11.6	-1.1	35.3	13.5
Gram	1.0	6.9	7.2	0.3	6.7	14.8	0.4	6.8	11.7
Pulses	0.2	23.0	3.5	1.1	22.1	6.5	0.4	22.7	5.1
Kharif crops	-0.6	80.1	3.8	0.05	73.4	3.4	-0.5	77.6	5.6
Rabi crops	0.8	45.8	2.9	0.7	48.7	5.8	0.65	46.9	5.2
Food grains	-0.2	125.8	2.4	0.3	121.7	3.4	-0.1	124.3	3.2
Groundnut	1.0	7.7	9.1	-2.2	6.8	9.4	-0.5	7.4	10.8
Rapeseed&Must.	3.1	4.8	21	-2.5	5.7	17.0	1.0	5.2	20.6
Soya bean	40.5	2.0	64.0	3.2	6.0	8.3	40.2	3.5	63.5
Sunflower	104	1.2	60.5	-0.6	1.6	22.6	66.0	1.4	47.0
Oil Seeds	2.9	21.4	15.4	-1.1	24.3	7.8	1.4	22.5	14.0
Cotton	0.1	7.5	5.3	-1.7	8.7	7.1	-0.1	7.9	9.5
Jute	-1.9	1.1	14.5	1.4	1.0	4.8	-0.8	1.0	12.4
Potato	3.1	0.9	11.0	2.6	1.3	5.5	3.6	1.0	19.4
Sugar Cane	3.0	3.3	9.1	-0.4	4.1	3.9	2.1	3.6	14.3
Onion	3.5	0.3	13.3	0.6	0.4	7.0	2.9	0.3	20.6
Tobacco	-1.0	0.4	10.0	-1.9	0.4	21.0	-1.1	0.4	15.0
Coconut	3.9	1.3	14.8	0.3	1.8	2.7	3.2	1.5	19.0
Non-food grains	2.8	53.6	12.4	0.4	65.9	1.6	2.3	57.5	14.0

Note: Mean Area in Million Hectares. CV in percentage.

Source: Calculated from the data taken from Agricultural Statistics at a Glance, various years.

There have been considerable changes in the area under food crops particularly, when compared between the two periods. The CGR of area under rice in period-2 has turned negative (-0.1 per cent) with variation going up marginally. In case of wheat though the positive nature of CGR has remained intact, the rate has decreased from 1.0 per cent in period-1 to 0.7 per cent in period-2. Nonetheless, in both these cases, the mean area allocated under these crops has gone up in period-2. Coarse cereals have not done any better since; the mean area has come down with higher variability in period-2 though the negative CGR has marginally decreased. The CGR of area under Kharif crops has turned positive from -0.6 per cent to 0.05 per cent but, the mean area has sizably reduced from 80.1 m.h. in period-1 to 73.4 m.h. in period-2. And the corresponding changes in the CGR of area under food grains are not quite remarkable. While the rate has turned positive in period-2 from -0.2 per cent to 0.3 per cent, the mean area has come down from 125.8 m.h. to 121.7 m.h. with an increased variability. On the other, the change in the CGR of area under non-food grains shows that though the rate has decreased from 2.84 per cent to 0.4 per cent, variability too has come down quite considerably during period-2, along with the improvement in the mean area from 53.6 m.h. to 65.9 m.h. These changes imply then increasing diversification of cultivating area towards the non-food crops, particularly at the cost of area under food grains.

Among non-food grains, oil seed crops have suffered. The CGRs of area under these crops have fallen quite sharply mainly due to liberalized imports, as noted above. Thus, only floricultural and horticultural crops are being brought under more cultivating area. The declining cultivating area under food crops need not be a cause for concern as long as the growth rate of production of food grains is maintained.

Changes in Production of Major Crops

Changes in cropping pattern do affect production of the crops concerned. Table-4 presents the analysis on CGR, mean and CV of production of major crops. There has been marked decline in the CGRs of production of the two basic food crops, rice and wheat. In case of the former the rate has decreased from 3.5 per cent and 1.4 per cent in period-1 and 2 respectively and 5.4 per cent and 1.8 per cent in case of

Table 4: CGR, Mean and CV of Production of Major Crops

Crops	Period-1 (1981-95)			Period-2 (1996-08)			Period-3 (1981-08)		
	CGR	Mean	CV	CGR	Mean	CV	CGR	Mean	CV
Rice	3.5	65.4	16.4	1.4	83.9	7.5	2.6	73.4	17.6
Wheat	5.4	49.4	16.8	1.8	69.3	6.1	4.1	56.9	21.2
Jowar	-0.9	10.9	12.8	-2.4	8.3	14.8	-1.2	9.9	18.7
Bajra	2.3	5.9	27.1	12.3	7.2	29.0	5.0	6.4	29.4
Maize	1.8	8.0	16.0	6.1	11.6	13.7	4.6	9.3	23.8
Coarse Cereals	0.2	30.1	12.0	3.3	31.5	11.2	1.3	30.6	11.7
Gram	3.2	4.8	14.6	1.8	5.3	17.3	1.4	5.0	16.4
Pulses	2.	12.5	8.8	2.6	13.2	11.3	1.8	12.8	10.0
Kharif crops	2.0	88.7	12.2	1.9	102.6	7.5	1.8	94.0	12.5
Rabi crops	4.9	68.9	15.8	1.9	95.3	7.0	3.8	78.8	20.4
Food grains	3.2	156.4	14.2	1.9	197.8	6.8	2.65	172.0	16.3
Groundnut	4.1	6.9	20.3	1.1	7.1	21.7	2.7	7.0	19.9
Rapeseed & Mustard	10.0	3.8	35.6	-0.3	5.3	17.0	6.4	4.4	32.1
Soya bean	52.8	1.7	82.0	6.0	6.1	18.3	70.1	3.4	73.6
Sunflower	11.0	0.6	66.7	-1.5	0.9	25.0	60.7	0.7	54.0
Oil Seeds	8.5	15.1	28.5	1.52	21.4	15.2	7.01	17.5	28.3
Cotton	4.6	8.8	21.6	0.8	11.5	16.5	4.0	9.8	23.0
Jute	0.7	8.6	16.3	3.0	10.7	8.3	1.5	9.4	17.0
Potato	5.3	13.5	20.0	2.8	22.2	11.3	6.1	16.8	30.0
Sugar Cane	5.2	205.6	17.0	-1.8	282.2	6.8	2.2	234.4	20.5
Onion	4.1	3.1	16.8	0.4	4.5	11.4	3.0	3.6	23.9
Tobacco	1.2	0.5	12.0	-1.1	0.6	20.0	0.1	0.5	15.1
Coconut	8.8	83.3	30.0	-1.0	125.6	3.0	4.7	99.2	28.8

Note: Mean in Million Tonnes [except Cotton and Jute (in Million Bales) and Coconut

(in '00 Million Nuts)] ; CV in percentage.

Source: Calculated from the data taken from Agricultural Statistics At a Glance, various years.

the latter. Nonetheless, mean production of both the crops has gone up in period-2 which has brought down the severity of variation. In case of coarse cereals, there has been a marked improvement in the CGR. It has gone up from 0.2 per cent to 3.3 per cent with a marginal increase in mean production. But the decline in the CGRs of the major cereals has been such that, they have pulled down the CGR of all three categories viz., Kharif, Rabi and total food grains. Decreasing area under food grains along with declining growth rate of production could spell a crisis as far as food availability is concerned, with the given rise in population.

Food Security Under WTO

Food security can be defined as the access by all people at all time to enough food for an active and healthy life. This implies that food should be available and the individuals should have entitlement to get food. However, mere availability of food at the national level leave alone at the international level does not guarantee food security at the individual level. Thus, food availability is only a necessary condition and not a sufficient condition for attaining food security.

The WTO, through its strictures on domestic support and market access, has seemed to have redefined 'food security'. Under the integrated world, food security is not attaining self-sufficiency in food production at the national level but, making food available from donor countries in time to target population to avert famine (Patnaik, 1996, p. 2446).

Developing countries tried to attain food self-sufficiency mainly through interventionist policies during the pre-WTO regime. But now, these countries cannot continue their supporting measures since, such policies are termed trade-distorting and should be done away with. When countries are made to concentrate only on those crops in which they have comparative cost advantage, they might succeed in attaining efficient resource-use whereas, their food security will suffer.

The WTO has included food security as a non-trade concern in the AoA. It supports those measures aimed at ensuring food security. But this measure exempts only the expenditure made on public stockholding of food grains from the calculation of AMS. This will be allowed only if these stockholding activities form an integral part of a food security programme identified by national legislation. It is also stipulated that the stockholding expenditure should include the price difference between the procurement price and the ruling international price. Moreover, the beneficiaries of such measure should be identified by a clearly defined criterion related to nutritional objectives (Dhar and Chaturvedi, op.cit., pp.20-21). It is clear that under the WTO regime, the Government is compelled not only to reduce its public stockholding of essential crops but has to increase the level of issue price too in order to reduce its expenditure and keep it under the stipulated AMS. Table-5 explains the changes taken place in procurement and public distribution of major cereals in India during the last 25 years.

Table 5: Procurement and Public Distribution of Major Cereals

(in million tonnes)

Year	*Procurement*	*Public Distr.*	*P.D.as % of Proc.*	*Year*	*Procurement*	*Public Distri.*	*P.D.as % of Proc.*
1981	13.0	13.0	100	1996	19.8	18.3	92
1982	15.4	14.8	96	1997	23.6	17.8	75
1983	15.6	16.2	104	1998	26.3	18.6	71
1984	18.7	13.3	71	1999	30.8	17.7	57
1985	20.1	15.8	79	2000	35.5	13.0	36
1986	19.7	17.3	88	2001	42.6	13.2	31
1987	15.7	18.7	120	2002	40.3	18.1	45
1988	14.1	18.6	132	2003	34.5	22.5	65
1989	18.9	16.4	86	2004	41.1	22.5	55
1990	24.0	16.0	67	2005	N.A.	N.A.	Nil
1991	19.6	20.8	106	2006	N.A.	N.A.	Nil
1992	17.9	18.8	105	2007	N.A.	N.A.	Nil
1993	28.1	16.4	58	2008	N.A.	N.A.	Nil
1994	26.0	14.0	54	2009	N.A.	N.A.	Nil
1995	22.6	15.3	67				

Note: N.A. – Not Available.

Source: Economic Survey, 2008-09.

There has been a considerable decline in the volume of off-take of cereals though their quantum of procurement has been on the rise. Obviously, the volume of off-take as a percentage of total procurement has been falling with lot of inter-temporal variations and it has touched an all-time low of 31 per cent in the year 2001. Not only in relative terms, even in absolute terms, was the volume of off-take among the lowest at 13.0 m.t. in 2000. This is identical with that of 1981 though, in that year procurement too was 13.0 m.t. Clearly, the continuous rise in the issue price under the WTO regime, has taken its toll. While the off-take through the public distribution system is on the decline, the amount of public stockholding is also on the decline. This need not surprise since, in the decade under the WTO, exports of rice and wheat are at the highest.

Table 6: CGR, Mean and CV of Net Availability of Food Grains

Crops	*Period-1 (1981-95)*			*Period-2 (1996-08)*			*Period-3 (1981-08)*		
	CGR	*Mean*	*CV*	*CGR*	*Mean*	*CV*	*CGR*	*Mean*	*CV*
Rice	0.8	203.2	7.0	-1.3	203.5	6.7	-0.3	203.3	6.7
Wheat	2.2	148.7	9.1	0.2	163.5	9.1	1.6	153.8	10.1
Other Cereals	-1.8	79.3	14.9	-3.5	60.7	13.2	-2.2	72.8	18.9
Cereals	0.6	431.2	4.3	-1.0	428.1	6.2	-0.1	430.2	4.9
Gram	0.8	12.8	15.4	-3.3	11.2	20.4	-1.6	12.3	17.9
Pulses	0.1	38.9	6.9	-1.4	33.1	8.7	-1.0	36.8	10.6
Foodgrains	0.6	450.1	19.6	-1.0	461.3	6.2	-0.2	454.0	16.0

Note: Mean availability of grains (per capita per day) in grams; CV in percentage.

Source: Calculated from the data taken from Agricultural Statistics At a Glance, various years.

Net Availability of Food Grains during Post-WTO Period

Declining off-take on the one hand and falling public stockholding on the other will have their repercussions on the per capita net availability of food grains. Table-6 presents an alarming picture regarding the changes in the per capita per day net food availability over the periods. Except in wheat, the CGRs of all other categories have become negative in period-2. The CGR of per capita net availability of cereals per day has declined from 0.6 per cent in Period 1 to -1.0 per cent in period 2. Similarly, the CGRs of pulses and total food grains too have entered the negative zone, from 0.1 per cent to -1.4 per cent and from 0.6 per cent to -1.0 per cent in periods 1 and 2 respectively. The absolute volume of per capita net availability of many of the crops too is at historical low. For example, rice at 183.4 grams is the lowest in the last 20 years; cereals other than rice and wheat at 44.9 grams and pulses at 29.1 grams are the lowest in the independent India.

To attain food security through increased food availability, developing countries can either try to bridge the yield gap and/or import the shortage. Increasing the yield level is difficult since, developing countries are constrained by the huge presence of small and marginal farmers and hence the possibility of farm mechanization and adoption of new techniques on a considerable scale are limited. The barriers (particularly financial and environmental) in increasing net irrigated area through new projects any further compels the sector depends mostly on the Nature's mercy and finally, increasing land demand due to population pressure and diversification towards industrial sector, further push down the availability of cultivable land. Hence, without state intervention, it will not be possible even to attain food self-sufficiency, leave alone food security. Importing food crops too is an untenable argument since, the meagre export earnings by the developing countries have other unavoidable compulsions including debt-servicing.

Market-oriented production approach through liberalization cannot be the panacea. As the study by Azad (op.cit.) has shown, such an approach has deteriorated food security both at the household and individual levels and the worst affected were the poorest and women in the tribal households. Women's control over food supply has got diluted and the cultivation of cash crops has put the households at the mercy of middlemen. Thus, agricultural self-reliance is quite vital for the growth of the economy of the agrarian developing countries as good agricultural production provides purchasing power to a large majority of the population and in turn spurts industrial growth. Hence, developing countries should be given the requisite flexibility within the AoA to attain food security.

Conclusion

The analysis shows that in the post-WTO regime, export of food grains has increased while the huge import of vegetable oils which is encouraged in the name of efficient resource-use has adversely affected the domestic agro-processing industry. Also, in the last ten years, the CGR of area under food crops has decreased, giving place to increased cultivation of horticultural and floricultural crops among the non-food crops. The CGRs of rice and wheat production too have decreased in a marked way during the post-WTO period. Though the CGR of coarse cereals has gone up that of food grains as a whole, has come down in this period. While, procurement of major cereals is on the rise of late, their off-take through the PDS was at the lowest in 2000 and 2001. More importantly, per capita net availability of food grains is at historical low. This is quite disturbing since food availability is only a necessary condition in attaining food security. It needs a new strategy in conformity with the WTO, to avoid the impact of this market-oriented production approach. The poorest and the women in the rural households, who form the most vulnerable group, should be given alternative livelihood strategies.

REFERENCES

Azad, Nandini, (1996), Engendeed Mobilisation – the Key to Livelihood Security: IFAD' Experience in South Asia, IFAD, Rome.

Bapna, S.C., (1997), Macro Policies and Food Security in South East Asia, Indian Institute of Management, Ahmedabad.

Bhalla, G.S., (1995), "Globalisation and Agricultural Policy in India", *Indian Journal of Agricultural Economics*, Vol, 50, No.1, January-March, pp.7-26.

Bhattacharya, B., and Pal, Parthatratim, (1999), *Uruguay Round: Impact on India's Food Security and Environment*, Indian Institute of Foreign Trade, New Delhi.

Desai, B.M., and Namboodiri N.V., (1999), *Farmer's Response, Prices and Government Expenditure Analysis Under WTO Framework for Developing Agriculture*, Indian Institute of Management, Ahmedabad.

Dhar, Biswajit and Chaturvedi, Sachin, (1999), *WTO Agreements and Agricultural Sector: Implications and Options for India*, RIS, New Delhi.

Gill, S.S. and Brar J.S., (1996), "Global Market and Competitiveness of Indian Agriculture: Some Reflections", *Economic and Political Weekly*, Vol.31, No.32, Aug. 10, pp.2167-77.

Government of India, Agricultural Statistics At a Glance, various years, Department of Agriculture and Co-operation, Ministry of Agriculture, New Delhi.

Government of India, *Economic Survey*, various years, Ministry of Finance, New Delhi.

Gulati, Ashok and Narayanan, Sudha (2003), "Rice Trade Liberalisation and Poverty", *Economic and Political Weekly*, Vol 38, No.1, January 4, pp.45-51.

Gulati, Ashok and Sharma, Anil (1997), "Freeing Trade in Agriculture: Implications for Resource Use Efficiency and Cropping Pattern Changes", *Economic and Political Weekly*, Vol, 32, No.52, December 27, pp.A155-64.

Patnaik, Utsa (1996), "Export-Oriented Agriculture and Food Security in Developing Countries and India", *Economic and Political Weekly*, Vol.31, Nos.35-37, Special No., September, pp.2429-49.

Nayyar, Deepak and Sen, Abhijit (1994), "International Trade and Agricultural Sector in India", *Economic and Political Weekly*, Vol. 29, No.20, May 14, pp. 1187-1203.

11

Indian Agriculture: A Discussion With Special Reference to WTO Agreement

Kakali Majumdar

Introduction

Agriculture continues to be the mainstay of the Indian economy and ironically it is this sector that the country lags behind most. Even now 70% of its total population, directly or indirectly, depends on agriculture and cultivates about 184 million hectares [Bansil, 2002] but its contribution to GDP is only 24%. Pre-independent India with its stagnant agriculture was hard hit by the ravages of repeated famines, floods, droughts, faulty distribution, food shortages etc.

Agricultural growth frequently stimulates broader economic development in low-income countries by generating growth of employment and income in other sectors through backward and forward linkages with agriculture. Accelerated growth along with its spread effects in other sectors does invariably lead to a significant reduction in poverty and income inequality. The failure of agricultural output to respond to the increasing needs of rising population places a limit to the overall growth of an economy and thus hastens the emergence of a stationary state.

The active march towards agricultural development in

India started mainly under the five-year plans. In the beginning of the plans, the main policy thrust of Indian Government was on agrarian reforms as well as modernizing agriculture through large-scale investment on irrigation and on infrastructure. However, it was with the beginning of the 4th five-year plan that agriculture got its due importance in the sectoral economic plan. The emphasis shifted from institutional to technological factors the result of which we saw in Green Revolution of 1968-1978. Double cropping was the primary factor for the Green Revolution. The artificial monsoon came in the form of huge irrigation facilities which enabled double and later, multiple cropping.

Historical data shows that before the Green Revolution, area growth was the major source of agricultural produce and yield growth was given comparatively less importance. Though overall performance of Indian agriculture during the Green Revolution period was satisfactory, there remained considerable inter-regional inequality in growth. There was much concern over the fact that the bulk of the increase in agricultural production had come from a relatively small area, the so called Green Revolution belt. Green Revolution was basically concentrated in the North-Western states like Punjab, Haryana, Uttar Pradesh etc. and was confined mainly to wheat. Punjab was the greatest beneficiary of the Green Revolution in India.

Economic reforms introduced in India since 1991 focused mainly on industry. Agriculture was kept outside of GATT till 1995. One of the important issues of WTO agreement was the inclusion of agriculture under its umbrella, implemented from first January 1995.

The Uruguay round Agreement on Agriculture (AOA) of 1995 was the first step towards the reforms in agriculture, especially agricultural trade. It marks a new chapter in the history of multilateral trade negotiations. The WTO Agreement on Agriculture contains provisions in three broad areas of agriculture viz Market access, Domestic support and Export subsidies. Market access includes tariffication, tariff reduction and access opportunities. For domestic support policies, subject to reduction commitments, the total support given in 1986-88 was measured by the Total Aggregate Measure of Support

(AMS). The Agreement related to Export subsidies contained provisions regarding member's commitment to reduce Export Subsidies. Developed countries were required to reduce their export subsidy expenditure by 36%. For developing countries the percentage cuts were pegged at 24%.

The AOA recognized free and market oriented trade of Agriculture. It legitimized the various trade distorting practices of the developed countries. AOA also prohibited countries not using subsidies during the years 1986-88 from introducing any new subsidies in the WTO regime. It was expected that implementation of the AOA would benefit agro based countries like India. The Doha Declaration states that the agricultural negotiations should try to achieve substantial improvements in market access with the reductions of all forms of export subsidies and substantial reductions in trade-distorting domestic support (WTO 2001, Para 13).

India's policy adjustment to meet the obligations of WTO was rather slow. A good number of studies focused on the benefits of WTO (Sharma & Jain, 2005). Those who support trade liberalization of Indian Agriculture maintained that India had a strong competitive advantage in agriculture over most of the developed world and that WTO induced trade liberalization has made agricultural export more attractive and remunerative. This advantage is said to be strong in the case of high value crops such as fruits, floriculture products and vegetables, Basmati rice and cotton. However, those who are against the globalization of India's agriculture opine that liberalization of agricultural trade would destabilize prices and expose Indian market to violent fluctuation in the international market. Their view is that liberalization of agricultural exports would change the cropping pattern away from food to nonfood items. There will be a chance of hike in the food grain prices that will create problems for the mass people below poverty line and also for the small and marginal farmers those who mostly were food-grain producers.

Under this background the present paper tries to highlight the Indian Agricultural scenario with special reference to production and export of Indian food-grains under WTO agreement.

METHODOLOGY

Objectives of the Study

The Specific objectives of the present study are as follows:

O1. To study the change in production pattern of major agricultural product during WTO regime.

O2. To study the change in the export pattern during WTO era.

O3. To study the implementation of AOA in India

Hypotheses of the Study

H1. There would be an influence of time on agricultural output.

H2. There would be sharp changes in the growth rates of output

H3. There would be an influence of time on export.

H2. There would be sharp changes in the growth rates of export

Study Period

The period chosen for this study is 1983 to 2008. The WHO period has been subdivided into two sub-periods, pre WTO era i.e. 1983 to 1995 and post WTO era, i.e. from 1996 to 2008.

Data Type and Sources

The data used for this study are of secondary type. The basic sources are CMIE, Ministry of Agriculture, Govt. of India and Economic Survey for various years.

The present work considers food grains data both for the study of the performance of agricultural output and export in India. Food grains in India, mainly includes rice, wheat, barley, gram and other pulses. Rice is the main food crop of the nation. Basically Aus, Aman and Boro are the three main important varieties of rice in India. Other pulses constitute Arhar, Mug, and Maskalai etc.

MEASUREMENT OF GROWTH

Calculation of Sub-period Growth Rates

Kinked Exponential model (Majumdar, 2005) has been used to study the growth rates. The sub-period growth rates can be measured either by estimating them separately or by fitting them into a single equation. However, in case of independent estimation the trend line are likely to be discontinuous and because of that, some time disparity may arise in between the sub-period and whole period growth rates [Boyce, 1987]. Kinked models that impose linear restrictions, so as to eliminate discontinuity between sub-periods, provide a superior basis for comparisons of sub-period's growth rates. For the present study the sub-periods are 1983 to 1995 (Pre WTO era) and 1996 to 2008(Post WTO era).

Kink Exponential Model: $\ln Y_t = a + b_1D_{1t} + b_2D_{2t} + u_t$,------------------1

Derivation of the model: Let us start from a discontinuous exponential model for two sub-periods that can be get just by adding the two separate exponential trends ($\ln Y_1 = a_1D_1 + b_1D_{1t}$ and $\ln Y_2 = a_2D_2 + b_2D_{2t}$) as

$\ln Y_t = a_1D_1 + a_2D_2 + b_1D_{1t} + b_2D_{2t} + u_t$-------------- 2

The possibility of discontinuity can be eliminated by a linear restriction such that the two lines intersect at the break point K. In mathematical term it is like

$a_1 + b_{1K} = a_2 + b_{2K}$-----------------3

After solving equation-2 with this restriction (Equation-3) one can easily get the restricted model as $\ln Y_t = a_1 + b_1 (D_{1t} + D_{2K}) + b_2 (D_{2t} - D_{2K}) + u_t$--------------4. Putting t = 0 at K, the simplified form of equation-4 can be derived as $\ln Y_t = a + b_1D_{1t} + b_2D_{2t} + u_t$, which is nothing but the Kink exponential model for the present study. where Y_t = Foodgrains production/Export/Import. a, bi, ci are the parameters estimated on the basis of observed data, t is the time period, Djs are the dummy variables and Dj = 1 for the jth sub-period, = 0 otherwise. i,j = 1, 2. The coefficients b_1 and b_2 in equation 1, multiplied by 100 will give the relative growth rates for the two sub-periods of the study.

2.5.2 *Test of Trend Breaks*

Equation of trend break

Significance of the trend breaks has been calculated by replacing the value of b_2 by $(b_1+ b)$ in the regression of the kink trend equations.

$$\ln V_t = a_1 + b_1 t(D_1 + D_2) + bD_2 t + \mu_t \text{ -----------5}$$

The significance level of b is the indicator of the significance level of the trend break from pre to post WTO era.

Results and Discussion

Output Performance: Estimated Kinked Exponential model for output is as $\ln Y_t = 12.16 + .026D_{1t} + .01D_{2t}$ Adj R2 =.85. Both the coefficients (b_1 and b_2) are observed significant at 1% and 5% levels respectively and thus hypothesis H_1 is justified. The sub-period-wise exponential growth rates of food grains production estimated from the selected trend lines are presented in Table 3.

As already mentioned, first sub-period starts from 1983 and continues up to 1995, the second from 1996 to 2008. Results show during the Pre WTO era the food grains output growth in India was higher than the post WTO era. As shown in Table-3, the exponential growth rate was Rs 2.6% per annum during the first sub period which decreased to 1% during second sub-period.

As mention in the methodology part, to study whether there is any significant change in the performance between the two sub-periods, exponential kinked model has been adjusted so that the significance level of the new co-efficient b (equation-5) may serve the purpose. As indicated in Table -4 the significant negative trend break is there for output growth of Indian agriculture.

Export Performance: Estimated Kinked Exponential model for export is as:

$\ln Y_t = 7.92 + .197 D_{1t} + .089 D_{2t}$ Adj R2 =.87.The trend of export growth (Table-3) is observed similar to the output growth that means decrease from first to second sum period. However, both the rates of export are quite high than that of the output. Here the figures are 19.7% and 8.9%, respectively. The trend breaks are also observed negatively significant in this case(Table-4).

AOA and Indian Agriculture

As mentioned earlier, the WTO Agreement on Agriculture contains provisions in three broad areas of agriculture, viz. Market access, Domestic support and Export subsidies. So far as the market access is concerned quantitative restrictions were not converted into tariff in Indian. For the country, ceiling binding was allowed and India fixed the ceiling tariff at 100% for the primary products, 300% for edible oils and for processed foods, 150%.

The provisions related to export subsidies under AOA were not extended in India. Rather certain subsidy schemes were continued to be in place for Agricultural and Processed Food Products Export Development Authority (APEDA) to encourage export of some agricultural products.

Domestic support as already mentioned, is the support to the farmers that was largely targeted to the developed countries under AOA. In India, product specific support is largely negative. However non-product specific support like subsidies on agricultural inputs etc. is in existence and the percentage is below the permissible level, i.e. ten percent of agricultural output. Thus it can be inferred that so far as domestic support is concerned, India is almost outside the AOA.

Interpretation

So far as the food-grains production is concerned the main reason of the fall in the output growth from the pre to post reform period is the fall in productivity growth. One possible reason of this unsustainable growth could be the reduction in soil fertility. Another big problem Indian agriculture faces today is the debt trap. Increase in the input costs, the plummeting price of produce and a lack of proper credit facilities, which makes farmers turn to private moneylenders who charge exorbitant rates of interest. In order to repay these debts, farmers borrow again and get caught in a debt trap. The biggest input for farmers is seeds. Before liberalization, farmers across the country had access to seeds from state government institution. The seed market was well regulated, and this ensured quality in privately sold seeds too. With liberalization, India's seed market was opened up to global agribusinesses like Monsanto, Cargill and Syn Genta. Also, following the deregulation guidelines of the IMF, 14 of the 24 units of the APSSDC's seed processing units were closed down in 2003.

The Agreement on Agriculture (AOA), under WTO, placed more emphasis on export as an instrument of growth. However, the growth rate of agricultural export declined during the post WTO era. From the present study it is clear that both production and export performance of food grains was better during pre WTO era. During the initial years of liberalization i.e. 1991 to 1994 the international prices of agricultural goods were higher than the domestic prices. Due to this advantage India gained significantly from export. Further reduction in tariffs and removal of quotas also helped to boost the export of agricultural produce of India. However, the performance has changed since 1996. The biggest problem for the developing countries in the post WTO period was unforeseen decline in international agricultural prices of some important products which caused adverse impact on farmers' income, employment and livelihood security. Developing countries faced threats from developed markets in the form of non-trade barriers like Sanitary and Phyto-Sanitary Measures (SPS) and Technical Barriers to Trade (TBT). Thus India does not stand to gain much from WTO. Exports are becoming increasingly competitive. Among the domestic factors that continue to hamper the export growth of India are infrastructural constraint, high transaction cost, erratic climatic condition, policies relating to production, distribution etc. Out of the essential commodities, the fall in export was observed in milled paddy rice, cotton lint, wheat, sugar etc.

Farmers were encouraged to shift from growing a mixture of traditional crops to export oriented 'cash crops' like chili, cotton and tobacco. The export prospects however, were bit brighter with high value products, marine products, horticulture products etc yielding favourable return to the producers. The trade related challenges in India come not only from the developed countries, but from some of the developing countries as well.

Summary and Conclusion

From the foregoing analysis it is clear that WTO has not made any significant dent in the agricultural growth scenario in India. The reform policies have not focused sufficiently on what needs to be done for this sector. Significant levels of fall in the growth rates of food grains production have been noticed from the pre to post WTO period.

The changing scenario of Global agriculture, especially agri-trade in the post-WTO regime is much challenging for developing countries like India. India is agrarian country and its comparative advantage lies in this sector. At this juncture it is very much important to take steps to improve the competitiveness of Indian agricultural output. With a contribution of 13% to total export earnings, agri-exports have occupied an important position in Indian external trade. The problems of downward trend in exports, sharp year to year fluctuations in net trade etc. raise question marks about the future of WTO in India and also for the other developing countries and seek further discussion or policy prescription on this subject at the international level.

REFERENCES

Bansil, P.C. (2002): *Economic Problems of Indian Agriculture,* CBS Publishers & Distributors, New Delhi.

Bhalla, G.S. and Singh, G. (2001): Indian Agriculture: Four Decades of Development. Sage Publications, New Delhi. Boyce, Jamse.K. *Agrarian Impasse in Bengal, Institutional Constraint To Technological Change.* Oxford University Press, New York. 1987.

Mahendradev, S. (1987): "Growth and Instability of Food grains Production: An inter-state Analysis", *Economic and Political Weekly*, Vol. 22, No.39, pp.82-92.

Majumdar, Kakali (2005): Performance of Indian Agriculture: A pre and post Reform Analysis in V. V. Jugale (ed) *WTO and Indian Economic Reforms*, Serial Publication.

Sharma Geetanjali and Jain, Subhas (2005): "Agriculture and WTO-A Case Study of India's Agro Food Industry", in Sabanna Talwar (ed.), *WTO and the Agriculture*, Serial Publications.

World Trade Organization (WTO) (2001): Ministerial Declaration WT/MIN (01)/DEC/120, Ministerial Conference, Fourth Session, Doha, Qatar, 2001, 9–14 November.

Table 1: Progress in Food Grains Production in India (Million Tonnes)

Item	*1960-61*	*1970-71*	*1980-81*	*1990-91*	*1999-2000*
Food grains	82(100)	108.4(100)	130(100)	177(100)	209(100)
Total Cereals	69(84.15)	96.5(89.02)	119(91.54)	163(92.09)	196(93.78)
Total Pulses	13(15.85)	11.9(10.98)	11(8.46)	14(7.91)	13(6.2)
Rice	35(42.68)	35(32.23)	54(41.51)	75(42.37)	90(43.06)
Wheat	11(13.41)	11(10.15)	36(27.69)	55(31.07)	76(36.36)

Note: Figures in the parentheses represent percentage share in total food grains

Source: Economic review (various issues), Government of West Bengal

Table 2: Exponential Growth Rates of Food Grains Production in India and States

States	*Growth Rates*			
	1960-61 to 1969-70	*1970-71 to 1979-80*	*1980-81 to 1990-91*	*1991-92 to 1999-2000*
Andhra Pradesh	1.06	3.63	.9	1.98
Tamil Nadu	.71	1.12	2.9	.56
Karnataka	3.86	2.89	.5	2.28
Kerala	2.03	-.49	-2.1	-5.17
Assam	2.97	.82	2.7	1.24
Bihar	.35	.32	3.8	4.62

West Bengal	2.83	.83	6.5	2.06
Orissa	2.26	-.17	4.1	-3.61
Gujarat	3.65	1.93	-1.9	2.69
Maharashtra	-.09	1.74	1.2	1.51
Rajasthan	-.31	-.49	.9	5
Madhya Pradesh	-.26	-1.62	2	2.43
Haryana	5.10	3.35	4.3	3.66
Punjab	9.09	5.60	4	2.25
Uttar Pradesh	2.38	1.19	3.5	2.66
Himachal Pradesh	4.9	.55	3.8	.71
All India	1.84	2.05	2.7	2.28

Sources: Mahendradev (1987), CMIE (1993)

Note: Exponential growth rates of 1990-91 to 1999-2000 are calculated by the present author.

Table 3: Sub-Period-Wise Exponential Growth Rates of Food Grains Production and Export in India

Growth rate	*Pre WTO Era*	*Post WTO era*
Output	2.6*(.003)	1**(.004)
Export	19.7%*(.024)	8.9%*(.027)

Notes: (1) *and ** indicate significant at 1% and 5% levels respectively by one-tailed t test.

(2) Figures in the parentheses represent Standard Errors

Table 4: Trend Breaks of Relative Growth in Kink Exponential Framework

Item	*Trend break*
Output	-.016 (.003)**
Export	-1.08 (.046)**

Notes: (1) ** indicate significant at 5% level by one-tailed t test.

(2) Figures in the parentheses represent Standard Errors.

12

WTO Regime and Emerging Trends in Indian Agriculture

Sudhansu Sekhar Nayak

Introduction

Agricultural sector of India is now standing on the crossroads of development particularly after the introduction of economic liberalization in the country since 1991. Here the economic liberalization has made attempt to reduce government interferences and has removed unnecessary restrictions in economic activities and has been encouraging privatization of the economy. Under this new economic liberalization wave, the agricultural sector of the country is facing the challenges to rationalize its activities and to face international competition in marketing its products as well as in its factors market.

Under the present trend of globalization and the set up of international trade under World Trade Organization (WTO) regime, there will be considerable reduction in production subsidies paid by developed countries to their farmers and the rolling back of some of the non-tariff barriers which have restricted agricultural trade. These provisions will provide benefit to India as the agricultural exports of the country enjoy a comparative and competitive advantage. Therefore, India's agricultural exports will receive a welcome stimulus, at a time when the incentive structures in the domestic economy are beginning to work to their advantage. Agricultural subsidies in India are not facing any problem as value of such subsidies in India is not only far below the 10 per cent limit but also negative. But the major problem which the agricultural sector of the country is going to face is increase in the price of agricultural inputs like HYV seeds, fertilizers, pesticides etc. due to the introduction of the system of product patents.

Thus from the Indian perspective, the effect of globalization and WTO regime of Indian agriculture is a kind of mixed bag with the plus points outweighing the minus. No doubt the new WTO arrangements will definitely raise the prices of agricultural inputs but with this India's market opportunities in exports of agricultural commodities would increase. Thus Indian agriculture and agri-business should get the kind of boost it has never known by exposing itself to the larger world market. The farm lobby would see major growth in exports in superior rice, vegetable, fruits, fisheries and meat products, vegetable oil processed products and flowers. The reduction in export subsidies o agriculture by developed countries will make Indian agricultural exports more competitive in world markets.

Thus Mr. Bibek Debroy of Indian Institute of Foreign Trade (IIFT) was of the that "If agriculture is liberalized there will be higher input prices. But there will also be higher output prices and it is slightly unfair to look at hike in input prices alone."

Thus under the present context, it can be finally observed that under the new GATT agreement, whatever negative aspects the Indian agriculture will face that can be suitably neutralized by responding to its positive aspects. Thus if the Indian agriculture can meet the challenges and opportunities open to it and if the developed countries do not put any trade barrier before the flow of Indian agricultural exports then Indian will definitely be able to overcome this threat and also become successful to gain sufficiently from the new world trade regime.

Some Emerging Trends in Indian Agriculture

The following are some of important emerging trends in Indian agriculture as a result of economic liberalization introduced in the country:

1. *Raising the Production of Food grains:* India has been experiencing the increase in the production of foodgrains particularly after the introduction of new agricultural strategy (i.e., Green Revolution) in agricultural practices. Annual growth rate of 2.08 per cent was recorded during 1970s. Annual growth rate of 3.5 per cent foodgrains in 1980s is the hallmark of the green revolution that enabled India to become self sufficient in foodgrains and even a marginal exporter. The decade of 1990s could not maintain this pace and annual growth rate has fallen to 1:7 per cent, which is just about equal to annual population growth. Total production of foodgrains has increased from 176.39 million tones in 1990-91 to 204.6 million tones in 2004-05. With the increase in size of population and increase in income, the demand of foodgrains is likely to rise in near future. As per the latest estimate it is found that by 2010, the demand for foodgrains is likely to rise at the rate of 2.6 per cent. If the country can maintain 4 per cent growth rate in agricultural production then after meeting its domestic demand, the country can export the surplus amount of food grains to the foreign countries in which it has favourable position.
2. *Diversification of Agriculture:* Agriculture is not only meeting the demand for foodgrains but also other needs of development. In recent years, agricultural sector has been diversified to produce commercial crops and horticultural crops viz, fruits, vegetables, spices, cashew, arecanut, coconut and floricultural products like flowers, orchids etc., dairy and other animal husbandry products. The demand for these products has also been increasing. Liberalization of the economy has created ample scope for the

development of agricultural sector both in terms of increased production and trade.

3. *Increasing Trend in Horticultural Output:* The diversity of physiographic, climate and soil characteristics enables India to grow a large variety of horticultural crops which includes fruits, vegetables, spices, cashew nut, coconut, cocoa, arecanut, root and tuber crops, medicinal and aromatic plants etc. India is the largest producer of fruits, and second largest producer of vegetables. Total production of fruits has increased from 29.0 million tones in 1990-91 to 91.6 million tones in 2004-05. India is the largest producer of cashew. Total production of cashew has increased from 3.7 lakh tones in 1991-92 to 6.0 lakh tones in 2003-04. With the increase in the production of fruits, vegetables another horticultural products, the value of exports of these products is also increasing. Total value of exports of fruits, vegetables and pulses has increased from Rs. 216 crore in 1990-91 to Rs. 1,029 crore in 1997-98. The value of exports of fruits and vegetables alone stand at 414 crore in 1996-97. Thus horticultural exports of the country contributes nearly 25 per cent of the total agricultural exports.

4. *Increase in Floricultural Output:* Presently about 31,000 hectares of land spread over Karnataka, Tamil Nadu, Andhra Pradesh and West Bengal are under flower production. Since the inception of liberalization, commercial farming of floricultural activities has been increasing gradually. The demand for Indian cut flower is increasing continuously in the international market. Total value of exports of cut flowers has increased from Rs.28.7 crore in 1994-95 to Rs.60 crore in 1996-97. Under the liberalized regime, India is having a wide prospect of export of floricultural products in near future, which is expected to exceed Rs.200 crore mark by the year 2000. the total production of flower during 2001-02 was 0.57 million tonnes of loose flowers and 803.5 million tonnes of cut flowers.

5. *Free Trade:* Liberalization has removed all restrictions on the movement of agricultural produce within the country. This has facilitated expansion of trade in agricultural products, especially of food grains.

6. *Agricultural Exports:* Another important emerging trend of agriculture under liberalization is the increasing volume of agricultural exports and its increasing prospects in near future under the WTO regime. India is favorably placed in respect of agricultural exports as the agricultural sector is subjected to low import content, low cost of labor, favorable climatic conditions, and low unit cost of inputs. Agricultural exports are playing an important role in expanding the activities of agricultural sector along with generating increasing number of employment opportunities and also in diversifying agricultural operations. The Export Import Policy (Exim) 1992-97 has provided ample opportunities for increasing the volume of agricultural exports. The policy has permitted exports of agricultural goods like oilseed, edible oil, sugarcane, pulses, coconut, etc. which were prohibited earlier. Accordingly, the total value of agricultural and allied exports of India has increased from Rs. 6,295.2 crore in 1991-92 to Rs. 38,079 crore in 2004-05 which was nearly 10.2 percent of country's total exports as compared to that of only 10.59 percent in 1992-93.

7. *Food Processing:* Economic liberalization has made ample scope for the development and expansion of food processing industry in India. Fruits and vegetables being perishable in nature are facing a huge loss worth Rs.3,000 crore every year. In order to prevent such losses, the National Horticulture Board is making necessary steps for providing infra-structure and for the packaging, storage and transportation of horticultural products. The production of processed fruits and vegetables are providing huge number of employment and improving agricultural productivity by raising the prospects of agricultural exports. The Government is also offering necessary incentives by

exempting the industry from excise duty. In order to invite foreign capital into this industry the Government has permitted 51 percent foreign equity partnership and also offered prompt approval of foreign technology transfer to the food processing industry of the country.

8. *Rising Productivity of Agricultural Resources:* One of the important aims of liberalisation is to attain higher productivity of resources utilized for agriculture. Improvement in the productivity of resources is being done through better allocation of resources between different areas and also with the application 01latest technology. In the present regime of liberalisation, there is an emerging trend to emphasise on export; oriented policies, applying new improved technologies in food processing and marketing and giving stress on planting crops as per geographical suitability.

9. *Developing Agriculture in Backward Areas:* In the post-Green Revolution period, application of new agricultural strategy, research and technology was very much restricted in the production of foodgrains, i.e. only wheat and rice. But under the liberalisation wave, with the growing demand for agricultural exports, many new areas of agricultural operations have become favourable and lucrative. In the agriculturally backward I areas, having no irrigation system, dry land farming has been initiated. The other activities like horticulture, floriculture, animal husbandry, fishery etc. have been encouraged. Application of in modern improve techniques in these areas has resulted in the development of many backward areas which were previously subjected to wide spread poverty.

10. *Developing New Biological Techniques:* During the period of green revolution, increasing application of chemical fertilisers and pesticides here encouraged extensively in order to meet the growing demand for food required to feed the rising population. Rising population, ever-increasing demand for food and unlimited exploitation, of natural resources have created a grave threat to

the environment as well as to the agricultural sector. In order to save and protect the environment as well as the agricultural sector from any further damage, increasing use of biological technology for agricultural operation has been emphasised and more emphasis is being given to develop new biological technology.

11. *Growing Trend of Unemployment in Agricultural Sector and its Solution:* Green revolution and increasing mechanisation of agriculture have resulted fall in employment opportunities, resulting in a serious problem in the rural areas. Although many special employment programmes have been introduced to serve as a security net but increasing potentiality of the agricultural sector as emerged from the liberalisation wave should be exploited properly. The growing trend in agricultural exports, increasing demand for horticultural and animal products in the export market has created ample opportunities and scope for employment of huge number of population. This allied sector being labour intensive can provide a hosting solution to the rural unemployment problem of the country.

12. *Growing Volume of Subsidies:* In India, the volume of subsidies granted to agriculture, in respect of fertilizer, irrigation and electricity charges etc. has been increasing. Aggregate subsidies provided by the Central Government are estimated at Rs. 22,025 crore in 1998-99 as compared with Rs. 19,664 Crore in 1997-98. Out of these total amount about 75 per cent is allotted in the area of fertiliser and foodgrains. Under the present era of liberalisation, although there is a move to reduce the volume of subsidies in the budget but political compulsions have prevented the government to undertake that move.

13. *Growing Trend of Investment in Agriculture:* Agricultural sector is experiencing a growing trend in the volume of its investment during the post-liberalization period. But the volume of public sector investment in the agricultural sector is declining.

14. *Institutionalization of Agricultural Credit:* Under the present wave of liberalization there is growing trend of institutionalization of agricultural credit. In the initial stage of post-independence period Indian farmers were depending too much on unorganized sources of agricultural credit, i.e., on village moneylenders, landlords, traders etc. But such non-institutional credit is very much damaging farmers' interest as they charge exorbitantly higher rate of interest. But with the passage of time, there is growing trend to institutionalize the flow of agricultural credit mainly through commercial banks cooperative and regional rural banks. Agricultural credit provided by various agencies rose from Rs. 16,494 crore in 1993-94 to Rs. 1,15,243 crore in 2004-05. In 2005-06, it is likely to rise to Rs. 1,17,898 crore. Thus under the present era of liberalisation, ihe tanners are showing much interest to collect loan from institutional sources and the recovery of agricultural advances has also increased from 56 per cent in 1993-94 to 63 per cent in 2000-01.

ANALYSIS

Table 1 shows the trend of public and private sector investment in agriculture.

Table 1: Gross Capital Formaton in Agriculture

Year	*Total Investment*	*Public Sector*	*Private Sector*	*Percent Share Public Sector*	*Percent Share Private Sector*	*Investment in Agri. As % of GDP*
			(At: 1980-81 prices)			
1981-81	4,636	1,796	2,840	38.7	64.3	N.A.
1990-91	4,594	1154	3440	25.1	74.9	N.A.
1995-96	6961	1268	5693	18.2	81.8	N.A.
1996-97	6999	1132	5867	16.2	83.8	
			(At: 1993-94 prices)			
1993-94	13523	4467	9056	33.0	67.0	1.6

1999-00	16582	4112	12470	24.8	75.2	1.3
2000-01	16687	3919	12768	23.5	76.5	1.28
2001-02	17219	4969	12250	28.9	71.1	1.24
2002-03	18240	4359	13881	23.9	76.1	1.27
2003-04 (C)	20510	5249	15261	25.6	74.4	1.31
		(At: 1999-00 prices)				
1999-00	43473	7754	35719	17.5	82.2	2.2
2000-01	38176	7018	31158	18.4	81.6	1.9
2001-02	46744	8529	38215	18.2	81.3	2.2
2002-03	45867	7849	38018	17.1	82.9	2.1
2003-04	47833	12809	35024	26.8	73.2	2.0
2004-05 (Q)	43123	12591	30532	29.2	70.8	1.7

(*Source:* Economic Survey, 2004-05, p. 184 & Economic Survey, 2005-06, p. 170)

Table 1 given above reveals that total volume of investment made in agricultural sector of the country at 1980-81 prices has declined from Rs. 4,636 crore in 1980-81 to Rs. 4,594 crore in 1990-91 and then subsequently increased to Rs. 6,999 crore in 1996-97. During this period the share of public sector investment which was 38.7 per cent in 1980-81 gradually declined to 25.1 per cent in 1990-91 and then subsequently to 16.2 per cent in 1996-97, i.e. from Rs. 1,796 crore in 1980-81 to Rs. 1,154 crore in 1990-91 and then to Rs.1,132 crore in 1996-97. The main reason behind the downward trend in public sector investment was the withdrawal of investment resources in favour of investment in terms of current expenditure incurred through subsidies. Such a decelerating trend is a matter of concern. However, the private sector investment has grown substantially in the 1990s. Total volume of private investment in agriculture which was Rs.2,840 crore in 1980-81 gradually increased to Rs.3,440 crore in 1990-91 and then considerably increased to Rs.5,867 crore in 1996-97.

However, the volume of total investment in agriculture at 1993-94 prices has increased from Rs. 13,523 crore in 1992-93 to Rs. 27,510 crore in 2003-04. The share of public sector investment has declined from 33.0 percent (Rs. 4,467 crore) in 1993-94 to 25.6 per cent (Rs. 5,249 crore) in 2003-04. On the other hand, the share of private sector investment in agriculture has increased considerably from 67.0 per cent (Rs. 9,056 crore) in 1993-94 to 74.4 per cent (Rs. 15,261 crore) in 2003-04. The main factors responsible behind such increase in private investment are the incentives and encouragement being provided to the development of agricultural sector and the favourable changes being made in trade policies under the post-liberalisation period and also clue to favourable prospects of agricultural exports in India under the path of globalisation.

Moreover, investment in agriculture declined from 1.6 per cent of GDP in 1993-94 to 1.3 per cent both in 1997-9P, and also in 1001-02. This decline was due to fall in public investment in agriculture in recent years.

Again the volume of total investment in agriculture at 1999-00 prices increased from Rs. 43,473 crore in 1999-2000 to Rs. 43,123 crore in 2004-05 (Q). The share of public sector investment has increased from 17.8 per cent (Rs. 7,754 crore) to 29.2 per cent (Rs. 12,591 crore) in 2004-05. On the other hand, the share of private sector investment in agriculture has decreased relatively from 82.2 per cent (Rs. 35,719 crore) in 1999-2000 to 70.8 per cent (Rs. 30,532 crore) in 2004-05. The main reasons behind the such decrease in private investment are the increasing flow of institutional credit, especially from public sector banks, to agricultural sector and :l-,c relative slump in the prices of agricultural products.

Moreover, investment in agriculture declined from 2.2 per cent of GDP in 1999-2000 to 1,2 per cent in 2004-05. Such decline in the share of the agricultural sector's capital formation in GDP is a matter of concern. This declining share was mainly due to the stagnation or fall in public investment in irrigation, particularly since mid-1990s. However, there is indication of a reversal of this trend with public sector investment in agriculture reaching the highest level of Rs, 12,591 crore in 2004-05 since the early 1990s.This is no doubt an encouraging trend.

Conclusion

It is observed that liberalisation has created several favourable impacts on the agricultural sector of the country. The emerging trends in agriculture which are very much prominent in the post-liberalisation period include the rising productivity, growing investment, diversification of the sector, application of modern techniques, development of horticulture and floriculture, growing volume of exports and development of food processing industry, India with its rising population are in an advantageous position to develop its agricultural and allied sectors which arc mostly labour intensive. Liberalisation has provided ample scope for the modernisation and development of the agricultural sector and also to reap the maximum benefit from the increasing scope of agricultural export arising out of the path of globalisation adopted by the economy.

REFERENCES

1. Singh, Gurmeet, "Problem of Rural Indebtedness", Kurukshetra, *A journul on Rural Development*, Vol. 56, No. 6, p. 22, April-2008.
2. Dhingra, I.C., *Rural Economics*, Sultan Chand & Co, New Delhi, 1998.
3. Conference volume, *Indian Economic Association-2007*, Kashmir.
4. Patnaik, B. Eswar Rao, "Problems and Prospects of Agricultural Development in Koraput District", Thesis unpublished.
5. Dutt, Ruddar and Sundaram, K.P.M., *Indian Economics*, Sultan Chand & Co, New Delhi, 2007.
6. Muhammad Yunus, Grameen Bank, Micro Credit & Millennium Development Goals, *Economic & Political weekly*, Sept. 04-10,2004, Vol.XXXIV, No.36.
7. *Economic Survey*, Govt. of Orissa, Bhubaneswar, 2006-07 & 2007-08.
8. Stastitical Abstract of Orissa, Bhubneswar, 2005 & 2008.
9. *Kurukshetra, A Journal on Rural Development*, Vol.56, No. 7, May 2008.
10. District at a Glance, Govt. of Orissa, Bhubaneswar, 2008.

13

Impact of WTO Agreements in Indian Agriculture

G. Jayasankar

Agriculture is the main story of the Indian economy as its performance is dependent upon the growth of agriculture sector. It contributes nearly 22% of India's Gross Domestic Product (GDP) and 13% of total exports. It provides employment to 57% of the country's work force and livelihood security to more than 650 million people.

The new economic policy 1991 was initiated with objective of LPG of the economy and later in 1994, accordingly GATT accord signed by 125 countries including India. This accord aims at substantial progressive reduction in support and protection so as to prevent restrictions and distortions in the world market, it includes establishment of WTO which came into force on 1st January 1995 including other proposals relating to agriculture such as market assess domestic support and export subsidies, removal of quantitative restrictions. Here in this way neo-liberalists succeeded in stepping into the aspects related to the agricultural sector also.

Adoption of new technology, mechanization and HYV seeds under Green Revolution, subsidies, easy accessibility to credit, public investment have helped in implementing and successfully in achieving the largest during 1950-1990.

As a result, at present Indian agriculture accounts for about 1/4th of the GDP and source of livelihood for more than 2/3rd of the population. Food production has also increased by more than the increase in the population leading to food security. Under these circumstances, what is the need to deviate from the protectional policies?

Does a WTO agreement really offer a helping hand to farming community counting at 91% small farmers and 8% of medium farmers? Or does it protect the interest of only 1% largest farmers in India? In this paper we have made an attempt to examine the impact of WTO agreements on agriculture development in India.

Agriculture Growth

Agricultural production has two components - food grains and non-food grains. The former contributes approximately two-thirds of total agricultural production. Agricultural growth analysis presents the fact that there has been a decline in average annual growth rate during pre-reform and post-reform period i.e., from 3.9 per cent per annum to 3.6 per cent. Growth rate in Food grains during 1980-1990 was 2.9 per cent and it has declined to 2.0 percent during the same period i.e. pre-reform and post-reform periods as shown in Table 1

Table 1: Pre & Post Globalisation Growth in Agriculture Sector

(Average Growth rate)

Sl.No.	Crop	1980-1991	1991-2000	2002-2007
1.	Agriculture and allied activities			
	a) Agriculture	3.6	3.9	1.2
	b) Forestry	4.2	3.7	-
	c) Fishing	-0.1	0.8	6.8
2.	Crop			
	a) Food Grains	2.9	2.0	6.1
	b) Cereals	3.1	2.1	-
	c) Rice	3.7	2.2	3.7

d)	Wheat	3.6	3.6	12.5
e)	Coarse Cereals	0.0	-1.6	-
f)	Pulses	1.4	0.8	-
g)	Non-food grains	4.3	2.4	-

Source: Economic Survey 2000 - 2001

Plan Allocations

Plan outlays on Agriculture and allied activities have been gradually declining during the plan from 14.9 percent in the first plan to 5.2 percent by the tenth plan. This is clearly shows Government withdrawal from the agricultural sector development (Table-2)

Table 2: Plan Outlay in Agriculture and Allied Sectors (Rs. in Crores)

Plan	*Total Outlay*	*Agriculture & Allied sectors*	*Percentage of agri & allied sectors*
I Plan	2378	354	14.9
II Plan	4500	501	11.3
III Plan	8577	1089	12.7
IV Plan	15779	2320	14.7
V Plan	39426	4865	12.3
VI Plan	97500	5695	5.8
VII Plan	180000	10525	5.9
VIII Plan	434100	22467	5.2
IX Plan	859200	42462	4.9
X Plan	398890	20668	5.2
XI Plan	3644720	674105	18.5

Source: Tenth Five Year Plan - 2002 – 2007.

Capital Formation

Gross domestic capital formation in agriculture has been undergone a secular decline due to steady erosion in the share of public investment. The increasing private capital formation has been concentrated in inputs like power and other inputs are available uninterruptedly and with large subsidy. In fact more and more investment must be fueled into farm sector in the fields of research, extension, infrastructure development, marketing etc. to attain higher production and productivity. It would raise the income position of rural population.

But Public investment in agriculture was at higher levels in the initial years of the planning while, in the later years it had been declining in particular after 1980's. Investment in agriculture as a percentage of GDP has remained at 1.6 percent during 1993-1996 after that it has gradually declined to 1.3 percent by 1999 and same level has continued up to 2001. This fall is due to the decline in Public Investment from Rs.4467 crores in 1993-94 to Rs.3869 crores in 1998-99 (Table-3).

Table 3: Gross Capital Formation in Agricultural Sector, (At 1993-94 Prices)

Year	*Gross Capital Formation*			*Investment in agri*
	Public Sector	*Private Sector*	*Total*	*as % of GDP*
1993-94	4467(33.0)	9056(67.0)	13523(7.47)	1.6
1994-95	4947(33.0)	10022(67.0)	14969(6.51)	1.6
1995-96	4849(28.9)	10841(69.1)	15690(5.56)	1.6
1996-97	4668(28.9)	11508(71.1)	16176(6.51)	1.5
1997-98	3979(25.0)	11963(75.0)	15942(4.77)	1.4
1998-99	3869(26.0)	11026(74.0)	14895(6.18)	1.3
1999-00	4112(24.8)	12470(75.2)	16582(6.18)	1.3
2000-01	4007(24.2)	12470(75.8)	16545(6.02)	1.3
*2004-05	12591(29.2)	30532(70.8)	43123	1.7

*New Series (at 1999-2000 Prices).

Source: Central Statistical Organization, New Delhi.

Since private investment seems to be compensating for decline in public investment in agriculture, voices are being raised in some circles that there is no need to expand public investment in agriculture. But public investment and private investment cannot be considered to be mutual substitutes in view of their current composition. Public investment is mainly made in medium and major irrigation projects, rural roads etc. in contrast private investment is essentially taking place for short term asset building, ground leveling etc.

In the name of macro economic stabilization of the economy, many measures have been introduced, though these liberalization measures would do nothing to raise the level of investment. And the present rate of capital formation is far below the rate that is required to transform India's low-level agricultural economy into high-level agricultural economy. Instead of making investment in agricultural sector, Government itself is withdrawing from the sector.

Rural Employment

Agricultural un-employment may be classified into seasonal, disguised, chronic and usual status unemployment. According to NSS, current daily status rural unemployment rate for male workers was 4.58 percent in 1987-88. Since then unemployment among rural male workers has been 7.2 percent in 1999-00 as against 5.64 percent in 1993-94.

Table 4: Rural Employment Growth

Employment	*1987-88 - 1993-94*	*1993-94 - 1999-00*
Total Employment (PS+SS)	2.14	0.66
Agricultural Employment (PS+SS)	2.17	0.18
Non - Agricultural Employment (PS+SS)	2.02	2.34

Source: Human Development in South Asia 2002.

Table 4 depicts that the agricultural employment has declined from 2.17 to 0.18 in between 1987-94 and 1994-2000 and total employment also has shown a decline to 0.66 from 2.14 during the same time period. Therefore we can conclude that the globalization has failed even in improving employment position in agricultural sector.

Agricultural Exports

The share of agricultural exports in total exports was 44.2 percent in 1960-61 which was declined to 19.4 percent in 1990-91 and by 2005-06 it has further declined to 10.8 percent.

The information in Table-5, clearly shows that especially since 1995-96, the share of agricultural exports gradually declined till the end of 2005-06. It is clear that though agriculture provides almost 25 percent of India's GDP, agricultural exports are insignificant.

Table 5: Agricultural Exports ($ Million)

Year	*Agricultural Exports*	*Total Exports*	*Agri. Exports as % of total Exports*
1960-61	596	1246	44.2
1970-71	644	2031	31.7
1980-81	2601	8486	30.6
1990-91	3521	18143	19.4
1995-96	6320	31797	19.8
1997-98	6840	35006	18.5
1998-99	6205	33218	18.2
1999-00	5773	36682	15.2
2000-01	6246	44560	13.5
2005-06	61194 Crs	456418 Crs	10.8

Source: Economic Survey of Various Issues.

India had expected that with the dismantling of domestic support in developed countries and widespread reduction in export subsidies by these countries, market access for Indian agricultural products in developed countries would expand. The developed countries have played their cards very cleverly and have taken effective steps to block agricultural exports from developing countries including India behind various loopholes in AoA and allied agreements.

Concluding Remarks

Indian farm sector is on one side neglected by reducing plan allocations by Government itself and on the other side globalization has led to declining share of agricultural exports in total exports and fall in capital formation, and decline in rural employment. Subsidies have been withdrawn. In the case of agricultural exports no subsidies were offered in India. But developed countries have been providing higher level of subsidies. The quantitative restrictions on imports have been withdrawn. Due to globalization of international trade has proved to be beneficial to the developed economies rather than developing economies like India.

However, it is clear from the detailed discussion above, the developed countries have played their cards very cleverly and have taken effective steps to block agricultural exports from developing countries including India behind various loopholes in AoA and allied agreements. Therefore to protect the Indian agriculture and Indian farmers from evils of globalization, the Indian agricultural policy needs be built-up with adequate "Safety-nets". This is possible only under interventionist policies of the Government

REFERENCES

1. Gulati, Ashok, and Narayan Sadhu: (1999) Indian agriculture in the global economy: what should India Negotiate in Seatle why? Focus WTO Sept, IIFT, New Delhi.
2. Chadha, G .K. (2000): Indian Economy under WTO Regime: Happiness and Missing Links, IEA Conference (83rd) Vol. of the Millennium 2000.
3. Chand, Ramesh (2000): Trade Liberalization WTO and Indian Agriculture, EPW March 10th 2000.
4. Mathur, V. C (2003): "Indian agriculture in the New Regime of Global Trade: Issues and Concerns" *WTO and New International. Trade Regime* Ed by Vasisht & Alka Singh, Advance Publishing Concept, New Delhi.
5. Dutt, Ruddar and K.P.M. Sundaram, *The Indian Economy*.
6. *Southern Economist*, January 1st 2006.
7. *Economic Survey* 2000-01.
8. Tenth Five Year Plan 2002-2007.
9. Dinghara, I.C. *The Indian Economy Environment & Policy*.

14

Impact of WTO Development of Indian Agriculture

P.K. Punjabi & Ram Singh Rathor

Introduction

The WTO and its predecessor, the General Agreement on Tariffs and Trade (GATT) have been enormously successful over the last 50 years at reducing tariff and trade barriers among an ever-increasing number of countries. The predecessor to the WTO began in 1947 with only 23 members, today it has 148 members, comprising approximately 97% of world trade WTO, the successor to GATT, is rapidly establishing itself as the third pillar of the Bretten Woods institutions alongside the World Bank and IMF.

WTO agriculture was among the most distorted sectors in international trade. The principal source of these distortions was the co-existence of very high level of domestic and export subsidies. The Urugway Round observed that these was an " urgent need to bring more discipline and predictability including those related to surpluses so as to reduce instability. Most Agricultural goods are price and income countries tend to have as stagnant demand for such commodities. Over production and stagnant demand for agricultural goods lead to structural surpluses in developed countries farm subsidies distort the production structure of a country by raising crop prices in a country's market. Higher prices induce over production of the subsidized crop.

Agriculture in India still engages about 58% of the work forces and contributes about a quarter of the GDP. A large majority of the cultivations belongs to the category of small and marginal holders. The number and holding constituted 68% of the total operations holding in 1971-72 but 80% increases in 1995-96. Total cultivated area is increased 10.2 in 1991-92.Small farms produce 41% of the India's total grain (49% of rice, 40% of wheat, 29% coarse cereals and 27% of pulses). Their contribution to incremental wheat and rice production is 62%.

The growth rate in 2005-06 was 8.4% and expectations are what India will be able to achieve a 10% rate of growth in immediate future. Trade already account for more than 30% of India's GDP, an increase of almost 10% points since 2002. Therefore, the final outcome of the WTO negotiations would be an important determinant of overall economic growth in India.

Objectives

1. To provide the understanding of operations and impact of WTO Agreements related to agriculture.
2. Assess the implication on Indian trade policy reform in agricultural trade barriers.
3. Review of agricultural trade policies in India.
4. To improve competence of Indian agriculture and trade sector.

Review of Literature

Anderson and Tyres, Subramanian,Parikh et al. analyses a paper "WTO Agreements and India Agriculture: Retrospection and prospectus (2006)" Subramaniam's (1995) study India stand to gain from higher world prices in the long run as India also liberalizes agricultural trade, however, the increase in the domestic food prices skews the distribution of gains only in favour of large farmers.

Parikh et al.(1995) study show that if agriculture alone is liberalized, then term of trade will improve for Indian agriculture by about 2% if both agriculture and non agricultural sectors are liberalized, then the Terms of Trade (TOT) will improve for agriculture by 27% gains to agricultural sector as portrayed by the studies mentioned earlier will not materialize. It is improve in irrigation research,extension and transport facilities that will do more for agriculture. Moreover, expenditure on such items will not be inflationary as it will promote agricultural productivity. Anderson and Tyres(1995) use macro techniques like computable general equilibrium models to study the effects of policy liberalization. They predict that Indian farmers including landless rural laborers, will benefit to the tune of 1.6 billion.

Binod K. Karmacharya (2005) analyses a paper "India's Agriculture Trade Policy reform under WTO Agreement". Per capita income of US$ 250 per year, India is a developing country in the work. There poverty remains wide spread 25% of the population living below the poverty line. International trade could help India grow faster. The proposed study aims to examine the impact on agriculture trade of India's trade policy reforms in agriculture sector same in developed countries that may result existing under WTO suggestions.

Methodology & Data Sources

To assess the implications of Indian trade policy reform in agriculture on Indian economy. The data collection based on secondary data. The policy induced changes in the relative demand of different factors of production, particularly labour. As a result, wages and household income react.

According to 11th Plan (2007-12) and world trade report (2006), the estimation of Indian trade policy (2004-09) impacts of India's agricultural trade reforms will comprises three steps: Firstly, changes in the domestic prices of imports and exports in India induced by agricultural trade reforms in developed countries and hence US and EU(European commission) will be assessed. Secondly wage price-elasticities will be estimated that will measure the response of India wages to the price changes, Finally simulated policy induced agricultural production will be used to predict the foreign trade income that would hypothetically be earned by each Indian household after the reform.

Beghin et. al. (2002) perform a CGE study of the response of international prices of agricultural goods to a foreign trade reform that includes the elimination of both trade protection and domestic support. The finding of these studies will be used to estimate the extent of pass through of foreign trade liberalization to foreign earning of agricultural goods in India.

Doha Negotiations: Agriculture

In 1955, the united states obtained a permanent waiver from substantial obligations in agriculture. The European union implemented an elaborate system of protection for its farmer through subsidies. This resulted in severe Distortions in the production and trade of agriculture products when the Doha round launched, it was expected that a significant reduction, if not full elimination of the distortions. Would be achieved in the negotiations. Opinion on the utility and effectiveness of the WTO as a forum for negotiating rules on agricultural tariffs and subsidies is split. In most developing countries agriculture is not so much a matter of commerce as one of livehood. A contrary view also exists which perceives WTO negotiations as the only available vehicle for seeking a reduction in developed country subsidies, which have significantly distorted global trade and agricultural production.

India's Agricultural Export

India's export of agricultural and allied products including plantation are of the order of Rs.360 billion. Export of these products have grown at a CAGR (compound annual growth rate) of 12.22% in the first 4 years of the 10th five year plan. During 2005-06, the Export of these products accounted for 9% of the total exports from India. Share of Agricultural &Processed Food Products Export Development Authority (APEDA) products in total agro exports is increasing over the years whereas share of agro exports in the total merchandise exports from the country is going down. The agro export from the country constituted 14.8% of the total exports out of India in 1999-2000. This share has come down. To about 9% into the year 2005-06. During the same period the share of APEDA products in the total agro exports has gone up from 30% to 42.3%.

Table 1: Major Export-Import for the Agro Products Monitored by Agricultural Department

Year	*Export (Value in Billions)*	*Import (Value in Billions)*
2001-02	297.2	162.6
2002-03	346.5	176.1
2003-04	372.7	219.7
2004-05	416.0	228.1
2005-06	492.2	215.0
2006-07	624.1	296.4
2007-08	777.7	297.8

Source: Agricultural Statistical at a Glance 2008.

India's Share in Global Trade

Food products (excluding fish) from about 64% of the total export of agriculture products. The export of agricultural products from India 2004 was of the order of US$ 7.06 billion ranking 22nd in the world with a market share of 1.16%. India's share in global exports seem to be very small considering that India has 184 million hectare of arable land and is the 3rd largest producer of food in the world. However, this may be largely attributed to the fact that we are also one of the largest consumers for most of the products.

Table 2: %Share Agri-Exports Monitored by APEDA in the Total Exports to Different Countries

Country	*%Share*	*Country*	*%Share*	*Country*	*%Share*
Bangladesh	15.69	Nigeria	03.95	Ivory coast	01.87
Saudi Arabia	14.14	U.K.	03.67	Yamen A.R.	01.85
UAE	07.44	Srialanka	03.44	Germany	01.85
Malaysia	05.97	South Africa	03.35	Indonesia	01.81
U.S.A.	04.74	Kuwait	02.63	India	1.16(22nd Rank)

Sources: www.indiastat.com/india/Data 2006

Growth of Exports of India compared with Global Trade

If one compares the growth of exports from India during the 4years of the tenth plan with the growth in the corresponding period in the global trade for the same commodities it would give an idea as to whether the growth is in real terms or not.

The Growth in the exports from India in the case of wheat and rice is much lower than the global growth which indicates that the share of India in global trade in these commodities has gone down.

Table 3: Agriculture Exports of India

Commodities	*2002-03*	*2003-04*	*2004-05*	*2005-06*	*2006-07**
I- Plantations	2626.04	2723.26	2909.38	3209.16	-
1.Tea	1652.07	1637.35	1840.30	1632.09	-
2. Coffee	993.98	1085.92	1069.08	1577.07	-
II-Agri & Allied products	22848.97	24844.48	28276.93	32797.32	-
1.Cereals	7682.17	6956.68	9022.57	8244.35	
(a) Rice	5831.24	4167.98	6768.92	7074.35	8470.00
(b) Wheat	1759.87	2391.15	1459.82	557.12	-
(C) others	91.06	397.55	793.83	512.88	522.00
2. Pulses	345.02	328.60	602.57	1102.62	675.00
3.Tobacco	1022.89	1096.47	1254.61	1330.11	1450.00
4. Spices	1655.49	1544.18	1883.18	2218.09	-
5. Nuts & Seeds	2690.68	3003.45	3809.84	3864.37	-
6. Oil Meals	1487.35	3348.41	3177.60	4826.07	-
7. Sugar & Mollasses	1814.54	1235.97	155.05	584.38	-
8 Processed foods	2929.00	3485.06	3430.94	4154.15	-
9. Meat & Preparations	1377.19	1714.41	1905.27	2647.50	3370.00
10.Poultary & Diary products	358.52	415.15	740.75	1112.07	1225.00
11. Floriculture	180.77	250.47	222.92	304.69	365.00
12. Spirit & Beverages	119.06	121.92	139.31	271.14	324.00

Source: Indian Planning Commission (11th Plan).

The strength on the demand side is India's huge domestic market with a growing middle-class with rising income fuelling consumption. Gulf countries and the countries in the SAARC region form the major market for Indian agro products. By 2010,. Since the bulk of the world population lives in the developing and emerging markets these would continue to be significant consumers of the agro products. Estimates suggest that an additional 1.2 billion consumers across the world will buy packaged foods for the first time, by 2010, bulk of which will be from the developing and emerging markets in Asia and Africa. India would have tremendous scope of increasing the export of agro products to these markets particularly after the domestic support and export subsidies are reduced by the EU and USA under WTO commitments by 2013.

Current WTO Negotiations on Domestic Subsidies and its Impact on India

During the Uruguay Round, initial projections suggested that the reform measures initiated by the AoA would open up new opportunities for developing countries. Early analysis of the likely effect of the AoA on world markets predicted that reduction in domestic support and export subsidies in the developed countries would lead to a deepening of world trade in agriculture, a spatial redistribution of agricultural production, an increase in the share of developing countries in global agricultural exports and more transparency in agricultural trade. A recent WTO Secretariat paper39 has analyzed agricultural trade performance by developing countries for the period 1990-2003. The Table shows that between 1995 and 2003.

Developing countries have only managed to increase their share in global agricultural trade by 2 percentage points. A closer look at the regional trade patterns shows that 'Developing Asia' has not gained any market share during this period and its market share has stagnated at around 16.5 percent for the entire period. The table also shows that the 2 percent gain in market share experienced by developing countries happened mostly because of good export performance of countries from Latin America and the Caribbean (mainly due to good export performance of Brazil, Argentina and Mexico).

Table 4: Share of Developing Countries in World Agricultural Exports by Region, 1990-2003 (Percentage)

	1990	*1995*	*1996*	*1997*	*1998*	*1999*	*2000*	*2001*	*2002*	*2003*
All Developing Countries	39	39.5	39.5	40	41.5	42	40	40	41	41.5
Africa	6	5.5	5.5	5	5.5	5.5	4.5	4.5	5	5
Developing Asia	15	16.5	16	15.5	16	16.5	16	15.5	16.5	16.5
Latin America Caribbean	16	15.5	16	17.5	18	17.5	17	17.5	17.5	17.5
Middle East	2	2	2	2	2	2.5	2.5	2.5	2.5	2.5

Source: WTO Secretariat

Calculations based on the data provided in the WTO document shows that India's share in world agricultural exports has increased marginally from 1.77percent in 1995 to 1.87 percent in 2003. In fact the table shows that for the UR AoA implementation period (1995- 2001), India's share in total agricultural exports was on a decline, India registered a decline in agricultural exports over the period 1995 to 2001.India's farm exports have marginally recovered in the last two years reported in the WTO study.

Conclusion:

Aimed at making Indian agriculture not only globally more competitive but also domestically more progressive by using knowledge as a strategic resource so that agriculture sustains livelihoods of millions of households dependent upon it in an environmentally sustainable manner. The major contention is that India should not view the challenges posted by WTO as if it will remain always an importing country and that it has no substantive offer to world market. Agricultural development continues to remain the most important objective of Indian planning and policy. The agriculture development is existing systems of delivery of agriculture inputs and marketing of agriculture output have not been efficient in reaching the benefits of technology to all the sections of farmers. There is plenty of distress sales among farmers both in agriculturally developed as well as backward region.

An analysis of the global trends after WTO indicates unprecedented decline in the global prices of agricultural commodities, severely hitting earnings from agricultural exports of the countries. India too could not gain much from WTO and global liberalization, though India generally performs better than the other countries when the international price situation is favourable. As the exports are becoming increasingly competitive, it is not possible to promote exports without improving produce quality, efficiency and cost reduction. India is facing challenges in traditional export items; the challenge is not from the developed countries, but from the developing countries; major import of vegetable oils are from the developing countries (Malaysia and Indonesia); and India has done well in export of high value products to the developed countries.

The ongoing Doha round of the WTO negotiations, India has been pushing for greater liberalization of Mode 4 and Modes1&2. However, services negotiations have taken a back seat to negotiation in agriculture and non-agricultural market access. India should push for reduction of regulatory barriers in the on going Doha Round since most developed countries are now replacing market access barriers with regulatory barriers which are more difficult to identify and address.

REFERENCES

Acharya, S.S. (2000): "Economic Reforms Programme: A case of Agricultural policies in India", in Bhalla, G.S. (Ed.) *New policies for a New India,* ICSSR and Haranand Publication.

Beghin, J.C., D. Roland-Holst and D.Vander Mensbrugghe (2002): "Global Agriculture Trade and the Doha Round: What are the Implications for North and South?", Working paper 02-WP 308, Centre for Agricultural and Rural Development, Iowa State University.

Gill, S.S. and J.S. Brar (1996): "Global Market and Competitiveness of Indian Agriculture: Some Issues", *EPW,* August 10, 2175.

Desai, B.M and N.V. Namboodiri (1999): "Farmers' Response, Prices and Government Expenditure Analysis under WTO Framework for Developing Agriculture," in *Impact of WTO on Indian Agriculture*, edited by S.K. Datta and S.Y. Deodhar, Delhi: Oxford and IBH Publishing Company Pvt. Ltd.

Dutta, Ruddar and Sundharam, K.P.M. (2005): *Indian Economy*, S.Chand & Company Ltd., New Delhi.

Geithner, T. and G. Nankani (2002): "Market Access for Developing Country Exports", IMF.

Hathaway, D.E. and M.D. Ingco (1995): Agricultural Liberalisation and the Uruguay Round, Paper presented at the World Bank Conference on The Uruguay Round and the Developing Economies. Washington, January 26-27.

ITN (1999): "WTO Rules Against India in Import Restrictions Dispute," *India Today News*, internet edition, April 8.

Konandreas, P. and J. Greenfield (1996): "Uruguay Round Commitments on Domestic Support: Their Implications for Developing Countries," *Food Policy*, vol. 21, No.4/5 pp. 439.Konandreas, P., R. Sharma, and J. Greenfield (1999): "Some Issues that May Arise in the Continuation of the Reform Process in Agriculture," Round Table on Follow-up to the Uruguay Round Agreement on Agriculture, New Delhi, India, January 18-19.

NCAER (1997): India's Agricultural Exports in the Post-Uruguay Round Set Up: Implications, Prospects and Policies, A report for the Ministry of Commerce, Government of India. Parikh, K., N. S. S. Narayana, M. Panda, and A. Ganesh Kumar (1995): "Strategies for Agricultural Liberalisation: Consequences for Growth, Welfare, and Distribution," Economic and Political Weekly, September 30.

Planning Commission (2006): An Approach to the 11th Five Year Plan.

Sharma, S. (1997): "The World Trade Organisation and Implications for Developing Countries,"*SAIS Review*, Summer/Fall.

Subramanian, S. (1993): Agricultural Trade Liberalisation and India, Paris: OECD.

WTO (1995): The Results of the Uruguay Round of Multilateral Trade Negotiations - The Legal Texts, http://www.wto.org/wto/legal/

WTO (1997): Annual Report, 1997, pp. 12 and 51, Geneva: World Trade Organisation.

15

Differentials in Agricultural Productivity in India

Sukhjeet K. Saran & Mini Goyal

Agriculture being the backbone of Indian economy, concerted efforts have been made for its improvement in the post independence period. The green revolution has solved the food problem of the country but has created the regional imbalances in agricultural development. Agricultural development is a complex process and has multi-dimensional structure depending upon its resources in general and infrastructural facilities in particular. It is necessary to have a group of indicators to measure it. Food grains availability and agricultural development not only provides strong foundation to the national economy but can also resolve the inherent problem of income, poverty, employment and over all development in the country. Since any attempt to restrict the study to the aggregative level alone will tend to conceal the distinctive characteristics of the individual states, so the present paper attempts to analyze the differentials in the growth of productivity of food grains and non-food grains between different states of India and the factors responsible for the differential growth in the productivity.

Methodology

The secondary data have been collected from the various

issues of Statistical Abstracts of Punjab for the year 1965-66, 1989-90 and 2004-05. The limitation of the data was that 16 states have been taken and information of the variables taken into account contributed more than 96 percent to the agricultural productivity of India. Moreover, the data for the states of Bihar and Jharkhand, Madhya Paradesh and Chattisgarh and Uttar Pradesh and Uttaranchal have been merged and these states have been taken as Bihar, Madhya Pradesh and Uttar Pradesh. Food grains include rice, jowar, bajra, maize, wheat, barley, other cereals, gram and other pulses. Non-food grains include oil seeds, cotton, chillies and tobacco. Since the absolute data were adjusted with reference to the existing boundaries of the States, it was fairly comparable over time. The linear function of the type $y = a+b_t$ was fitted to the three year moving average of yield data. This averaging was done to smoothen the uneven nature of data that had arisen due to different methods of yield estimation in the State. The liner function was chosen for this purpose because it gave a better fit to the scatter of productivity data for these years.

Based on this function, the trend values of productivity of different crops were estimated for the years 1965-66, 1989-90 and 2004-05 for each State and for the India as a whole. These values were then transformed into indexes by taking the India value of the corresponding years as base 100. This brought all the states to a common base and made it easy to visualize and trace the changes in productivity of different States relative to the India average since 1965-66 through 2004-05. Obviously, these indices reflect the levels of development of a variable at the beginning and at the end of sample period. Since the level of development at the end of sample period depends upon the growth performance of a variable during the entire period, so it needed to be associated and supplemented by the growth rates. Compound annual growth rates for the post-green revolution period and post liberalization period have been worked out by using the following functional form:

$Y = ab^t e^u$ where, r (growth rate) = $(b-1) \times 100$

Factor responsible for this differential growth of productivity were also explored to the extent possible in this study.

Results and Discussion

The level of productivity of food grains by states is encompassed of food grains, cereals, pulses, and non-food grains. All these indicators of agricultural development in food grains production have been analyzed separately.

Food grains

Table 1 represents the productivity levels of food grains by States according to ranks during the period 1965- 66 to 2004-05. The performance of nine states was above the national level in the beginning of the sample period but during 1989-90, all these states, except that of Himachal Pradesh, which showed practically no growth, continued to fall in this category. Among these states, Punjab and Madhya Pradesh maintained their previous ranks i.e. first and eighth respectively, despite recording 3.57 and 3.01 percent which were above the all India level. The states of Haryana and Uttar Pradesh could succeed in improving their ranks from fourth and seventh to second and fifth respectively by registering an impressive growth rate. On the other hand, the states of Kerala, Tamil Nadu, Jammu & Kashmir and West Bengal failed to do so since the growth of productivity in these states remained below the all India level. A mixed pattern has been noticeable in the performance of the states that remained below the national level. However, none of these states has showed any improvement in its rank position.

During the period 2004-05, nine states performed above the national level, out of which, eight states retained their previous performance and the state of Himachal Pradesh has shifted upward by registering an impressive growth rate of 3.85 percent. Though the Punjab and Haryana states have maintained their previous ranks but their growth rates have decelerated from 3.51 percent and 4.31 percent to 1.32 per cent and 2.62 percent respectively. The position of Gujarat state has improved by registering a superb growth rate of 6.16 percent but its performance remained below the national level. Other states, whose performance have been below the national level have not shown any significant improvement in their rank position since the growth of productivity of Gujarat, Karnataka, Orissa and Rajasthan remained well above the all India level. This indicates that the comparative position of the performance of a state at the end of study period has determined partly by its state of performance in the base period and partly by its growth during the entire period. It will be wrong to rush to conclusions on the basis of one alone.

These results highlight that during 1965-66, 54 per cent of the states had productivity above the national level but during 1989-90, only fifty percent of the states could achieve that and during 2004-05, more than 56 percent have produced above the national level. While the relative performance of some of the states has improved, it has deteriorated in case of others and remained unaffected in the case of still others during later periods. It is pertinent to note that Punjab along with Haryana has emerged into the developed states of India during the period from 1989-90 to 2004-05 but growth productivity of both the states has decreased during the period. On the other hand, Madhya Pradesh, Maharashtra and Rajasthan continued to remain the least developed states so far as food grain production was concerned.

Since the food grain sub-sector is a composite group of cereals and pulses, so in order to see whether the states have performed equally well in both, a separate analysis has been carried out.

Cereals

Table 2 reveals that in the beginning of the sample period the performance of eleven states was above the national level whereas during 1989-90 only eight states did so. Of these eleven states, the four states of Karnataka, Bihar, Himachal Pradesh and Orissa, due to poor growth of productivity, failed to retain their previous category. In contrast, the states of Punjab and Haryana raised their ranks from seventh and tenth to first and second respectively by registering an impressive growth rate of 3.83 and 4.90 percent per annum. Andhra Pradesh could improve its rank only marginally despite recording a growth rate as high as 3.12 percent per annum. But the states of Kerala, Tamil Nadu, West Bengal and Jammu & Kashmir failed to retain their previous ranks, though in Tamil Nadu growth rate exceeded the all India level. Among the five states which performed below the all India level during 1965-66, Uttar Pradesh was the only state which could manage to change its category by registering an impressive growth rate of 3.56 percent per annum. Rest of the states showed deterioration in their respective ranks.

During the period 1989-90 to 2004-05, eight of the states performed above the national level. The state of Jammu & Kashmir could not retain its position of the period 1989-90, though registering a growth rate above the all India level. The state of Uttar Pradesh could succeed in improving its rank from fifth to first by registering a superb growth rate of 6.99 percent per annum. During 1989-90, the states which performed below the all India level, Himachal Pradesh was the only state that could step up one stair by registering an impressive growth rate of 3.80 per cent per annum. The position of other states in their respective ranks almost represented a little bit change.

The results highlight the consistent efforts made by the states of Uttar Pradesh, Punjab and Haryana to emerge as the leading states of India. The states of Rajasthan, Bihar, Madhya Pradesh and Maharashtra, however, continued to be the least developed despite their best efforts.

Pulses

During the period 1965-66, the performance of the states in pulses was relatively poor (Table 3). Only five states performed above the all India level during this period. This number has, however, increased to eight as the states of Kerala, Bihar and Orissa have also succeeded in joining this category during 1989-90. Of these three states, Kerala and Bihar have made tremendous improvement and raised their respective ranks to third and fourth by recording growth rates of 3.63 and

3.48 percent but growth rate has been relatively low in Orissa. Uttar Pradesh along with Punjab has emerged as the leading states but Himachal Pradesh and Tamil Nadu have lagged behind in the developmental process.

Comparing the performance of different states during the periods 1989-90 and 2004-05, two states Jammu & Kashmir and Orissa have slipped down below the national level. The state of Uttar Pradesh has maintained its previous position but Punjab has shifted from rank second to rank fourth. The state of Tamil Nadu has shown impressive improvement by shifting upward to the third rank and by registering a growth rate of 4.47 percent per annum. Other states falling under both the categories have shown mixed pattern of the shifts of their respective ranks. Though the performance of Himachal Pradesh remained below the national level but registered a remarkable growth rate of 10.66 percent.

All these results highlight that during the later period; fifty percent of the states have performed above the national average in regard to cereals and more than fifty percent to pulses. Further the relative performance of a particular state in regard to productivity of food grains depended primarily on its performance in the cereals sub-group. This is not surprising since this sub-group commands to a large weight in the food grains sub-sector.

Non-food Grains

Table 4 exhibits that in the sub-sector of non-food grains, performance of the eight of the states remained above the national level during the period 1965-66 and 1989-90. However, during the period 1988-90, Kerala and Bihar slipped down as they showed poor growth. Rajasthan and AP shifted up by registering a growth rate of 4.69 and 2.91 percent per annum. The states of Punjab and Haryana retained their previous ranks, i.e. first and second even though Haryana registered a growth below the national level. Remaining states showed a mixed pattern in the changes of their respective ranks. During the period 2004-05, out of the nine states, only five states could retain their previous level whereas Punjab and Haryana have been still leading states in the production of non-food grains. During the period, the state of Gujarat shifted to third rank from the fifth rank by registering an excellent growth rate of 8.83 percent per annum. Among the eight states which performed below all India level during 1989-90, Kerala was the only state which could manage to change its category by registering an impressive growth rate of 4.41 percent during 2004-05. During the period 2004-05, only 37 percent of the states showed the productivity above national level, whereas Punjab and Haryana maintained their first and second ranks throughout the study period.

The study reveals that relative performance in the food grain as well as non-food grain sub sectors varies among the states during the entire study periods. The states of West Bengal, Himachal Pradesh, Andhra Pradesh, Uttar Pradesh and Kerala performed above the national level in the food-grain sub-sector during the study period but failed to do so in the non-food grain sub-sector. Similarly Gujarat and Tamil Nadu performed above the national level during the entire study period in the non-food grain sub-sector. It was interesting to note that the two states of Punjab and Haryana have emerged as leading states by their performance in both the sub-sectors but the states, at the other extreme were not the same in these two sub-sectors.

As agricultural productivity depends upon a number of other factors, technological and institutional, therefore, it becomes essential to assess these to evaluate the performance of a particular State.

Factors Responsible for the Differential Growth in Productivity

There can possibly be many factors responsible for the growth of productivity. The productivity of a crop may change due to level of fertilizer use, intensity of cropping, irrigated area, area under HYV and agricultural machinery. In the Indian economy, by and large, the use of these agricultural inputs has been restricted to foodgrain sub-sector which has pre-dominated the Indian agricultural scenario. An attempt has been made to compare the performance of the states in this sub-sector and also the use of each of these inputs.

Intensity of Cropping

Table 5 indicates that, during 1965-66, the intensity of cropping was above the national average in eight states, where this number rose to nine during 1989-90 as the state of Madhya Pradesh joined this category. The state of Punjab has recorded the highest growth rate as 1.99 percent per annum. Uttar Pradesh and Punjab have marginally improved their ranks and Kerala has drifted down from second rank to sixth rank. Haryana and Orissa have succeeded in maintaining their previous ranks. The other two states of Himachal Pradesh and Jammu & Kashmir showed a downward shift in their ranks. The states below the national average also exhibited a mixed pattern in the changes of their ranks.

During the period 2004-05, out of nine states, only one state i.e. Madhya Pradesh drifted down in its performance. No doubt, Punjab has retained the first rank but growth of intensity of cropping has declined. Haryana has shifted one rank ahead whereas Kerala drifted down from sixth rank to eighth rank representing the deterioration in its performance. The other states above the national average showed the marginal changes in their ranks. Among the eight states which performed below the all India level during 2004-05, the performance of Gujarat has worsened whereas other states exhibited slight changes in their previous performance.

It may be noted that, by and large, the states in which the intensity of cropping was above the national average also had productivity of food grains above it during the study period. But this does not apply to the states of Tamil Nadu and Andhra Pradesh in either of three periods. The states of Punjab and Haryana were leading in these characteristics during the entire study period. But in Himachal Pradesh, intensity of cropping does not seem to have contributed to higher productivity to the same extent.

Irrigation

Since water is one of the crucial inputs in the agricultural sector and assured irrigational facilities play a multipurpose role in defense against the vagaries of monsoon, boosting the productivity of existing inputs with the existing technology and aiding in the use of improved seeds and new technology. An analysis of the irrigation area reveals that it was above the national average in nine states during 1965-66 (Table 6). But during 1988-99, it was so in seven states because Kerala and West Bengal had drifted down. During 2004-05, it rose to eight states as Madhya Pradesh state has shifted up by registering an impressive growth rate of 7.58 percent but the state of Jammu & Kashmir could not manage its previous performance, slipped down with negative growth.

During the period 1965-66 to 1989-90, Kerala occupied the lowest rank. The states of Haryana, Uttar Pradesh and Bihar have improved their ranks from fourth, fifth and eighth to second, third and seventh respectively are registering a growth rate well above national level. Punjab and Andhra Pradesh have succeeded in retaining their previous ranks despite recording growth below the national level. Similarly, a mixed pattern was noticeable among the states which stood below the national average. All states, except Bihar, having irrigated area above the national average, and also have productivity of food grains above it during both the periods. During the period 2004-05, Punjab has slipped down to rank fourth from rank first by registering a negative growth rate having decrease in the irrigated area. The other states which stood below the national average showed marginal changes in their respective ranks.

Area Under High Yield Varieties

Table 7 shows that per unit area under HYV was above the national average for eight states during 1965-66, but this number has increased to nine during 1989-90. However, during the later period while Kerala has slipped downward, Bihar and Andhra Pradesh shifted up. Also while some of the states have managed to improve, others have lost their previous ranks during the later period, in both the categories. The states of Punjab and Haryana have, however, succeeded in raising their respective ranks to first and fourth by registering a tremendous growth rate of 11.97 and 20.59 per cent per annum respectively. During 2004-05, seven of the states performed above the national level. Punjab maintained its previous rank by registering a growth rate of 0.17 per cent per annum. Among the states, which had per unit area under high yield varieties below the national average, the states of Maharashtra, Gujarat, Karnataka and Kerala drifted down in ranks. A comparative analysis of the performance of the states in regard to the area under HYV and the productivity of food grains showed the states, which had per unit area under HYV above the national average also had productivity of food grains above it during 1965-66, 1989-90 and 2004-05. But this was not so for the states of Himachal Pradesh and Bihar during 1989-90 and Bihar and Orissa during 2004-05.

Consumption of Fertilizer

Application of fertilizers is one of the most effective methods of increasing fertility of soil. As soils losing its fertility over time, become poorer, crop yield become more dependant on the use of fertilizer (Chopra, 1986). Perusal of table 8 shows the performance of different states in the consumption of fertilizer where it accounted that during the period of 1965-66, per unit consumption of fertilizers was above the national average in five states. This number has increased to seven during 1989-90. Of the former five states, Kerala, Jammu & Kashmir and Maharashtra have drifted down wards during later period. Andhra Pradesh has just stuck to its previous rank while Tamil Nadu has come down from the first to the second rank. The states of Punjab, Uttar Pradesh, West Bengal, Haryana and Karnataka, which had per unit consumption of fertilizers below the national average, have improved tremendously and crossed the national average during the period 1989-90. During the period 2004-05, the states of Punjab, Andhra Pradesh, Uttar Pradesh and West Bengal retained their previous ranks. The per unit consumption of fertilizer of the state Haryana has increased during this period and this state has shifted to second rank from the sixth rank whereas Tamil Nadu has taken place of Haryana by shifting from second to sixth rank. The position of Madhya Pradesh and Gujarat has improved and crossed the national average by registering the growth rates of 5.09 and 0.17 per cent respectively. The other states below the national average represented a mixed pattern in the changes of their ranks.

A comparative analysis of the performance of the states in the consumption of fertilizers with their respective agricultural productivity in general showed that the states which have performed above the national average in the former have also achieved a higher productivity of food grains.

Agricultural Machinery

Technological breakthrough in agriculture has made it imperative to speed up the agricultural operations lest the impact of the former should be washed away. Therefore, the use of agricultural machinery in the states has also been examined (Table 9). This characteristic examines the use of tube-wells and tractors per unit of total cropped area.

Tractors

The per unit number of tractors above the national level was in four states only during 1989-90. These states have succeeded in maintaining their previous ranks during the period 2004-05 whereas Rajasthan managed to shift up from sixth rank in 1989-90 to fifth rank in 2004-05. The states below the national average also presented a mixed pattern in the changes of their ranks. The state of Tamilnadu has recorded the highest growth rate as 17.99 per cent during the period 1989-90 to 2004-05 though its performance was below the India level.

Tube-Wells

During 1989-90, seven states were above the national level regarding per unit number of tube-wells. During the period 2004-05, out of seven states, one state i.e. Haryana drifted down the India level. Kerala and Karnataka have shifted respectively two and three ranks ahead and registered the growth rate of 2.87 and 3.00 per cent per annum, whereas Punjab and Maharashtra have receded and drifted down one and two ranks respectively.

It may be noted that in Rajasthan and Gujarat though per unit number of tractors remained above the national average but this did not seem to have contributed to productivity to the same extent. In case of tube-wells, it has happened so in the states of Karnataka, Maharashtra and Rajasthan.

Conclusion

The proceedings analysis clearly reveals that there is an uneven growth in agricultural productivity in the states. During the period under study, relative performance of some of the states has improved while it deteriorated in the case of others. The two states of Punjab and Haryana have emerged as leading states by their performance in the sub-sectors of food grains and non-food grains. West Bengal, Himachal Pradesh, Andhra Pradesh, Uttar Pradesh and Kerala performed above the national level in the food-grain sub-sector. Madhya Pradesh, Maharashtra and Rajasthan continued to remain the least developed states so far as food grain production was concerned. Gujarat and Tamil Nadu performed above the national average in the non-food grain sub-sector. Overall study reveals that the performance of the states in regard to productivity of food grains depends upon fertilizer consumption, irrigation facilities, cropping intensity, high yielding varieties and machinery. However, the performance of a particular state seems to be determined by the use of multiple rather than one single agricultural input. During the periods under study, relative performance of some of the states has improved, while it deteriorated in the case of others and remained unaffected in the case of still others.

Policy Implications

With the green revolution, increased production has brought food sufficiency to the country. But the differentials in growth of productivity of food grains and non-food grains in different states of India have resulted in regional imbalance among the states since the agricultural performance of a state depends on use of multiple factor inputs like high cropping intensity, irrigation facilities, use of high yielding varieties, fertilizers, agricultural machinery, etc. rather than one single agricultural input, it is necessary to strengthen infrastructural facilities uniformly in all over the states.

BIBLIOGRAPHY

Alag, Y.K. and Sharma, P.S. (1980), Growth of Crop Production: 1960-61 to 1978-79- Is It Decelerating?, *Indian Journal of Agricultural Economics*, 35(2), April-June.

Chatak, S. and Ingercent, K. (1984), *Agriculture and Economic development*, Select Book Service Syndicate, New Delhi.

Chopra, R.N. (1986), *Green Revolution in India, A Study of Punjab, Haryana, UP and Bihar*, Pub: Intellectual Publishing House, 23 Ansari Road, Daryaganj, New Delhi- 110 002: 47.

Kausik, K. K. (1993), Growth and Instability of Oil Seeds Production, *Indian Journal of Agricultural Economics*, 48(3), July-Sept.

Mahendra, S. (1987), Growth and Instability in Food Grains Production; An Inter- State Analysis, *Economic and Political Weekly*, Sept. 26.

Roy, Soma (2008), A study of Crop Fluctuation in India During Post Green Revolution Period, *Indian Journal of Regional Science*, 40 (1): 53-66.

Shukla, Narendra and Sandeep Dhagat (1999), Disparities of Economic Development in India- A Factor Analysis Approach, *Indian Journal of Regional Science*, 31(1):13-18.

Debapriya, A. and M. K. Mohanty, Inter-districtVariations in the Levels of Industrial Development of Orissa, *Asian Economic Review*, 48 (1).

Debapriya, Aryashree and Manmath kumar Mohanty, Inter-district Disparity in the Levels of Development in Education and Health Care Facilities- A Case of Orissa, *Indian Journal of Regional Science*, 40 (1)118-123

Table 1: Levels of Productivity of Food Grains by States According to Ranks, 1965-66 to 2004-05

Rank	*1965-66*	*1989-90*	*Growth Rate*	*1989-90*	*2004-05*	*Growth Rate*
			Abov^ the India Level			
1	Punjab	Punjab	3.57	Punjab	Punjab	1.32
2	Kerala	Haryana	4.31	Haryana	Haryana	2.62
3	Tamil Nadu	Kerala	1.18	Kerala	West Bengal	2.50
4	Haryana and Jammu & Kashmir	Tamil Nadu	1.58	Tamil Nadu	Kerala	1.85

5	West Bengal	Uttar Pradesh	3.28	Uttar Pradesh	Andhra Pradesh	2.88
6	Himachal Pradesh	Jammu& Kashmir	2.02	Jammu& Kashmir	Uttar Pradesh	1.72
7	Uttar Pradesh	West Bengal	1.65	West Bengal	Himachal Pradesh	3.85
8	Andhra Pradesh	Andhra Pradesh	3.01	Andhra Pradesh	Tamil Nadu	0.60
9					Jammu& Kashmir	3.04
			Below the India Level			
1	Bihar	Bihar	1.88	Bihar	Gujarat	6.16
2	Karnataka	Karnataka	2.09	Karnataka	Karnataka	3.08
3	Orissa	Himachal Pradesh	0.004	Himachal Pradesh	Orissa	3.21
4	Gujarat	Gujarat	2.10	Gujarat	Bihar	1.14
5	Madhya Pradesh	Orissa	0.41	Orissa	MP	1.69
6	Maharashtra Pradesh	Madhya	1.86	Madhya Pradesh	Rajasthan	3.86
7	Rajasthan	Maharashtra	2.54	Maharashtra	Maharashtra	0.44
8		Rajasthan	2.03	Rajasthan		
	All India		2.51			2.04

Table 2: Levels of Productivity of Cereals by States According to Ranks, 1965-66 to 2004-05

Rank	*1965-66*	*1989-90*	*Growth Rate*	*1989-90*	*2004-05*	*Growth Rate*
			Above the India Level			
1	Kerala	Punjab	3.83	Punjab	Uttar Pradesh	6.99
2	Tamil Nadu	Haryana	4.90	Haryana	Punjab	1.21
3	Himachal Pradesh	Tamil Nadu	2.96	Tamil Nadu	Haryana	2.42
4	West Bengal	Kerala	1.16	Kerala	Andhra Pradesh	3.47
5	Jammu & Kashmir	Uttar Pradesh	3.56	Uttar Pradesh	West Bengal	2.42

6	Orissa	Jammu & Kashmir	2.10	Jammu & Kashmir	Kerala	1.73
7	Punjab	West Bengal	1.52	West Bengal	Tamil Nadu	0.47
8	Bihar	Andhra Pradesh	3.12	Andhra Pradesh	Himachal Pradesh	3.80
9	Andhra Pradesh, Karnataka					
10	Haryana					
	Below the India Level					
1	Uttar Pradesh	Himachal Pradesh	0.68	Himachal Pradesh	Karnataka	3.70
2	Gujarat	Karnataka	2.40	Karnataka	Jammu& Kashmir	2.48
3	Madhya Pradesh	Bihar	1.97	Bihar	Gujarat	6.40
4	Rajasthan	Gujarat	2.39	Gujarat	Orrissa	1.20
5	Maharashatra	Orrissa	0.78	Orrissa	Rajasthan, Bihar	4.51 1.66
6		Madhya Pradesh	2.19	Madhya Pradesh	Madhya Pradesh	1.87
7		Maharashtra	2.89	Maharashtra	Maharashtra	-1.06
8		Rajasthan	2.23	Rajasthan		
	All India		2.76			2.21

Table 3: Levels of Productivity of Pulses by States According to Ranks, 1965-66 to 2004-05

Rank	*1965-66*	*1989-90*	*Growth Rate*	*1989-90*	*2004-05*	*Growth Rate*
	Above the India Level					
1	Punjab	Uttar Pradesh	3.21	Uttar Pradesh	Uttar Pradesh	0.70
2	Haryana	Punjab	-0.46	Punjab	Kerala	1.06
3	Uttar Pradesh, Jammu& Kashmir	Kerala	3.63	Kerala	Tamil Nadu	4.47
4	West Bengal	Bihar	3.48	Bihar	Punjab	1.49
5		Haryana	-0.49	Haryana	Haryana	3.79
6		West Bengal	2.19	West Bengal	West Bengal	0.96

Rank	1965-66	1989-90	Growth Rate	1989-90	2004-05	Growth Rate
7		Jammu& Kashmir	-0.12	Jammu& Kashmir	Madhya Pradesh	1.65
8		Orissa	0.70	Orissa	Gujarat, Bihar	5.05 0.00
			Below the India Level			
1	Himachal Pradesh	Madhya Pradesh	1.08	Madhya Pradesh	Himachal Pradesh, Andhra Pradesh	10.66 1.56
2	Orissa	Gujarat	1.90	Gujarat	Jammu & Kashmir, Maharashtra	1.05 0.24
3	Bihar	AP	4.37	AP	Orissa	-1.56
4	Madhya Pradesh	Karnataka	1.05	Karnataka	Karnataka	0.00
5	Rajasthan	Rajasthan	0.61	Rajasthan	Rajasthan	2.10
6	Karnataka	Maharashtra	0.90	Maharashtra		
7	Maharashtra	Tamil Nadu	2.55	Tamil Nadu		
8	Gujarat	Himachal Pradesh	-2.40	Himachal Pradesh		
9	Kerala					
10	Tamil Nadu					
11	Andhra Pradesh					
	All India		0.42			0.76

Table 4: Levels of Productivity of Non-Food Grains by States According to Ranks, 1965- 66 to 2004-05.

Rank	*1965-66*	*1989-90*	*Growth Rate*	*1989-90*	*2004-05*	*Growth Rate*
			Above the India Level			
1	Punjab	Punjab	2.89	Punjab	Punjab	2.49
2	Haryana	Haryana	1.41	Haryana	Haryana	2.81
3	Kerala	Tamil Nadu	0.66	Tamil Nadu	Gujarat	8.83
4	Tamil Nadu	Jammu & Kashmir	2.06	Jammu& Kashmir	Tamil Nadu	1.24
5	Gujarat	Andhra Pradesh	2.91	Andhra Pradesh	Kerala	4.41
6	Jammu & Kashmir	Gujarat	0.49	Gujarat	Andhra Pradesh	1.20

7	Bihar	Orissa	1.82	Orissa		
8	Orissa	Rajasthan	4.69	Rajasthan		
			Below the India Level			
1	Andhra Pradesh	Karnataka	2.76	Karnataka	Rajasthan	3.40
2	Karnataka	West Bengal	2.75	West Bengal	Jammu & Kashmir	1.92
3	Maharashtra	Kerala	-1.98	Kerala	West Bengal	0.90
4	Uttar Pradesh	Bihar	0.93	Bihar	Uttar Pradesh	3.54
5	Himachal Pradesh	Maharashtra	1.58	Maharashtra	Maharashtra	2.90
6	Madhya Pradesh	Uttar Pradesh	0.58	Uttar Pradesh	Madhya Pradesh	2.86
7	Rajasthan	Madhya Pradesh	1.63	Himachal Pradesh	Bihar, Orissa	1.61, 0.07
8	West Bengal	Himachal Pradesh	-0.75	Himachal Pradesh	Karnataka	0.88
9					Himachal Pradesh	9.04
	All India		1.71			2.74

Table 5: Levels of Cropping Intensity by States According to Ranks, 1965-66 to 2004-05

Rank	*1965-66*	*1989-90*	*Growth Rate*	*1989-90*	*2004-05*	*Growth Rate*
			Above the India Level			
1	Himachal Pradesh	Punjab	1.99	Punjab	Punjab	0.71
2	Kerala	Himachal Pradesh	0.13	Himachal Pradesh	Haryana	1.05
3	Haryana	Haryana	1.01	Haryana	Himachal Pradesh	0.39
4	Punjab	Uttar Pradesh	0.52	Uttar Pradesh	West Bengal	1.23
5	Uttar Pradesh	West Bengal	0.87	West Bengal	Orissa	0.50
6	West Bengal	Kerala	0.06	Kerala	Uttar Pradesh	0.08
7	Orissa, Jammu&	Orissa	1.07	Orissa	Jammu& Kashmir	0.27

Rank	1965-66	1989-90	Growth Rate	1989-90	2004-05	Growth Rate
	Kashmir					
8		Jammu& Kashmir	1.01	Jammu& Kashmir	Kerala	0.32
9		Madhya	0.46	Madhya Pradesh		
			Below the India Level			
1	Madhya Pradesh, Bihar	Gujarat	0.24	Gujarat	Bihar	-0.13
2	Tamil Nadu	Maharashtra	0.36	Maharashtra	Madhya Pradesh	0.66 0.72
3	Gujarat	Bihar	-0.03	Bihar	Maharashtra	0.67
4	Maharashtra	Karnataka	0.29	Karnataka	Rajasthan	0.58
5	Karnataka	Rajasthan	0.22	Rajasthan	Karnataka	0.23
6	Rajasthan	Andhra Pradesh	-0.14	Andhra Pradesh	Andhra Pradesh	-1.08
7	Andhra Pradesh	Tamil Nadu	-0.69	Tamil Nadu	Tamil Nadu	0.29
8					Gujarat	
	All India		0.43			0.38

Table 6: Levels of Total Irrigated Area as Percentage of Total Cropped Area by States According to Ranks, 1965-66 to 2004-05

Rank	*1965-66*	*1989-90*	*Growth Rate*	*1989-90*	*2004-05*	*Growth Rate*
			Above the India Level			
1	Punjab	Punjab	1.15	Punjab	Uttar Pradesh	4.13
2	Tamil Nadu	Haıyana	3.06	Haryana	Bihar	3.80
3	Jammu& Kashmir	Uttar Pradesh	2.77	Uttar Pradesh	Madhya Pradesh	7.58
4	Haryana	Tamil Nadu	0.32	Tamil Nadu	Punjab	-0.33
5	Uttar Pradesh	Jammu& Kashmir	0.62	Jammu& Kashmir	Haryana	9.86
6	Andhra Pradesh	Andhra Pradesh	1.33	Andhra Pradesh	Tamil Nadu	1.56
7	Kerala	Bihar	2.89	Bihar	West Bengal	1.75
8	Bihar				Andhra Pradesh	0.69

9	West Bengal					
			Below the India Level			
1	Himachal Pradesh	Gujarat	5.29	Gujarat	Gujarat	2.57
2	Orissa	West Bengal	0.39	West Bengal	Jammu& Kashmir	-0.32
3	Rajasthan	Orissa	2.15	Orissa	Rajasthan	2.21
4	Karnataka	Rajasthan	2.63	Rajasthan	Karnataka	1.94
5	Gujarat	Karnataka	2.47	Karnataka	Orissa	-1.38
6	Maharashtra	Himachal Pradesh	0.04	Himachal Pradesh	Maharashtra	2.12
7	Madhya Pradesh	Maharashtra	3.55	Maharashtra	Kerala	1.23
8		Madhya Pradesh	4.60	Madhya Pradesh	Himachal Pradesh	0.43
		Kerala	-3.00	Kerala		
	All India		2.27			1.31

Table 7: Levels of Area Under HYV per Unit of Total Cropped Area by States According to Ranks, 1965-66 to 2004-05

Rank	*1965-66*	*1989-90*	*Growth Rate*	*1989-90*	*2004-05*	*Growth Rate*
			Above the India Level			
1	Himachal Pradesh	Punjab	11.97	Punjab	Punjab	0.17
2	Punjab	Himachal Pradesh	20.69	Himachal Pradesh	Himachal Pradesh	-0.08
3	Tamil Nadu	Jammu& Kashmir	13.32	Jammu& Kashmir	Jammu& Kashmir	-0.26
4	Jammu& Kashmir	Haryana	20.59	Haryana	Bihar	-0.35
5	Kerala	Bihar	17.94	Bihar	Uttar Pradesh, West Bengal	0.00, -1.19
6	West Bengal	Uttar Pradesh	12.59	Uttar Pradesh	Haryana	0.44
7	Uttar Pradesh	Tamil Nadu	10.61	Tamil Nadu	Orissa	-0.13
8	Haryana	Andhra	17.15	Andhra		

		Pradesh		Pradesh		
9		West Bengal	15.00	West Bengal		
		Below the India Level				
1	Gujarat	Maharashtra	14.90	Maharashtra	Madhya Pradesh	-0.71
2	Maharashtra	Gujarat	18.05	Gujarat	Tamil Nadu	0.32
3	Karnataka	Madhya Pradesh	23.55	Madhya Pradesh	Maharashtra	-1.86
4	Andhra Pradesh	Karnataka	16.63	Karnataka	Rajasthan	-1.51
5	Rajasthan	Orissa	16.66	Orissa	Karnataka	-0.72
6	Orissa	Rajasthan	18.09	Rajasthan	Andhra Pradesh	-2.54
7	Bihar	Kerala	3.17	Kerala	Gujarat	-1.90
8					Kerala	-4.51
	All India		13.98			-0.64

Table 8: Levels of Consumption of Fertilizer per Unit of Total Cropped Area by State According to Ranks, 1965-66 to 2004-05

Rank	*1965-66*	*1989-90*	*Growth Rate*	*1989-90*	*2004-05*	*Growth Rate*
		Above the India Level				
1	Tamil Nadu	Punjab	12.89	Punjab	Punjab	0.32
2	Kerala	Tamil Nadu	8.66	Tamil Nadu	Haryana	1.28
3	Andhra Pradesh	Andhra Pradesh	9.66	Andhra Pradesh	Andhra Pradesh	-0.60
4	Jammu& Kashmir	Uttar Pradesh	12.97	Uttar Pradesh	Uttar Pradesh	0.46
5	Maharashtra	West Bengal	12.00	West Bengal	West Bengal	0.18
6		Haryana	14.88	Haryana	Tamil Nadu	-1.78
7		Karnataka	12.28	Karnataka	Madhya Pradesh	5.09
8					Gujarat	0.17
		Below the India Level				
1	Orissa	Kerala	5.32	Kerala	Bihar	-0.61
2	Gujarat	Gujarat	11.52	Gujarat	Karnataka	-1.44
3	Punjab	Maharashtra	8.90	Maharashtra	Jammu& Kashmir	0.55

4	Bihar	Bihar	10.09	Bihar	Maharashtra	-1.01
5	Karnataka	Jammu& Kashmir	7.64	Jammu& Kashmir	Kerala	0.38
6	Uttar Pradesh	Himachal Pradesh	10.89	Himachal Pradesh	Himachal Pradesh	1.30
7	Himachal Pradesh	Madhya Pradesh	14.59	Madhya Pradesh	Orissa	0.86
8	Rajasthan	Orissa	8.41	Orissa	Rajasthan	0.96
9	Madhya Pradesh	Rajasthan	13.13	Rajasthan		
10	West Bengal					
11	Haryana					
	All India		10.77			-0.22

Table 9: Number of Tractors and Tubewells per Unit of Total Cropped Area by States according to Ranks, 1965-66 to 2004-05

Rank	*1989-90*	*2004-05*	*Growth Rate*	*1989-90*	*2004-05*	*Growth Rate*
		Tractors			*Tubewells*	
		Above the India Level				
1	Punjab	Haryana	6.98	Tamil Nadu	Tamil Nadu	3.80
2	Haryana	Punjab	3.16	Andhra Pradesh	Andhra Pradesh	5.70
3	Uttar Pradesh	Uttar Pradesh	7.80	Maharashtra	Kerala	2.87
4	Gujarat	Gujarat	7.66	Punjab	Karnataka	3.00
5		Rajasthan	10.02	Kerala	Punjab, Maharashtra	5.42
6				Haryana	Rajasthan	1.53
7				Karnataka		4.96
		Below the India Level				
1	Bihar	Tamil Nadu	17.99	Gujarat	Gujarat	3.87
2	Rajasthan	Madhya Pradesh	9.45	Madhya Pradesh	Haryana	3.17
3	Madhya Pradesh	Jammu& Kashmir	8.04	Uttar Pradesh	Madhya Pradesh	1.88
4	Karnataka	Bihar	3.51	Bihar	Uttar Pradesh	1.15

5	Himachal Pradesh	Karnataka	7.32	Rajasthan	Bihar	11.66
6	Jammu& Kashmir	Maharashtra	7.84	Bihar	Bihar	1.55
7	Kerala	West Bengal	4.89	Orissa	Himachal Pradesh	3.36
8	Maharashtra Pradesh	Andhra Pradesh	5.47	Himachal	Jammu& Kashmir	7.86
9	West Bengal	Himachal Pradesh	1.42	Jammu& Kashmir	Orissa	10.54
10	Andhra Pradesh	Orissa	6.74			
11	Orissa	Kerala	0.13			
12	Tamil Nadu					
	All India		7.00			3.50

16

The Status of Agriculture Sector in the Post-Reform Period in North-East India

Subhabrata Chakrabarti & K. K. Bagchi

Introduction

In the reform period manufacturing sector is supposed to grow significantly. It apparently seems that the examination of the performance of the agriculture sector is not so important during that period. But actually it is not so. In our traditional literatures like Fisher and Clark (1940), Rostow (1960), Kuznet (1965) and Chennery (1975) it is suggested that there will be gradual expansion of manufacturing sector along with the decreasing contribution of agriculture sector during the economic transition. They have also suggested that there will be transformation of labour force in the same direction. Now the identification of any period of economic transition is not an easy task. Nevertheless, it can be said that growth of manufacturing sector can not give indulgence to the deterioration of economic status of agricultural labour in terms of their average productivity.

Objective and Methodology

The main objective of this paper is to understand whether

the agriculture sector in north-east India is neglected or not in the post-reform era.

The Methodologies Applied in the Present Study are:

1) For the trend of different sub-sectors the null hypothesis is there is no change of income shares in those sectors over time. Similarly in the regression analysis of two sectors our null hypothesis is there is no relationship between them in terms of their income shares.
2) For the estimation of employment elasticity and average productivity of workers under different sub-sectors $Y_t = Y_0 (1 + r)_t$ equation is used.
3) Labour productivity is obtained through dividing the sectoral domestic product by number of workers absorbed in that sector (Hari, 2003).

Trend of Sectoral Distribution

Table 1: Sectoral Distribution in the Post-Reform Period

SIKKIM	*93-94*	*95-96*	*96-97*	*97-98*	*98-99*	*99-00*	*00-01*	*01-02*	*02-03*	*03-04*	*04-05*	*05-6*
Agriculture	36.26	34.33	33.9	30.8	29.48	21.9	21.82	21	22.51	22.36	21.58	21.47
Manufacturing	5.61	5.14	4.74	4.09	3.86	4.3	4.08	3.8	3.48	3.24	3.06	2.88
A.PRADESH												
Agriculture	35.51	28.55	30.7	31.2	30.56	29.2	31.09	27.66	26.45	26.06	24.58	
Manufacturing	3.16	3.37	4.5	3.1	3.3	3.11	2.64	2.8	2.48	2.31	2.28	
ASSAM												
Agriculture	37.26		35.4	37.3	35.65	34.4	32.46	34.74	33.17	30.88	30	27.95
Manufacturing	8.42		8.27	9.02	7.97	8.54	7.98	7.2	7.3	7.56	7.8	8.36
MANIPUR												
Agriculture	31.19		27.6	26.3	26.3	22.3	27.7	25.75	24.41	24.38	23.13	
Manufacturing	7.39		6.97	6.5	9.62	9.94	7.5	8.1	8.48	8.82	8.87	
MEGHALAYA												
Agriculture	26.05	26.56	27.5	26.2	24.8	26.5	25.47	24.83	24.21	23.12	22.3	
Manufacturing	2.57	2.81	2.92	2.33	1.9	2.08	2.09	1.82	2.73	2.69	2.66	
NAGALAND												
Agriculture	20.87	18.39	19.2	22.5	24.9	28.2	30.31	33.32	34.32			
Manufacturing	• 3	5.59	6.34	5.93	2.15	0.78	0.66	0.8	0.64			
TRIPURA												
Agriculture	31.43		28.7	26.5	26.43	25.2	20.79	22.27	20.63	19.35		

Manufacturing	3.26	2.66	2.42	1.07	1.92	3.66	2.6	1.66	1.57
MIZORAM									
Agriculture	27.72	27.4	27.5	27.25	21.6	27.28	24.54	22.52	
Manufacturing	2.74	3.14	1.59	1.23	1.22	1.05	0.96	0.86	

Source: Calculated from October 2004 & January 2006 Databank Quarterly Journal NEDFI

The data have been collected over the period 1993-2005. In terms of changes in percentage share of sectoral contribution Sikkim, Arunachal Pradesh, Assam, Tripura and Mizoram have experienced a negative trend regarding manufacturing sector estimated as -2.73, -0.88, -0.06, -1.69 and -1.88 respectively. On the other hand agricultural sector in these states have shown negative trends as -14.49, -10.93, -9.31, -12.08 and -5.2 respectively. In Manipur and Meghalaya the contribution of manufacturing sector has increased marginally along with the falling share of agricultural sector.

Table 2: Results on the Simple Linear Trend of Agriculture (A), Manufacturing (M), Secondary (S) and Tertiary (T) Sectors

Sikkim	*t statistic*	*R2*	*p value*
A Sector	-5.088*	.742	.001
M sector	-8.794*	.896	.000
Arunachal Pradesh			
A Sector	-3.428*	.595	.009
M sector	-4.355*	.703	.002
Assam			
M sector	-1.472	.213	.179
Manipur			
A Sector	-1.877	.335	.103
M sector	1.193	.169	.272
Meghalaya			
A Sector	-5.832*	.810	.000
M sector	-.152	.003	.883
Nagaland			
A Sector	22.761*	.989	.000

M sector	-4.71*	.787	.003
Tripura			
A Sector	-7.928*	.913	.000
M sector	-.457	.034	.663
Mizoram			
A Sector	-1.779	.388	.135
M sector	-3.098**	.658	.027

Note: (*) indicates significant at 1% level of significance; (**) indicates significant at 5% level of significance; (***) indicates significant at 10% level of significance

Table 3: Annual Growth Rate of Sectoral Income Shares

	Sikkim	*Arunachal Pradesh*	*Assam*	*Manipur*	*Meghalaya*	*Nagaland*	*Tripura*	*Mizoram*
A sector	-2.17%	-0.89%	-1.09%	-0.59%	-0.79%	4.28%	-2.37%	-1.19%
M sector	-2.17%	-2.56%	-0.39%	1.005%	-0.09%	-15.71%	-1.09%	-7.5%

Source: Calculated from Table 1.

Table 3 suggests growth rate of agriculture sector's income share is negative in all states except Nagaland. On the other hand, among all the states Manipur only has experienced positive growth of manufacturing sector's income share. Though not shown, it has been observed that, because of the rising share of the construction sector, in Sikkim, Meghalaya and Tripura, the growth rate of secondary sector's income share is positive where as the same for manufacturing sector's income share is negative. By the same logic in Arunachal Pradesh, Assam, Nagaland and Mizoram the income share of secondary sector is reduced at a lower rate compared to the rate by which income share of manufacturing sector is reduced. Thus, in Manipur only we notice positive growth of manufacturing sector during post-liberalisation period though, to be remembered that the rising trend of manufacturing sector in this state is not statistically significant (Table 2).

Agricultural Output in North-Eastern States

Apparently from the experience of north-eastern states

mentioned above in the pre-reform period, it will not be wise to conclude that secondary sector has been much influenced by the primary sector with its usual trend of falling importance in total domestic product. We have noticed from the very beginning (70's or 80's) tertiary sector has occupied a lion share of domestic product, it may be considered as the tertiarisation without being dependent on secondary sector or it may be called tertiarisation bypassing the secondary sector. The dynamics of the shares can not be the only clue to the causes underlying economic progress. It must be accompanied with quantam rises in the aggregate value of GDP for economic development to take a firm hold. As per report of the world development indicators 2004 the share of agriculture sector of Japan, UK, USA are only 1%, 1%, and 2% respectively. Keeping in mind the issue of self sufficiency in food supply, development can take place, even if there is low and declining share of primary sector.

Let us have a look on the production status of food grain in the northeastern states. Table 4 suggests that except Manipur and Meghalaya in all other states growth rate of production of foodgrain over 1985-2000 is lower than the growth rate of productivity. Moreover in the decade of 1990's growth of foodgrain production in Assam (17.6%), Manipur (31.46%), Meghalaya(35.29%) and Mizoram(49.36%) have maintained a balance with the population growth in between 1991-2001. On the other hand, Tripura and Arunachal Pradesh have experienced negative growth of foodgrain production. Besides, Nagaland having highest growth rate of population during 1991-2001(64.46%), had foodgrain production growth of only 45.49%. Thus per capita foodgrain availability has decreased for Tripura, Arunachal Pradesh and Nagaland in the decade of 1990's.

Table 5 exhibits production of fruits and vegetables subject to three reference periods. Figures given within the brackets are the growth rates with respect to previous reference periods. It is to be noticed that during 2001-05, four states, viz, Arunachal Pradesh, Assam, Mizoram and Nagaland have registered negative growth in the fruit and vegetable output. Moreover, during 1991-2002 fruit and vegetable output growth was 23.63%. Where as, growth of productivity (MT/ha) of the same was 10.03%. The entire northeast region has been identified with crop diversification or shifting in the agricultural pattern from food grain production towards fruit and vegetable production. Food grain output by its share in total agricultural output has decreased from 71.8% (1990-91) to 64.41% (2003-04). The same for fruits and vegetables has increased from 9.88% to 12.92%

Table 4: Production ('000 tonnes) & Productivity (kg/ha) of Foodgrain During 1985-2000

	1985-86	*1990-91*	*1999-2000*	*Growth (85-00)*
A.Pradesh	173-Production	220	205	18.5%
	1071-Productivity	1173	1126	5.13%
Assam	3031-Prodction	3442	4048	33.55%
	1112-Productivity	1249	1406	26.43%
Manipur	347-Production	286	376	8.36%
	2038-Productivity	1673	2238	9.81%
Meghalaya	160-Production	153	207	29.37%
	1152-Productivity	1147	1556	35.06%
Mizoram	51-Production	77	115	125.5&
	926-Productivity	1296	1474	59.17%
Nagaland	111-Production	211	307	176.58%
	677-Productivity	1166	1420	109.74%
Tripura	395-Production	515	513	29.87%
	1371-Productivity	1783	2138	55.94%

Source: NEDFi Quarterly Journal; April 2004.

Table 5: Production of Fruits and Vegetable ('000 MT) in NE States

	1991-92	*2001-02*	*2005-06*
Arunahal Pradesh	127.2	208.8(64.15%)	182.03(-12.82%)
Assam	3018.7	4270.(41.48&)	3201.5(-25.02%)
Manipur	93.3	200.1(114.46%)	426.96(113.37%)
Meghalaya	437.3	452.8(3.54%)	471.42(4.11%)
Mizoram	66.6	107.5(61.41%)	66.50(-38.13%)
Nagaland	76.1	588(672.66%)	132.42(-77.47%)
Sikkim	64.9	70.3(8.32%)	94.46(34.36%)
Tripura	625.9	805.3(28.66%)	855.42(6.22%)

Source: NEDFi Quarterly Journal; January 2006.

We have mentioned earlier that development process has to compromise with many given factors of any economy, which go against this process. Agricultural practices in northeast India have not become feasible in a full-fledged manner for many reasons. Soil erosion, deforestation, landslide and other natural calamities are common characteristics of these hill states. Irrigation in the hills is difficult. Besides, horizontal capillary movements of soil moisture of the hills also play a negative role against smooth agricultural practice.

The diversities in the agro-climatic condition have influenced the crop pattern in the hills. Subba and Upadhaya(1995) have identified mainly two types of climates in northeastern states, i.e., per humid to humid and humid to per humid. In the per humid to humid climate soil types, viz., brown hills, red sandy laterite acid soil, alluvial red heavy tarai soil are available. Under these types of soils farmers prefer to cultivate Rice, Maize, Ragi, Potato, Rapeseed, Wheat, Jute etc. On the other hand, in humid to per humid climate with an alluvial red heavy type of soil, farmers prefer to cultivate rice, Jute, Rapeseed and Wheat.

Another reflection of declining share of agriculture is the falling share of outlay on this sector in total planned outlay in all northeastern states over the successive planning periods (Table 6). Mechanization in the hills is almost impossible. So the scopes of agricultural reform are limited and are mainly dependent on the steps such as bringing additional area for cultivation, various state sponsored schemes, giving training to the agricultural workers to have more skill, generation of additional employment, application of fertilizers etc.

Table 6: Outlay on Agriculture during Different Plan Periods

	6th Plan	*7th Plan*	*8th Plan*	*9th Plan*
A. Pradesh	37.04%	29.51%	22.89%	21.00%
Assam	15.90%	19.0%	11.04%	11.09%
Meghalaya	13.21%	18.27%	15.10%	15.66%
Nagaland	36.00%	34.98%	31.21%(1996-97)	
Tripura	24.89%	16.35%	18.00%	6.53%

Source: Government Reports of the respective States.

Employment Elasticity

Employment elasticity by definition of any sector is the ratio of percentage growth of employment to the percentage growth of income under that sector over any period. In this section employment elasticity is calculated during 1993-2000. At first annual compound growth rate of rural and urban main workers are calculated subject to the main worker levels provided by Census Reports 1991 and 2001 for each state. For that we applied the CAG formula $Y_t = Y_0 (1+ r)^t$. Thereafter the total numbers of rural and urban main workers are calculated corresponding to the reference periods 1993-94 and 1999-2000. Taking these figures into consideration total number of rural and urban workers on principal status basis in those two periods under agriculture (A), manufacturing (M), construction (C), trade hotel and restaurant (THR), transport storage and communication (TSC) and other service (OS) sectors are obtained with the help of NSSO reports of 1993-94 and 1999-2000 which give per 1000 distribution of workers in the above mentioned sectors. Summing up rural and urban figures we get total number of workers on usual status basis in any individual sector corresponding to 1993-94 and 1999-2000.

Table 8: Percentage Growth of Different Sub-sectors and Corresponding Employment over the Period 1993-2000

States	*A*	*M*	*C*	*THR*	*TSC*	*OS*
Arunachal	42.7	16	115.96	221.12	-83.63	49.28
Pradesh	6.31	6.15	-13.73	101.70	-10.33	77.75
Manipur	79.44	-4.45	-11.2	61.81	50	18.27
	15.03	54.80	118.79	39.71	27.69	53.24
Meghalaya	55	38.6	46.04	19.34	100	0.096
	55.33	26.24	89.72	47.87	55.97	41.52
Mizoram	-21.29	18.75	101.23	55.45	155.56	27.28
	65.56	NG	238.79	32.90	152.57	167.02
Nagaland	29.06	135.89	-34.5	-28.53	38.18	17.68
	74.43	NG	63.66	7.15	18.11	21.22

Sikkim	21.68	47.19	86.3	198.36	233.33	93.92
	NG	5.85	52.34	132.71	NG	96.62
Tripura	-0.32	-28.15	27.27	28.33	-18.85	17.83
	25.35	-7.77	192.27	53.64	38.04	71.56

Source: Calculated from NSSO 50th, 55th round, Employment unemployment situation in India and NEDFi Journal 2006.

[*Note:* In each column 1st figure is employment growth and 2nd figure is SDP growth under respective sub-sectors ; NG means negative growth of income share in the respective sub-sector]

Based on the Table 8 we get the employment elasticity in any sector for each state during 1993-2000 in the Table 9. This is not always less than unity as it is expected to be because productivity of a person is supposed to increase over time, which implies "employment increases proportionately lower than output" (Mathew, 2006). In some cases sub-sectoral growth is negative, for example, Agriculture sector in Sikkim, manufacturing sector of Mizoram and Nagaland and Transport storage & communication sector in Sikkim. In the Table 9, ## indicates the sub-sectors which have shown negative growth in employment but positive growth in SDP share. For instance, transport, storage and communication of Arunachal Pradesh and manufacturing of Tripura exhibits negative growth. Other service sectors include banking and insurance, real estate, ownership of dwelling and business services, public administration and other sub-sectors. In this sector for all states employment growth is much lower compared to SDP growth. Apart from that the sub-sectors which have experienced the same trend like other service sector are agriculture (Nagaland and Tripura), manufacturing (Manipur and Tripura) construction (Manipur, Meghalaya, Nagaland and Tripura), trade, hotel and restaurant (Meghalaya, Nagaland andTripura) and transport, storage and communication (Arunachal Pradesh and Tripura).

Table 9: Employment Elasticity over the Period 1993-2000

States	A	M	C	THR	TSC	OS
Arunachal Pradesh	6.77	2.60	Negative growth of SDP share	2.17	##	0.63
Manipur	5.28	-0.08	-0.09	1.55	1.80	0.34
Meghalaya	0.99	1.46	0.51	0.40	1.78	0.002
Nagaland	0.39	Negative growth of SDP share	-0.54	-3.99	2.10	0.83
Sikkim	Negative growth of SDP share	8.06	1.64	1.49	Negative growth of SDP share	0.97
Tripura	-0.012	##	0.14	0.52	-0.49	0.24

Source: Calculated from previous table.

Labour Productivity (1993-2000)

Table 10: Growth Rate of Labour Productivity During 1993-2000

States	A	M	C	THR	TSC	OS
Arunachal Pradesh	-0.26	-0.09	-0.6	-0.72	11.32	0.19
Manipur	-0.35	0.62	1.46	-0.21	-0.06	0.29
Meghalaya	0.0021	-0.089	0.29	0.306	-0.26	0.26
Mizoram	1.06	-0.21	0.68	-0.14	-0.011	1.09
Nagaland	0.35	-0.85	1.49	0.65	-0.22	0.03
Sikkim	-0.28	-0.28	-0.18	-0.67	-0.30	.013
Tripura	0.25	0.28	1.29	0.07	0.89	0.45

Labour productivity can be obtained through dividing the sectoral domestic product by number of workers absorbed in that sector. Normally it gives a broad idea of the trend prevalent in the productivity (Hari, 2003). We computed labour productivity for 1993-94 and 1999-2000 of different subsectors and corresponding growth rates subject to constant price level of 1993-94 (Table 10). We observe that in both the periods labour productivity under agricultural sector is lowest among all sub-sectors in all states. Similarly, in many cases the same is highest in construction sector. Agriculture sector has shown negative growth in labour productivity in Arunachal Pradesh, Manipur, Sikkim and Tripura. Manufacturing sector also has shown negative trend in all states except Manipur and Tripura. Only Arunachal Pradesh and Sikkim have experienced falling trend in construction sector. Besides, the states having decreasing profile of trade, hotel and restaurant sector are Arunachal Pradesh, Manipur, Mizoram and Sikkim. On the other hand, all states except Arunachal Pradesh and Tripura have been identified with negative growth of labour productivity in transport, storage and communication sector. It can be noticed that only other service sector in all states has got a trend of positive growth in all states. In most of the states construction sector has achieved the maximum growth of labour productivity. It seems on the basis of usual status (PS+ SS) workers levels, construction and other service sectors have received much more benefits compared to any other sub-sectors.

Conclusion

Agriculture sector has shown negative trend for most of the northeastern states in terms of contribution in SDP, employment elasticity and growth rate of average productivity. We have also seen the growth of agricultural output in all states has a decreasing trend. One of the reasons behind this fact is falling share of planned outlay on agricultural sector. There is no any clear evidence that falling productivity of agriculture sector has become helpful to flourish manufacturing sector (though it is beyond of our analysis in this paper). Basically service sector has been benefited from the growth process of all northeastern states in term of income share, employment elasticity and average productivity.

REFERENCES

1. Clark, K. (1940): *The Condition of Economic Progress;* Macmillan.
2. Chenery, H. (1960); Patterns of Industrial Growth; *AER*, September.
3. Chenery, H. and M. Syrquin (1975): *Patterns of Development 1950-70;* OUP.
4. Chenery, H. (1979): *Structural Change and Development Policy;* OUP.
5. Das, Gurudas (edited) (2005): *Structural Change and Strategy of Development: Resource-Industry Linkages of North-East India,* Akansha Publication; New Delhi; paper by Gurudas Das, Paper by Anil Bhuimali & Kanak Kanti Bagchi, paper by Butola, paper by Rabindranath Bhattacharyya.
6. Fischer, A.G.B. (1933): Capital and Growth Knowledge; *Economic Journal,* September.
7. Fischer. A.G.B. (June 1939): Production-Primary, Secondary and Tertiary; *Economic Record.*
8. Hari, K.S (2003): Structural Transformation in an Agrarian Economy- A Case Study of India 1970-2000; *The Indian Journal of Labour Economics*; Vol. 46; No. 4.
9. Joseph, Mathew (2004): *Northern Vs. Southern States - A Comparative Analysis;* Working Paper No.134; Indian Council for Research on International Economic Relations.
10. Joshi, P.C. & Rao, C.H. Hanumanth edited (1980): *Reflections on Economic Development and Social change;* Allied Publisher; New Delhi.
11. Joshi (2004): Tertiary Sector Driven Growth in India, Impact on Employment and Poverty; *EPW;* September 11.
12. Jorgensen, D. (1966): Testing Alternative Theories of the Development of a Dual Economy in "The Theory and Design of Economic Development" Edited by I.Adelman and E. Thorbecke; Baltimore, John Hopkins University Press.
13. Kuznet, Simon (1965): *Economic Growth and Structure.*
14. Mathew, E.T. (2006): *Employment and Unemployment in India;* Sage Publication; New Delhi.
15. Mundle, S. (1993): Unemployment and Financing of Relief Employment in a period of Stabilisation of India 1992-94; *EPW;* Vol. XXVIII; No. 5; January.

16. Rostow, W. W. (1960): The Stages of Economic Growth; *Economic History Review;* Cambridge University Press.
17. October 2004 *NEDFi Databank Quarterly Journal;* Issue IV.
18. Annual Report 2001-02; Department of Development of North-East Region (DONER).
19. Annual Report 2004-05; Department of Development of North-East Region (DONER).
20. April 2005; *NEDFi; Databank Quarterly Journal;* Vol.4.
21. Census Report 1971.
22. Census Report 1981.
23. Census Report 1991.
24. Census Report 2001.
25. *Yojana;* Special issue on North-East; December 2005.
26. EPW Research Foundation Report- Estimation of SDP 1960-61 to 2000-01.
27. Government of Sikkim (2001): Sikkim and the Noth-Eastern States - A Statistical Abstract-2001; Planning & Development Department.

17

Problems and Prospects of Agriculture in Sikkim: A Critical Appraisal

Anjan Chakrabarti & Sanchari Roy Mukherjee

Introduction

Economic growth has continued to remain at the core of modern development discourse which is an off-shoot of 'post-war era'. Western development economics thus remained engaged in prescribing various mechanisms through which a country can either become an industrialized nation or can catch up with the advanced industrialized countries. To dovetail the concept of modernization with the development thinking, 'political modernization' in the form of nation building was added. As a consequence, from nineteenth century to late twentieth century, philosophy of development gradually moved from 'structuralist perspective' (that emphasized on macro structure) to 'agency oriented view'. It is the 'agency oriented view' that incorporated attributes like pro-poor growth, limit to growth, sustainable development, etc. The common synergy has been developed between global agenda for development and various attributes of local developmental policy interventions for various countries and again within the countries, in various regions and the process continues unabated. The progress of 'agency oriented view' is monitored by various multilateral international agencies. With the decline of welfare economics, the so called distinction between developing and developed societies has been blurred **(Pieterse, 2010)**. Instead of remaining as 'self contained units' countries are now dependent on actions taken by one another. The new terminology 'global issues' has been coined to justify various common problems/ constraints that the inter-related world system is now facing.

Therefore, achieving high economic growth rate, continuous rise in per-capita income, structural change in terms of decline in share of agriculture in national income and rise in share of industry and services, allowing market to operate freely by removing internal government restrictions and removing barriers to facilitate international trade, have become most used attributes of development. This is a truism for India since 1991. However, it cannot be undermined that 'ever since humankind domesticated plants and animals, the relations of men and women to land, water, forests and pastures have largely determined their state of well-being'(Bagchi, 2002).

Agriculture in India in Post-Liberalisation Period

For India and for most of her states the fact is that seventy per cent plus population derive their livelihoods from agriculture and allied activities in spite of being tagged as one of the fastest growing economy in the world. In 1999-2000, 72 percent of population and 76 percent of the workforce were rural (Reddy & Mishra, 2008). Since early 1990s, more precisely after the adoption of neo-liberal path of globalization, rural India has become a cause of concern with the continuing rise in rural-urban disparities (Bhalla, 2005). High proportion of rural folk (more than 70 per cent) as a percentage of total population are confronting declining share of national income/ product. No significant improvement has been observed in the rural non-farm sector employment (Reddy & Mishra, op.cit). Since the introduction of economic reforms, there has been a substantial increase in landlessness among the rural population in India (Reddy 2006a). This indicates that the casualisation of the rural workforce and engagement in low-paid works is on the rise during the reforms period (Rao and Hanumappa, 1999).

During the reforms era, gross capital formation also declined substantially. The public sector gross capital formation in agriculture declined to one-third in 1999-2000, in comparison to the level attained in 1980-1981 (Reddy 2006b). Agrarian investment scenario precipitated further with the decline in the growth of private investment in agriculture (Sen, 2003). NSS 59th Round revealed that almost 50 percent of the farming households are indebted. The rise in prices of various agricultural inputs has raised the cost of cultivation across the country. As a matter of fact, the fertilizer price index increased from 99 in 1990-91 to 228 in 1998-99 at a compound annual rate of growth of 11 percent (Acharya, 2004).

According to the observations of Planning Commission, Government of India (2001) during the 10th Plan, agricultural GDP grew at an annual rate of mere 2.1 percent against the targeted growth rate of 4 percent and this was possibly as a consequence of stagnation and decline in agricultural productivity over the last decade. Agriculture Strategy for Eleventh Plan (2007) has categorically mentioned that a particular area of concern is food grains, whose production during 10th plan was less than that of 9th plan. Per capita annual production of cereals had declined from 192 kg in 1991/1995 to only 174 kg in 2004/2007 and of pulses from 15 kg to 12 kg in India. As a cumulative effect, in the recent past food security has emerged as a matter of concern in the national as well as in international arena.

In the aftermath of recent global meltdown, it is strongly felt that consumption demand from rural India can act as a stabiliser for the industry. It is expected that rural consumption demand can register an increase with commensurate increase in agriculture production and productivity. On the other hand, fall in agriculture production is expected to have a direct bearing on rural employment, income, access to food and food security and poverty.

Since a large section of the rural poor in India are either subsistence farmers or landless labourers and as they derive their livelihood either by acting as a producer or by selling their human labour, therefore, inadequate food grain production is bound to add misery among these sections of the rural populace. In addition to that, urban food insecurity is also on the rise. In the process, the so called high economic growth and rising per-capita income and concomitant structural change will lose its much touted relevance in development discourse, while, in the process, agrarian reforms may become more relevant a phrase than economic reforms. Against this backdrop, the paper chooses to re-examine the relevance of agriculture in the state of Sikkim in India.

Sikkim—A Macro Overview

Sikkim, located in the Eastern Himalaya, was a monarchy which was later annexed to India as the 22nd state in 1975. Sikkim has her own success story that has been achieved within a span of three and half decades after joining the Indian Republic. The most visible efforts were on the expansion of education and health care with the establishment of schools and hospitals across the state. According to Census 2001, the literacy rate of Sikkim stands at 69.98 percent (76.73 percent for males and 61.46 percent for females). This represents a sharp rise against the 1981 figures of 34.05 percent overall literacy rates (43.95 per cent for males and 22.20 per cent for females). Progress in this respect has been achieved by spending a large part of the central grant[1] to the State in the social sector. Creation of vast amount of human capital has been achieved within a short span of time (Chakrabarti, 2009). The value of human development index stood at 0.532 and infant mortality rate is 33 as against the all India figures of 60. Real average growth rate for Sikkim during 2000-01 to 2006-07 was at 7.8 per cent, which apparently looks impressive. Sectoral contribution shows that the contribution of primary sector towards GSDP is continuously falling while that of services is increasing. This trend resembles a development pattern experienced by the so called developed countries. Its real per-capita income stands at Rs. 25872 (in 2006-07) which is higher than the all India average.

Sector-wise distribution reveals that the primary sector, which is mainly propelled by agriculture and allied activities, has shown impressive growth during 1981-82 to 1984-85, a little sluggish thereafter, but has maintained a healthy growth rate from 1995-96 to 2006-07.

In the secondary sector, the growth is mainly propelled by construction activities. The manufacturing sector, which is supposed to be the backbone of the secondary sector, has registered as a very poor performer.

Tertiary sector, since 1984-85, has been growing at a satisfactory rate. Good performance of tertiary sector or services is mainly guided by the growth of public administration and other services. The economic growth rate of transport, communication, real estate, legal and business services have slowed down considerably in the late 1990s. In 1996-97 and thereafter, trade, hotels and restaurant business have shown an upsurge in the growth rate with expansion in the tourism industry as a possible attributing factor. In the new millennium, banking and insurance sectors are also achieving a healthy growth. Again, the growth rate of public administration and other services has slowed down since 1999-2000 in comparison to the 1980s, and this indicates that the rate of expansion of government services is gradually getting saturated (Tables 1.1, 1.2 and 1.3).

It is observed that growth is more pronounced in the sectors where government is directly involved. In the secondary sector, it is the construction, where the government plays a direct role, which has become the driving force. On the contrary, poor growth of manufacturing sector shows the mere absence of the private sector. The phenomenal growth of public administration and other services do suggest that the government remains as a sole provider of employment in the state. Poor growth rate of transport, communication, trade and commerce, banking and insurance, real estate etc. has reduced the scope of participation of entrepreneurs in the private sector (Chakrabarti, ibid).

Unlike many of the North-Eastern states, Sikkim is one of the most peaceful states in India. It is one of the greenest

Table 1.1: Growth of GSDP at Constant Price (%) By Industry of Origin from 1980-81 to 1992-93 in Sikkim (Base Year –1980-81)

INDUSTRY OF ORIGIN	*81-82*	*82-83*	*83-84*	*84-85*	*85-86*	*86-87*	*87-88*	*88-89*	*89-90*	*90-91*	*91-92*	*92-93*
AGRICULTURE & ALLIED ACTIVITIES	11.1	14.6	-1.3	16.1	-2.0	2.7	46.3	4.6	5.1	3.8	1.0	-9.9
FORESTRY & LOGGING	-1.9	93.2	37.3	-34.7	3.4	16.6	21.9	-62.1	-46.5	128.4	40.4	10.6
FISHING	6.9	125.4	-22.8	33.5	837.9	-90.1	-5.3	10.7	7.1	9.6	6.4	1.4
MININIG & QUARRYING	34.8	-61.1	44.2	-1.9	36.8	-60.6	-29	859.3	7.1	-49.4	33.0	-5.3
TOTAL PRIMARY	11.0	15.1	-0.5	14.8	-1.8	2.7	45.7	4.2	4.9	3.8	1.3	-9.7
MANUFACTURING	25.4	4.0	12.6	8.1	3.5	9.0	27.2	22.2	15.6	-26.0	5.1	8.1
CONSTRUCTION	-6.8	9.5	3.4	3.2	32.5	73.5	-13.7	4.5	9.3	2.8	8.1	8.2
ELCETRICITY, GAS & WATER SUPPLY	-15.4	-189.0	202.1	34.0	-6.5	-8.6	-14.7	-197.1	-304.2	-120.1	325.5	-57.7
TOTAL SECONDARY	2.9	11.3	9.5	6.1	20.3	50.7	-4.8	5.1	17.9	-11.1	4.7	10.3
TRANSPORT & COMMUNICATION	31.9	11.9	2.2	8.5	125.7	-0.1	68.9	6.5	15.7	11.3	42.8	6.5
TRADE, HOTELS & RESTAURANT	5.8	6.4	3.7	5.7	21.3	44.3	5.4	15.3	13.0	78.6	9.4	8.1
BANKING & INSURANCE	-39 2	-15.5	11.9	69.1	62.5	12.1	28.1	50.4	18.2	24.0	4.5	4.2
REAL ESTATE, LEGAL & BUSINESS SERVICES	1.04	10.4	10.8	10.9	11.5	11.6	11.7	12.2	-23.4	14.5	14.8	11.8
PUBLIC ADMINISTRATION	1.8	17.5	-14.5	35.0	6.3	13.5	7.6	25.0	1.9	25.1	13.6	4.9
OTHER SERVICES	2.6	2.8	32.3	19.7	22.4	19.0	-24.6	54.5	9.0	18.9	5.0	13.2
TOTAL TERITARY	4.2	9.3	4.8	19.9	21.1	18.5	5.4	25.2	3.3	32.0	12.5	8.2
GSDP	*6.3*	*12.7*	*2.9*	*14.4*	*9.4*	*18.2*	*18.4*	*10.6*	*7.0*	*9.6*	*6.3*	*1.4*

Source: Calculated from GSDP data at constant prices, State Domestic Product of Sikkim, Directorate of Economics and Statistics, Monitoring & Evaluation, Planning and Development Department, Govt. of Sikkim.

states in India and has emerged as one of the favourite tourist destinations for the people living within as well as outside India.

Table 1.2: Growth of GSDP at Constant Price (%) by Industry of Origin from 1993-94 to 1997-98 (Base Year 1993 – 94) in Sikkim

INDUSTRY OF ORIGIN	*94-95*	*95-96*	*96-97*	*97-98*
AGRICULTURE & ALLIED	-4.9	7.9	10.4	4.5
FORESTRY & LOGGING	3.7	4.0	4.0	6.3
FISHING	-1.5	44.6	-2.1	-24.0
MININIG & QUARRYING	-17.2	15.9	-24.3	-77.2
TOTAL PRIMARY	-4.4	7.8	9.7	4.2
MANUFACTURING	1.1	1.4	2.0	0.2
CONSTRUCTION	-7.4	41.6	11.2	44.9
ELCETRICITY, GAS & WATER SUPPLY	2.9	17.7	12.1	4.2
TOTAL SECONDARY	-3.6	26.0	9.2	29.1
TRANSPORT & COMMUNICATION	16.7	-8.9	43.3	-1.5
TRADE, HOTELS & RESTAURANT	2.1	3.5	7.5	7.9
BANKING & INSURANCE	6.5	31.7	1.5	24.6
REAL ESTATE, LEGAL & BUSINESS SERVICES	2.4	2.6	3.7	1.5
PUBLIC ADMINISTRATION	-7.7	10.3	3.4	28.2
OTHER SERVICES	6.7	9.2	26.0	16.3
TOTAL TERTIARY	1.6	6.5	12.8	14.0
GSDP	-1.5	10.6	10.9	13.9

Source: Calculated from GSDP data at constant prices, State Domestic Product of Sikkim, Directorate of Economics and Statistics, Monitoring & Evaluation, Planning and Development Department, Govt. of Sikkim.

Status of Agriculture in Sikkim

In Sikkim, almost 70 per cent of the total working force is engaged in agriculture and allied activities, and they cultivate around 16 percent of the total land area. Unlike the plain areas, in Sikkim, the agricultural lands are crescent shaped (4.5m to 7.5m long and 2.5m to 3.5m wide) and terraced (Dasgupta, 1992) and have a varied elevation of 300m to

Table 1.3: Growth of GSDP at Constant Price (%) By Industry of Origin from 2000-01 To 2006-2007 (BASE YEAR 1999-2000) in Sikkim

INDUSTRY OF ORIGIN	*2000-01*	*2001-02*	*2002-03*	*2003-04*	*2004-05*	*2005-06*	*2006-07*
AGRICULTURE	6.9	7.4	6.6	8.2	5.5	5.2	5.6
FORESTRY & LOGGING	0.9	2.1	-0.5	-0.2	-0.3	-0.1	-0.1
FISHING	0.0	0.0	0.0	0.0	0.0	0.0	0.0
AGRI & ALLIED	6.5	7.0	6.2	7.8	5.2	5.0	5.3
MININIG & QUARRYING	1.8	7.0	3.3	7.9	8.0	3.4	3.3
TOTAL PRIMARY	6.5	7.0	6.1	7.8	5.2	4.9	5.3
MANUFACTURING-REGISTERED	4.9	2.1	4.3	6.1	7.4	7.3	6.9
MANUFACTURING UNREGISTERED	4.4	0.2	4.1	7.3	6.2	9.2	8.2
MANUFACTURING	4.6	1.0	4.2	6.8	6.6	8.5	7.7
CONSTRUCTION	13.2	28.6	19.1	13.3	14.2	15.5	16.0
ELECTRICITY,GAS & WATER SUPPLY	88.6	3.8	-4.0	2.4	5.6	5.1	4.6
TOTAL SECONDARY	29.9	15.3	9.5	9.4	10.9	12.0	12.3
TRANSPORT & COMMUNICATION	5.8	6.9	11.2	15.2	14.1	12.0	11.3
TRADE,HOTELS & RESTAURANT	6.5	7.0	7.1	5.3	5.6	5.4	5.4
BANKING &INSURANCE	21.3	14.3	14.3	14.3	13.1	8.4	8.4
REAL ESTATE, LEGAL & BUSINESS SERVICES	3.4	3.4	3.3	3.4	3.4	3.4	3.5
PUBLIC ADMINISTRATION	-2.4	6.0	7.3	8.2	8.9	8.8	9.0
OTHER SERVICES	-2.1	3.2	5.7	5.7	5.5	6.3	6.3
TOTAL TERITARY	0.8	5.2	6.7	7.2	7.3	7.2	7.2
SDP	7.6	7.9	7.3	7.8	7.8	8.0	8.2
Per Capita Income	4.0	4.0	6.7	6.3	6.5	6.5	6.7

Source: Calculated from GSDP data at constant prices, State Domestic Product of Sikkim, Directorate of Economics and Statistics, Monitoring & Evaluation, Planning and Development Department, Govt. of Sikkim & http://www.mospi.nic.in

3000m. Diversity in ecological condition along with the varied elevation has brought considerable variation in agricultural practices in the State and a vast area is unsuitable for traditional agricultural practice. Out of the total land area of 7096km^2, 44.09 per cent area is under forest; another 40.02 per cent area is under permanent snow or alpine pasture. Thus only 15.69 per cent of total land area is presently under cultivation.

Trends in Agricultural Production, Productivity and Agricultural Growth in Sikkim and Its Possible Outcomes (1975-2006)

Total food grain production in the State has registered a healthy increase in absolute terms and a rising trend is witnessed both in productivity as well as in the area of cultivation from 1975-1976 to 1995-96. Among various crops, wheat and maize were the prime contributors. However, since 1995-96, production and area under cultivation of food grains has been declining. Precisely, the fall is more pronounced for wheat and other cereals. The coefficient of variation of rice output was high between 1970 and 1980 and this variability was primarily caused by changes in both area and yield. Between 1980 and 1990, the variability in rice output was primarily influenced by variation in yield level. However, the high coefficient of variation for wheat between 1970 and 1980 was caused by variability in area. Coefficient of variation for maize and other cereals were the highest again between 1970 and 1980 and those were primarily caused by rise in variation in yield level. For pulses, it was variability in area which was the prime contributor for the same period. For food grains, the high coefficient of variation between 1970 and 1980 was mainly attributed to the variation in the yield level (Table 1.4). Though maize has never been a staple food in Sikkim, its production has steadily increased over the periods, and it contributes half of the food grain production in the State. To provide a disaggregated view, crop wise compound annual rate of growth rates of output, area and yield have also been considered (Table 1.5). For rice, the growth rate of output has substantially fallen and had come down to 0.45 between 1996 and 2006, which was 5.51 during 1975-

1985 and 2.41 between 1985 and 1995. The growth rate of area under rice was negative (-0.75) in the period 1996-2006. The fall in growth rate of rice output could have been arrested had the growth rate of yield of rice been increased. However, the growth rate of yield had also declined from 2.15 percent in 1985-1995 to 1.21 in 1996-2006. The scenario for wheat is more depressing. Between 1975 and 1985, the growth of wheat output was phenomenal (49 per cent) and it was primarily achieved through the growth of area under wheat which was 44 percent for that decade. However, over the next two decades, a complete reversal of the picture has been observed and, in fact, the growth rate of output, yield and area of wheat, had been negative during 1996-2006. In case of other cereals, the growth rate of output, area and yield were always sluggish in comparison to other crops and finally all the figures of growth for other cereals had negative values between 1996 and 2006. For pulses, growth rates for output, area and yield have decelerated but remained positive. The cumulative impact was captured in the growth rate of output, area and yield for food grains in the state of Sikkim. The compound annual growth rate of food grains output and area thus became negative in the present decade (1996-2006). The cause for concern is that for most of the crops, the fall in growth rate in output had been accompanied by a fall in the growth rate of area and it was not compensated by the rise in the growth rate of productivity. If the farmers have gone for crop diversification, that is, moved towards cash crops from producing food crops then the plight of farmers may have lessened through better incomes. Other wise three possibilities become prominent, first, more and more agricultural land are being used for non agricultural purpose; second, farmers may fail to augment technical upgradation to raise productivity (both biological and mechanical) and this may also happen because of the fall in public expenditure on agriculture, and third, farmers are getting more and more marginalised and absence of non farm employment and failure to implement agrarian reforms may further complicate the situation.

Table 1.4: OUTPUT (In '000tonnes), AREA (In '000 Hectares) AND YIELD (In Kg/Hect) IN SIKKIM (1975-2006)

CROP/YEAR		*1975-1976*	*1985-86*	*1995-96*	*2005-2006*
RICE	OUTPUT	10	17.1	21.7	22.69
	AREA	11.4	15.5	15.9	14.74
	YIELD	891.4	1121.1	1386.9	1564.3
WHEAT	OUTPUT	0.2	11.2	15.3	9.2
	AREA	0.2	7.4	8.4	5.74
	YIELD	1016.2	1538.0	1850.9	1628.7
MAIZE	OUTPUT	16.5	49.3	56.6	61.1
	AREA	28.5	39	39.9	36.6
	YIELD	588.3	1284.6	1441.5	1696.4
OTHER	OUTPUT	4.5	6.98	8.06	7.01
CEREALS	AREA	7.2	7.8	8.3	7.3
	YIELD	635.0	909.2	986.7	975.7
TOTAL	OUTPUT	31.2	84.58	101.66	100
CEREALS	AREA	47.3	69.7	72.5	64.38
	YIELD	670.3	1233.1	1424.9	1578.4
TOTAL PULSES	OUTPUT	0.7	4.6	5.9	6.8
	AREA	1.7	5.5	6.7	6.8
	YIELD	418.4	849.9	894.9	1016.2
TOTAL FOOD	OUTPUT	31.9	89.18	107.56	106.8
GRAIN	AREA	49	75.2	79.2	71.18
	YIELD	661.6	1205.1	1380.1	1524.7

Source: Sikkim Human Development Report, 2001 and Economic Survey 2006-2007, Govt. of Sikkim.

As a matter of fact, the work participation rate or the ratio of labour force to population has also been declining consistently in the State of Sikkim. According to Census1971, the labour participation rate in Sikkim was 53.2 per cent, it declined to 41.4 per cent in 1981. In 1991 it was marginally reduced to 40.4 per cent and finally in Census 2001, the figure stood at 39.4 per cent (Calculated from Census Reports of 1971, 1981, 1991 and 2001). Lower work participation rate reflects difficulty of finding work and increased marginalization of workers (Patnaik, 2005).

Table 1.5: Crop-wise Compound Annual Rate of Growth (CAGR) and Coefficient of Variation (CV) Of Output, Area and Yield in Sikkim (1975-2006)

CROP		*1975-1985 (CAGR)*	*1985-1995 (CAGR)*	*1995-2006 (CAGR)*	*1975-1985 (CV)*	*1985-1995 (CV)*	*1995-2006 (CV)*
RICE	OUTPUT	5.51	2.41	0.45	37.1	16.8	3.15
	AREA	3.12	0.26	-0.75	21.6	1.8	5.35
	YIELD	2.32	2.15	1.21	16.1	15.0	8.50
WHEAT	OUTPUT	49.56	3.17	-4.96	136.5	21.9	35.21
	AREA	43.49	1.28	-3.74	134.0	9.0	26.60
	YIELD	4.23	1.87	-1.27	28.9	13.1	9.03
MAIZE	OUTPUT	11.57	1.39	0.77	70.5	9.7	5.41
	AREA	3.19	0.23	-0.86	22.0	1.6	6.10
	YIELD	8.12	1.16	1.64	52.6	8.1	11.49
OTHER	OUTPUT	4.49	1.45	-1.39	30.6	10.2	9.85
CEREALS	AREA	0.80	0.62	-1.28	5.7	4.4	9.07
	YIELD	3.65	0.82	-0.11	25.1	5.8	0.79
TOTAL	OUTPUT	10.49	1.86	-0.16	65.2	13.0	1.16
CEREALS	AREA	3.95	0.39	-1.18	27.1	2.8	8.39
	YIELD	6.29	1.46	1.03	41.8	10.2	7.23
TOTAL	OUTPUT	20.72	2.52	1.43	104.1	17.5	10.02
PULSES	AREA	12.46	1.99	0.15	74.6	13.9	1.05
	YIELD	7.34	0.52	1.28	48.1	3.6	8.98
TOTAL	OUTPUT	10.83	1.89	-0.07	66.9	13.2	0.50
FOODGRAIN	AREA	4.38	0.52	-1.06	29.8	3.7	7.54
	YIELD	6.18	1.36	1.00	41.2	9.6	7.04

Calculated from the figures of crop wise output, area and yield

In addition, the contribution of agriculture to gross state domestic product (GSDP) has continuously been declining though the dependence on agriculture has not declined over the periods. The share has declined from 48.7 per cent in 1980-81 to just 18.8 per cent in 2006-07 (Figure 1). This is bound to reduce the per-capita income of the people associated with agriculture. It also needs to be mentioned that there was huge rise in plan allocation in agriculture between the Vth (1974-79) and VIth Five Year Plan (1980-85). In terms of percentage, the plan allocation was highest for agriculture in VIth plan (26 per cent). It might be one of the attributes for the spectacular rise in production, area and productivity for most of the crops between mid-1970 to mid-1980. Thereafter, plan allocation has continuously declined and it is a clear indication of decline in public expenditure on agriculture (Table 1.6). It consequently led to the deceleration in production and productivity for food grains in Sikkim. In addition to this, the average compound annual rate of growth of population since 1980s has outweighed the growth of food grain production and the gap was further widened since the 1990s although it narrowed down during 2005-06 (Figure 2). This may have led to the creation of food scarcity within the State since Sikkim has registered the highest per capita PDS purchase (8.6 kg) in the country. The areas where PDS off take were relatively high were not only deficit in terms of cereal production but also tended to be areas of low cereal consumption (Swaminathan, 2003).

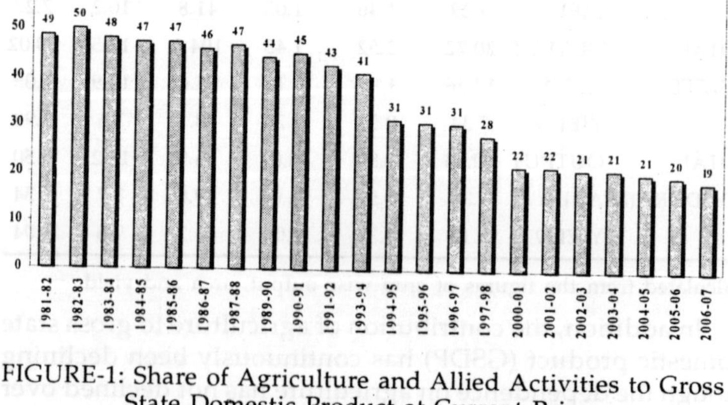

FIGURE-1: Share of Agriculture and Allied Activities to Gross State Domestic Product at Current Prices

Source: CSO, Govt. of India

TABLE-1.6: Plan Allocation on Agriculture and Forest (*in percentage*)

PLAN PERIOD	*EXPENDITURE (in %)*
I PLAN (1954-61)	21.5
II PLAN (1961-66)	20
III PLAN (1966-71)	15
IV PLAN (1971-75)	14.2
V PLAN (1974-79)	15.9
VI PLAN (1980-85)	26
VII PLAN (1985-90)	18.29
VIII PLAN (1992-97)	16.72
IX PLAN (1997-2002)	9.6
X PLAN (2002-2007)	12.37

Source: various plan documents, Govt. of Sikkim

Now the question arises why this deficiency has occurred- is this because of rising population pressure, or fall in productivity or reduction in cultivable area or are all these factors together affecting the production? It is observed that fall in cultivable land, fall in productivity and indeed rise in population are among the major factors affecting the food grain production adversely.

Figure-2: Compound Annual Rate of Growth (CARG) of Population and Food Grain Production in Sikkim

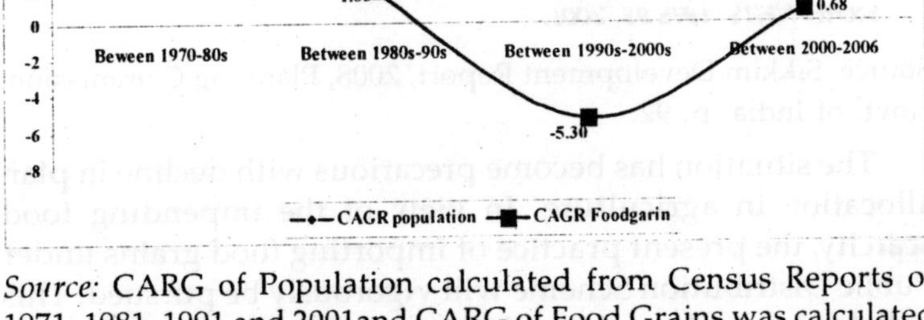

Source: CARG of Population calculated from Census Reports of 1971, 1981, 1991 and 2001and CARG of Food Grains was calculated from data available from Dept. of agriculture, Govt. of Sikkim.

Conclusion

Food grain production, agricultural productivity or yield and agricultural growth have started decelerating since 2000 in Sikkim. Share of agriculture to Gross State Domestic Product has continuously been declining although people depending on agriculture for their livelihood have not declined. It is evident that though no longer monarchic rule exists in Sikkim, the feudal elements still has its root in agrarian system and land distribution has remained skewed[2] (Chakrabarti, 2010). Growth rate of population has outweighed the growth of food grain production and thus the possibility of food insecurity is looming large on Sikkim. It can have an adverse impact on the nutritional level of rural and urban poor people of Sikkim (Table-1.7).

TABLE- 1.7: Nutritional Status (in percentage) in Sikkim

Women with Anaemia*	6[illegible]
Women with Moderate/Severe Anaemia*	23.8
Children Age 6-35 months with Anaemia*	76.5
Children Age 6-35 with Moderate/Severe Anaemia*	48.[illegible]
Children Chronically Undernourished (stunted)**	[illegible]
Children Acutely Undernourished (wasted)**	.48
Children Underweight**	20.6

Note: *–Anaemia-haemoglobin levels <11.0 grams/decilitre (g/dl) for children and pregnant women and <12.0 g/dl for non pregnant women. Moderate/severe anaemia haemoglobin level <10.0 g/dl. ** Stunting assessed by height for age, wasting assessed by weight for height, underweight assessed by weight for age.

Source: NFHS, 1998-99, 2001.

Source: Sikkim Development Report, 2008, Planning Commission, Govt. of India, p. 92.

The situation has become precarious with decline in plan allocation in agriculture. In view of the impending food scarcity, the present practice of importing food grains under Public Distribution Scheme will vigorously be pursued. This will further reduce the public expenditure on agriculture.

Again, this is bound to increase the incidence of rural poverty, both from nutritional point of view as well as in terms of declining employment opportunities in rural areas. It is indeed true that agriculture is providing sustenance to the majority of the people in the State, but rising population pressure on cultivable lands, physical constraints created by the terrain, limitations of terrace farming in terms of productivity, irrigation, cost of production, lack of infrastructural support, declining public expenditure, and complete absence of marketable surplus are also working as major obstacles for the growth of the agricultural sector. Therefore, attention should immediately be given to raise the agricultural productivity and production in the State and to do so institutional changes have become imperative. Mere references of high economic growth and high per-capita income otherwise will become misleading and will fail to reflect the true economic status of 60 percent of the work force who earn their living from agriculture. Serious efforts are to be made to bring more land into cultivation through appropriation of surplus land possessed by big land owners and enough space needs to be created within the economy where surplus agricultural workers can gainfully be employed.

REFERENCES

Acharya, S.S. (2004), "Fertilizer Subsidy in Indian Agriculture: Some Issues" in Bruno Dorin and Thomas Jullien (eds), *Agricultural Incentives in India: Post Trends and Perspective Paths Towards Sustainable Development*, Manohar, New Delhi and Centre de Sciences Humains.

Bagchi, Amiya (2002) *'Agrarian Transformation and Human development'*, in V.K. Ramchandran and Madhura Swaminathan (eds), Agrarian Studies: Essays on Agrarian Relations in Less Developed Countries, Kolkata, Tulika.

Bhalla, Sheila (2005), "India's Rural Economy: Issues and Evidence", Working Paper No.25, Institute for Human Development, New Delhi.

Census of India (1971)

Census of India (1981), Series- 19, PartXIII A&B

Census of India (1991), Series- 22

Census of India (2001), Provisional, Series- 21

Chakrabarti, Anjan (2009), *"Economic Development and Employment in Sikkim"*, Authors Press: New Delhi.

———(2010), "A Critical Review of Agrarian Reforms in Sikkim", *Economic and Political Weekly*, Vol XLV No 5, January 30, 2010, pp.23-26

Chakraborty, Anjan & Anup Seakhar Chakraborty (2010), "Emergent Development Approach: A Critique of 'Money-bags' Centre directed Dole Development in North-East India", *Indian Journal of Political Science*, Vol.LXXI, No.2, April-June 2010, pp. 547-559.

Dasgupta, Manas (1992), *Sikkim: Problems and Prospects of Development*, Indus Publishing Company: New Delhi.

Government of India (2001), *"Indian Planning Experience - A Statistical Profile"*, Planning Commission, New Delhi.

Government of India (2007), *"Agriculture Strategy for Eleventh Plan: Some Critical Issues"*, Planning Commission, New Delhi.

Government of Sikkim, "Economic Survey, 2006-2007.

NSSO (2005), Situation Assessment Survey of Farmers: Indebtness of Farmer Households, NSS 59th Round (January-December 2003), Report No. 498 (59/33/1), Ministry of Stattistics and Programme Implementation, Government of India, New Delhi.

Pieterse, Jan Nederveen (2010), *'Development Theory'*, Sage Publication India Ltd.: New Delhi, pp. 4-16.

Rao, V.M. H.G. Hanumappa (1999), "Marginalisation Process in Agriculture - Indicators, Outlook and Policy Implications", Economics and Political Weekly, 34(52), December 25-31

Reddy, D. Narasimha, Srijit Mishra (2008), "Crisis in Agriculture and Rural Distress in Post-Reform India", in R. Radhakrishnan (ed) *India Development Report*, Oxford University Press, New Delhi, IGIDR, Mumbai.

Reddy, D. Narasimha (2006a), "Changes in Agrarian Structure and Agricultural Technology: Is Peasant Farming Sustainable under Institutional Retrogression", in R. Radhakrishna, S.K. Rao, S. Mahendra Dev and K. Subba Rao (eds), *India in a Globalising World: Some Aspects of Macro economy, Agriculture and Poverty, Essays in Honour of C.H. Hanumantha Rao,* Academic Press, New Delhi, 2006.

———(2006b), "Economic Reforms, Agrarian Crisis and Rural Distress", 4th Annual Prof. B. Janardhan Rao Memorial Lecture, Prof. B. Janardhan Rao Memorial Foundation, Warangal, Telegana.

Sen, Abhijit (2003), "Globalization, Growth and Inequality in South Asia: The Evidence from Rural India", in Jayati Ghosh and C.P. Chandraseakhar (eds), *Work and Well-being in the Age of Finance*, Tulika Books, New Delhi.

Swaminathan, Madhura., (2003) "Strategies towards Food Security" *Social Scientist*, Vol. 31, No. 9/10, Sep. – Oct : 58-94.

Sikkim Development Report (2008), Planning Commission, Government of India, Academic Foundation, New Delhi, p.92.

Sikkim Human Development Report (2001), Government of Sikkim, Social Science Press: New Delhi.

Patnaik, Utsa (2005), "Theorising Food Security and the Poverty in the Era of Economic Reforms" *Social Scientist*, Vol. 33, No. 7/8, Jul.–Aug.: 50-81.

Planning Commission (2007): Agriculture Strategy for Eleventh Plan: Some Critical Issues

NOTES

1. Like all the North-Eastern states, Sikkim is also treated as special category state and receives substantial financial and non-financial support from the Central Government. It currently gets 90 per cent of its plan assistance as grants and the remaining 10 per cent as loans which is 30:70 for non Special category states. Special Category States receive preferential treatment in the distribution of normal central assistance from state plans. From the total central assistance available for State plans, funds are earmarked for externally aided projects and special area programmes (hill areas, tribal sub plans, border areas, North-East Council, etc.) (Chakraborty and Chakraborty, 2010).
2. After Sikkim became an Indian state in 1975, the first measure taken by the Government was the abolition of intermediaries. And it subsequently created the provision of land rights to

the landless tillers, enforced ceiling laws of landholding, distribution of surplus land and protection of tenancy rights through legislations like The Sikkim Cultivators Protection Act, 1975; The Sikkim Agricultural Land Ceiling and Reforms Act, 1978; and The Sikkim Land (Requisition and Acquisition) Act, 1978. Land rights of the indigenous Lepchas & Bhutias, which was protected earlier by the Revenue order No 1 of 1917, (it was mentioned there that the land owned by the Lepcha and Bhutia community can not be transferred to other communities), continued to be so after the merger of Sikkim with India because of the tribal status of those two ethnic groups. Imposition of land ceiling on agricultural holdings helped the State to acquire a substantial amount of agricultural land, demarcated, as 'vested land', however, complete abolition of feudal agrarian structure remained unfulfilled. Because of that, the ceiling was applied only to the agricultural land; no ceiling was imposed on non agricultural holdings. The kazis (a Persian word, 'qazi' meaning munsif, magistrate or equivalent) still hold considerable amount of land and many kazis are reported to have 1500 acres of land even today.

18

Regional Variations in Agricultural Productivity of West Bengal: An Analysis in Relation to Irrigation

Govinda Choudhury

Introduction

Revolutionary increase in agricultural production in India during the last four decades was made possible primarily due to technology advancement and appropriate institutional changes. Even now, when agriculture contributes less than twenty per cent of the national Gross Domestic Product, more than 65 per cent of the rural population in India are dependent on agriculture directly or indirectly (Masood & Tabassum 2007; Swaminathan, 2006). The growth of agricultural production in general and food grain production in particular therefore has a direct bearing on rural livelihood and food security of the nation (GOI, 2008b).

Inadequate supply of the wage-goods can stall the growth process of any country, and as a result our policy makers were prompted to encourage agriculture productivity by various means. Both price and non-price instruments were emphasised for the growth of agriculture. But, it appears that the cornerstone of policy measures has been 'incentive prices' backed by government procurement to encourage agricultural performance. An important lacuna of such a policy was that over the year's government procurement operations have been more or less restricted to 'fine cereals', only. However, study show that the output elasticity of food crops is influenced by rainfall, input availability (specifically irrigation, fertilizer and HYV seeds), and relative profits, in that order of importance (Kanwar, 2004). As a natural conclusion to such findings we are encouraged to prefer that our policy approach should be to expand irrigation, fertilizer and HYV seeds use, rather than increase output procurement prices year after years. This paper however, does not refute the role of price instruments in increasing agriculture output, but reckon that such operations can be expensive and inefficient as our experience has shown over the years.

Contrary to Gulati & Sharma (1990), Lahiri & Roy (1985), and Narayana & Parikh (1981) estimates, Kanwar (*ibid*) found that irrigation was relatively less important than rainfall in agricultural productivity. But, there is no denying of the fact that the most important policy variable to achieve a sustained growth of agricultural output is water. As rainfall is beyond our control, irrigation variable therefore becomes an important policy instrument. Irrigation has a direct effect in increasing the supply of output, and it also indirectly helps to reduce the yield risk due to variation in rainfall and to increase agricultural productivity. Agricultural sector continues to support more than half a billion people providing employment to almost half of the workforce in our country. There is little doubt that irrigation and associated changes in cropping intensity and crop patterns, together with improved seed varieties and use of chemical fertilizers and related inputs, have been the principal driving force behind the sustained and historically unprecedented growth of agricultural production during the last four decades in Indian economy.

It is because of adequate rainfall and expansion of irrigation that India has been able to increase foodgrains output over the last many years. The growth in output was made possible through increase in gross cropped area and increasing the yield rate made through expansion of irrigation facilities. Dhawan (1988) and Hanumantha (2005) in their studies observed that the productivity difference between irrigated and un-irrigated lands is substantial.

Inter and intra state variation in production and yield rates exits in agriculture sector. Such variations are natural in country like India due to its vast geographical and agro-climatic diversity, but lack of appropriate institutional infrastructure and inadequate availability of inputs are the major bottlenecks for increasing agricultural output. Lack of irrigation has been a major binding constraint in agricultural growth. In 2002-03 around 41 per cent (approximately) of the gross cropped area had irrigation facilities, that is, 59 per cent of the gross cropped area still continues to depend on monsoon (Haque[1], 2003).

Current Challenges in Agriculture Sector

Since 1966 India has been successful in increasing the food grain production, but planners and agricultural scientists are worried about the slow growth rate of agriculture production in the recent years. Declining public investments in agriculture sector over the years, slow development of technology, etc., are at the core of this slowdown. Although the slowdown did not have much adverse impact on the overall growth of the economy, this has implications for the majority of Indian population, who directly or indirectly depend on agriculture. The slow growth of agriculture has been explicitly noted as a matter of concern in the Approach Paper to the XI Plan, and accelerating the rate of growth of agricultural production is seen as central to a more inclusive growth, if not growth per se. Growth of agriculture output decelerated from 3.7% during 1991-92 to 1996-97 to around 2.5% for 1997-98 to 2006-07 (GOI, 2007b). The growth of foodgrains was only 1.2% for 1990-2009. During the same period the growth of rice and wheat production was less than the population growth rate. The euphoria and the confidence that followed the green revolution with regard to the food security are fast vanishing. The challenge before us now is enormous. The HYV[2] technology was rather simple, relatively easy to transfer and adopt and provided immediate result in output production.

Table 1: Distribution of Land Holding in India

Sl. No.	*Land Holding Size Group*		*No. of Operational Holding in '000*						
			1970-71	*1976-77*	*1980-81*	*1985-86*	*1990-91*	*1995-96*	*2000-01*
1	Marginal	Number of household	36200	44523	50122	56147	63389	71179	75390
	(Lessthan 1 ha.)	Operated Area	14599	17509	19735	22042	24894	28121	29807
2	Small	Number of household	13432	14728	16087	17922	20092	21643	22687
	(1 to 2 ha.)	Operated Area	19282	20905	23169	25708	28827	30722	32128
3	Semi-Medium	Number of household	10681	11666	12444	13252	13913	14261	14014
	(2 to ha.)	Operated Area	29999	32428	34645	36666	38375	38953	38174
4	Medium	Number of household	7932	8212	8068	7916	7630	7092	6573
	(4 to 0 ha.)	Operated Area	48234	49628	48543	47144	44752	41398	38194
5	Large	Number of household	2766	2440	2166	1918	1667	1404	1230
	(10.0 and above)	Operated Area	50064	42873	37705	33002	28659	24160	21092
6	All Holdings	Number of household	71011	81569	88887	97155	105287	115579	119894
		Operated Area	162138	163343	163797	164562	165507	163355	159394

Sources: All India Report on Agriculture Census (2000-01), Department of Agriculture & Cooperation, Ministry of Agriculture, GOI, p. 26.

There is no similar technology presently available for increasing agriculture yield at reduced cost that would not only enable farmers to achieve higher income but also increase livelihood opportunities in rural areas. The present mean yield levels for all crops and animals' productivity are much lower than that realized in other countries, and this provides a scope for further increase in agricultural productivity.

In India agriculture appears to be a complex economic activity. It is the largest private entrepreneurship engaging million of farmers and farm workers in about 119.9 million (excluding Jharkhand state) operational holdings, 81.8 percent of which are small and marginal land holdings (GOI, 2008a; 25-26). Even though, agriculture is in the concurrent list of subjects of our Constitution, but there is hardly any direct government intervention in the production and investment decisions of the farmers. However, State's policies do influence the environment in which farmers operate (Vaidyanathan, 1996).

Growth of population has led to continuous fragmentation of farm holdings in India. The average size of holdings for all sizes at the country level was 2.28 ha. in 1970-71, it fell to 2.00 ha in 1976-77, 1.84 ha in 1980-81, 1.69 ha 1985-86, 1.55 ha in 1990-91 and further declined to 1.41 ha in 1990-91 and 1.33 ha in 2000-01 (GOI, 2008a; 25). Decline in per capita land availability[3] and unceconomic farm size are responsible for the low productivity in farm sector. Small and marginal farm holders dominate the agricultural landscape in rural economy and provide largest source of subsistence in agricultural productivity, but they still remain highly susceptible to poverty and hunger because they neither produce sufficient food nor income to ensure household food security.

Advocates of the New Economic Policy 1991 were of the impression that, the benefits of liberalization would flow as cheaper agriculture inputs to the farmers. This would enable the small agriculture holdings to increase production, generate additional income and employment in the rural areas. As cultivation has become concentrated to small and marginal lands, the risk of production has also increased correspondingly. During the last two decades, disparities in productivity across regions and crops, and between rain-fed and irrigated areas have increased considerably. As a result, agriculture indebtedness has increased and the worst suffers has been the marginal and small farmers (Agriculture Statistics, 2006; 218-221). The diversification of agriculture has also raised concerns on food security. Producing food-crops is becoming a non-viable activity over the years. Further, the scope for increase in net sown area has been exhausted, and overuse of the agricultural land has resulted in land degradation in the form of depletion of soil fertility, erosion, water logging etc. There has been decline in the surface irrigation expansion rate and reduction in ground water table in many part of the country. Degradation of the groundwater resource base through over extraction and pollution are increasing rural poverty, social inequality and conflict in many parts of India. The problem is made worse by the fact that cheap power encourages farmers to use excessive water. The benefit of free power has been mostly captured by the wealthy and many small farmers and led highly inefficient water use practices. The small farmers on the other hand were forced to close down their wells because of huge increase in cost of irrigation.

In recent years, increase in global food prices has been serious concern to the policy makers. Increasing demand of food crops both for consumption and for the manufacture of bio-fuels along with fall in supply has pushed food prices. Increases in usage of crop for bio-fuel have reduced its availability for food and feed, and has exerted pressure on food prices. International prices of wheat, rice and maize increased significantly during the last two years, in fact; there was more than 100 per cent increase in price for some commodities. The present double digit inflation of food prices is therefore, a serious challenge for Indian economy in recent years.

Another major hurdle is that the Indian agricultural sector is lack of investment. Agricultural investment is needed to meet the expenses on irrigation, research and extension and building up rural infrastructure-roads and electricity, to further increase the productivity and strengthening the agricultural sector in India. Since mid 1990's the share of private investments in agriculture and allied sector of total gross capital formation has been declining and that of public investment is stagnant (GOI, 2007a; 38).

Trend in Food grain Production in India

The performance of the agricultural sector influences the growth of the Indian economy. Thus sustained growth in agricultural production and productivity is essential for overall stability of this country. India has taken notable strides in the agricultural sector during the last four decades of economic planning. After remaining a food-deficit country for about two decades since independence, the country has produced positive results in food-grain production dramatically in recent times.

Though growth in the agriculture sector has been less compared to the non-agriculture sectors, however, it has remained higher than the growth of population in the country. Between 1950-51 and 2006-07, production of foodgrains increased at an average annual rate of 2.5 per cent compared to the growth of population which averaged 2.1 per cent during this period. However, the rate of growth of foodgrains production during the period 1990-2007 decelerated to 1.2 per cent which was lower than average annual rate of growth of population at 1.9 per cent. As a result the per capita availability of cereals and pulses declined from a peak of 468 grams per capita per day in 1990-91 to 412 grams per capita per day in 2005-06. The per capita availability of pulses (a cheap source of protein) declined from 72 grams in 1956-57 to 42 grams in 1990-91 and further to 33 grams in 2005-06 (*Economic Survey*, 2008). Such decline in foodgrains and pulses availability adversely affects the health of workers and thereby their productivity and income. It was alternatively pointed out that such decline in foodgrains and pulses has been more than compensated by increased availability of horticulture and livestock products. But such an argument appear to be weak when there is no or little evidence to suggest that benefits of economic growth during the period have reached the poor, enabling them to attain an elitist consumption basket.

Figure 1: Gross Area under Major Crops (All India)

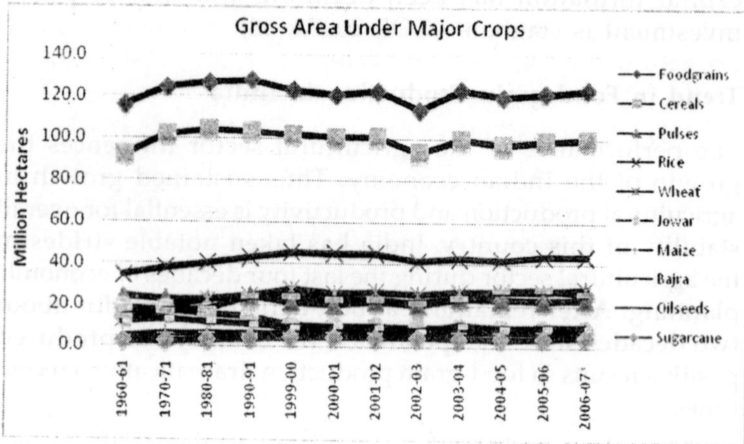

Source: Economic Survey, 2007-08.

The high growth rate of the agricultural sector in 1990s was achieved mainly due to three factors. First, diversification towards horticultural crops, livestock, fisheries etc., from foodgrain production. Horticultural crops attained a growth rate close to six percent, which helped agriculture sector to attain growth rate of 3.28 percent during the decade. Chand (2003a) study shows that in presence of a large difference in productivity per unit of land, a one percent shift in area from non-horticultural crops to horticultural crops raises overall output of crop sector by four percent. Second, the decade of 1990s has witnessed highest expansion in gross irrigated area. This expansion has been made through overexploitation of groundwater. Finally, a favourable terms of trade for agriculture during the 1990s.

However, this increased rate of growth of agriculture sector during 1990s should not be taken as a sustainable achievement as there are worrying signs of slowdown in growth rate of almost all the sub sectors of agriculture during the second half of 1990s. This deceleration has continued since then. It is alarming to note that overall foodgrain growth is only

1.3%, and that is less than growth in population (1.66%) during the period. The gap in the two rates of growth has adversely affected foodgrain availability per capita per day.

Under these circumstances increasing agriculture output is the only alternative to enhance income and foodgrains availability in the country. In India, the growth in gross area under all crops has increased from 122 million hectares (mha) in 1949-50 to 151 mha in 1964-65 and has presently reached a plateau around 167 mha (Figure 1.1). Any further increase in agriculture production is not possible by expanding area under agriculture; the thrust is now on increasing agricultural intensity. Before we discuss the role of various inputs in increasing agriculture production and productivity an assessment of the performance of the Indian agriculture sector over the years becomes essential.

Agriculture production has two components *viz.*, foodgrains and non-foodgrains. The former contributes almost two-third of total agricultural output. The most important component of the foodgrains is rice (weight 29.7) followed by wheat (weight 14.5), and in case of non-foodgrains, oilseeds constitute the most important group (weight 12.6). Foodgrains output increased from 50.8 million tonnes (mt) in 1950-51 to 187 mt in the Eight Plan (annual average) and further to 202.9 mt in the Ninth Plan (annual average) and remained at 202.22 mt during Tenth Plan. For convenience of our analysis we have divided the entire period into two parts – (i) period after Third Plan and up to 1991, and (ii) period after 1991. The later is often referred to as the post New Economic Policy period. During the second period growth in foodgrains output has stagnated. The increase in foodgrains has stagnated because of insignificant increase in the yield rate of major crops after 1991. Though the yield rate per hectare of all foodgrains had increased from 750 kg (approximately) to 1380 kg per hectare at a rate of 2.5 per cent (approximately) in between 1965-66 to 1990-91, it declined to less than 1 per cent during the period 1990-91 to 2006-07. The all India average yield rate for all foodgrains in the year 2006-07 stood at 1750 kg per hectare and this is much lower compared to many other countries. The productivity in India is not only lower than other countries but it is also much below than the potential estimated by the planning commission. The potential for rice is estimated at 4000/5810 kg per hectare but the actual yield has been 2127 kg per hectare in 2006-07 which is much below the potential, even in case of wheat, the actual productivity in 2006-07 was only 2671 kg per hectare as against the potential of 6000/6800 kg per hectare. This is true for all other crops.

Agricultural growth is essential for the overall growth of Indian economy. This growth rate is also a sort of essential condition for improving living standard of those who are dependent on agriculture. In this context, it may not be wrong to mention that the New Agriculture Policy (2000) target of attaining a growth rate in excess of 4 per cent seems too ambitious an objective, particularly, when we look at the historical rate of growth in Indian agriculture. The post independence average growth rate in agriculture has been 2.55 percent per annum. This growth rate includes contribution of technological breakthrough of Green Revolution and major expansion in irrigation and in area under cultivation. Out of these three sources of output growth the scope for expansion of cultivated area is much more limited in future compared to that experienced in the past.

Irrigation and Agriculture

Net area under cultivation has already reached a plateau and only a limited scope of expansion exists if we take steps to bring wastelands under cultivation. However, as an alternative cultivated area as such can be expanded by raising more number of crops on the same piece of land i.e. by raising crop intensity. This expansion depends heavily on extent of irrigation expansion.

Dhawan (1988) showed that for the expansion of crop output in India, irrigation has played the role of a kingpin. This is also true about its appropriate role in stabilising the production of wheat and rice, the two principal foodgrains that constitute the backbone of the foodgrains distribution system in the country. Thus, irrigation development as an instrument of agricultural growth and its stability has performed reasonably well. Nearly 70% of gross value of crop production (GDP) has come from irrigated areas and by the expansion of irrigated area per hectare yields of crops has also increased (Vaidyanathan, 2006). But it is true that for the growth of plants, water must be available in the appropriate quantities and at the right time, depending on the species of plants, the soil and other climatic conditions also (Jha, 1984). An important consideration in agriculture performance other than its rate of growth in production and yield is efficient use of scarce resources such as water.

Increase in productivity leads to agricultural growth and can help to reduce poverty in country like India where most of the people depend on agriculture for their livelihood. Since area under cultivation remaining constant, improving the productivity in necessary for strengthening the agriculture sector. In general, productivity has increased when output from a given level of input has increased. Water, is an essential input[4] in agricultural production. Since, rainfall is a beyond control and uncertain, stability of production is dependent on appropriate irrigation facilities. According to the ICAR, the production of crops in irrigated areas is on an average 50 to 100 percent higher than that of the unirrigated areas in the same locality. Improved water management (including irrigation and drainage) can probably do more towards increasing agricultural production both of foodgrains and other crops in the irrigated areas of the world than any other agricultural practice. The second-generation challenges of green revolution technologies also need serious attention and there is evidence that the high yielding varieties of seed and the chemical fertilizers have been largely beneficial in the irrigated farming system and use of these agro chemicals have been highly successful only in the irrigated areas (Kiran Kumar *et. al.,* 2008).

According to official estimates, available water resources can provide irrigation to 140 million hectares area (Tenth Five Year Plan Vol. 2 Ch. 8) which can provide irrigation to 72 percent of gross cropped area, assuming irrigated crop intensity to be 1.36, as compared to 40 percent area under irrigation at present. Further, productivity of one hectare of gross irrigated area is reported to be 2.75 times the productivity of unirrigated area (Dhawan, 1994). Prof R. Chand of IEG has done a simple exercise based on this information, which shows that if irrigation potential is fully exploited it would raise present level of output by 50 percent. This further implies that if the entire irrigation potential is exploited by the year 2020 it would enable the country to realize annual growth rate of the order of 2.00 percent per annum for two decades. This would require decadal increment in gross irrigated area by 31.8 million hectare, which is more than double the irrigation potential created during the decade of 1990s. In case the pace of irrigation development is maintained at the level of decade of 1990s, it would help in attaining only 0.78 percent growth rate in output.

The ultimate irrigation potential in the country has been estimated at 140 million hectare. This shows that tremendous efforts are needed in development of irrigation in the country to help attain growth rate stipulated in National Agricultural Policy. This would require very sharp increase in public investments in agriculture, which has either remained stagnant or declined during the last two decades. However, for creating such a gigantic irrigation capacity would require almost a threefold increase in public investments in real terms. Second, to meet such high targets through major irrigation projects is likely to face resistance from various environmental groups.

Expansion of irrigation and water management is an important strategy to raise agricultural output. Water is one of the key inputs for the agricultural productivity, and development of irrigation facility and water management was one of the core issues in Indian planning since independence. Despite remarkable gain of various irrigation projects, out of total net cultivated area, merely 40 percent of total cropped area is estimated to be irrigated, whereas remaining 60 percent are mainly dependent on rainfall. Indian agriculture is largely dependent on monsoon, the conventional ponds and tanks are no longer in use, the increased demand of water for non agricultural purposes, over exploitation of the groundwater has resulted in lowering of the water table in many area. Agriculture is the largest consumer of water.

If the present trend in agriculture water use continues, then the demand for water will exceed the available water in no distant time (see Table 2).

Table 2: Estimated Annual Requirement of Water in India by Different Uses

(Unit: b.c.m.)

Sl. No.	*Sector*	*Year* 2000	2010	2025	2050
1	Domestic	42	56	73	102
2	Irrigation	541	688	910	1072
3	Industry	8	12	23	63
4	Energy	2	5	15	130
5	Other	41	52	72	80
	Total	634	813	1093	1447

Source: Central Water Commission (BP Directorate) Report of the Standing Sub-Committee for Assessment of Availability and Requirement of Water for Diverse Uses in the Country August, 2000.

Efficiency in water use is as important as increasing the cultivable area under irrigation. The problems of water logging and soil salinity reduce the land productivity. Due to degradation problems, growth in total factor productivity has decreased across a substantial area of the country under major food crops.

Irrigation development was the cornerstone of the economic strategy in Indian agriculture planning. Substantial irrigation potential has been created through major, medium and minor irrigation schemes. The total irrigation potential in the country has increased from 81.1 million ha in 1991-92 to 102.8 million ha in 2006-07. Of the total potential created, however, only 87.2 million hectares (84.9 per cent) is actually utilized (*Economic Survey 2007-08*). Irrigation development in the country has been taken up in a big way through Major, Medium and Minor irrigation schemes since independence with the advent of First Five Year Plan. Huge investment was made for these schemes in successive plan period. But most of these large multi-purpose and irrigation river valleys projects have spilled over from one plan to another, mainly because of financial constraints being faced by the State Governments. As a result the performances of these projects are far below than their potential. The low-level performance of the existing irrigation systems is of serious concern to the farmers, the governments and other funding agencies that have made massive investment in their development.

The most severe problems encountered by large irrigation projects in the developing countries are the increasing costs of new schemes, the huge backlog of incomplete schemes, and the increasing neglect of existing systems. Large scale canal irrigation systems, in particular, are in poor condition: they are not properly maintained, operations are inadequate, water supplies do not reach the end of systems, and the timing of water supply is unreliable. The wide gap between actual and desirable performance threatens the sustainability of irrigated agriculture. This state of affairs warrants proper investment strategies with institutional reforms and comprehensive plans for developing irrigation systems, starting from micro-level or at grass-root level. Government agencies and farmers need to work together in this direction. Increasing irrigation facilities without ensuring equitable distribution and efficient use of water at the village level will not help growth of the agriculture sector.

Irrigation and Water Use Policy in India

In India a centralized model of planned economic development and governance gave rise to a highly centralized approach to water resource management. Its primary focus was on the construction of big reservoirs, multi-purpose projects and large irrigation systems. Minor irrigation was given less priority for water resources development. A comprehensive approach to water resources planning was first made under the Fourth Five Year Plan (1970-1974). In March 1983 the National Water Resources Council (NWRC) was set up to frame policy and coordinate action at the central level. The National Water Policy (NWP) adopted in 1987, called for water resources planning, development and conservation "on an integrated and environmentally sound basis". The NWP 1987 it gave highest priority to domestic water needs followed by irrigation for agriculture, hydropower, navigation, industrial and other uses. But this policy has been mainly criticized for poor implementation and remaining on paper (Chowdhury, 2009; p. 37).

As a result this policy was revised in 2002 mainly incorporate the growing environmental concerns, larger need for information and growing complexity of the projects which increase the need for integrated water resource management. It recognizes water as a crucial element in developmental planning, to be managed in a sustainable manner and guided by the national perspective. Rainfall, river waters, surface ponds and lakes and ground water are all part of water resource system. It acknowledges integrated and coordinated development of surface and ground waters and their conjunctive use, the socio-economic, environmental and sustainability issues in water resources development; and issues of equity and social justice in water distribution; and stipulates that all these concerns need to be addressed on basis of common policies and strategies.

The 73rd Amendment Act recommended 29 subjects – including drinking water supply, minor irrigation, water management and watershed development – to be transferred to Gram Panchayats. Yet, the new Water Policy of 2002 continues to emphasize government control over water, and totally ignored the nation's rich heritage of water resources harvesting and management by local communities. The National Water Policy in its present form appears to be a statement of intentions as it is not supported by any legislation and does not have an action plan.

To increase agriculture productivity, the stated strategies of the State Governments has been implementation of institutional reforms particularly the land reforms, and provide the beneficiaries of land reforms along with small and marginal farmers crucial non land inputs like credit, seeds, irrigation facilities, fertilizers, etc. Irrigation as mentioned is by far the most important non land input to attain a high growth rate of agricultural output. However, creating additional irrigation potential with limited resources and within short span of time is not possible through large river projects. Thrust on the development and expansion of irrigation by utilizing available surface as well as ground water sources has led to the birth of the concept of Minor Irrigation Schemes. Within minor irrigation emphasis needs to be placed on expansion of irrigation facilities through increased use of surface water as against ground water. Increase in surface water may be done by reclamation of ponds, lakes, canals to harvest rain water which will not only increase the storage capacity of excess rain waters in these bodies but will help to mitigate flood during monsoon.

Minor Irrigation Potential and Prospect in India

All irrigation schemes having upto 2000 hectares of cultivable command area have been classified as minor since 1978, but the criteria for classification of minor irrigation schemes has been changing from time to time. Since April 1993 all ground water schemes and surface water schemes (both flow and lift) having cultivable command area upto 2000 hectares individually are considered as minor irrigation schemes. The minor irrigation schemes provide control and timely irrigation to the farmers. These schemes do not require heavy investments for their installation and are quick maturing, so that the beneficiaries can be benefited in short period of times. As the surface water projects alone are not able to meet the full demand of water, farmers have installed wells and tube-wells in their command area to provide supplementary irrigation by exploiting ground water.

In India, irrigated area from major projects has increased to 3.47 times, from tanks 1.9 times, and from groundwater 6.3 times during 1951 to 2007. The ultimate irrigation potential from minor irrigation schemes has been assessed as 81.42 million hectares, out of which 17.3 million hectares is assessed to be contributed through surface water scheme. Out of this surface water minor irrigation schemes 11.9 million hectares has already been created as per the Third Minor Irrigation Census. The minor irrigation sector including groundwater schemes covers about two third of the country's total irrigation capacity. By 2004, a potential of 58.46 million hectares has been created from minor irrigation schemes out of the ultimate irrigation potential of 81.42 million hectares.

Over the years, Indian agriculture has been sustained by natural and man-made water bodies such as lakes, tanks, ponds and so on. It has been estimated that there are about five lakh water bodies/tanks used for irrigation in our country. Many of them have begun to disappear and there is an urgent need of restoration, repairs and improvements. These water bodies have been treated as an important source of minor irrigation in the country and even today two-thirds of irrigated agriculture is covered in our country under such minor irrigation schemes. The carrying capacity of tanks has decreased over a time for a variety of reasons and hence restoration and renovation of tanks and other local sources is a priority task (*ibid*, p. 43). In the Eleventh Five Year Plan, restoration of water bodies has been taken up in 24 districts of 14 States, namely, Andhra Pradesh, Chhattisgarh, Gujarat, Himachal Pradesh, Jammu and Kashmir, Jharkhand, Karnataka, Kerala, Madhya Pradesh, Maharashtra, Orissa, Rajasthan, Tamil Nadu, and West Bengal.

However, there is considerable inter and intra state variation in the development of minor irrigation schemes. Inter and intra state variation in production and yield rates exits in agriculture sector. Such variations are natural in country like India due to its vast geographical and agro-climatic diversity, but lack of appropriate institutional infrastructure and inadequate availability of inputs are the major bottlenecks for increasing agricultural output. Lack of irrigation has been a major binding constraint in agricultural growth. In 2002-03 around 41 per cent of the gross cropped area had irrigation facilities, that is, 59 (approximately) per cent of the gross cropped area still continues to depend on monsoon.

Agriculture Scenario in West Bengal

The Eleventh Plan proposes to develop irrigation in regions that lag in general and Eastern Region in particular. The Eastern Region comprises of four States namely, Bihar,

Jharkhand, Orissa and West Bengal. Share of agriculture in State GDP during 2004-05 in West Bengal was 19.9% which is almost equal to that of Jharkhand (19.6%) and is relatively lower than other states in the Eastern Region of India (GOI, 2007; p. 27). West Bengal is the highest producer of rice in India, but the yield of rice per hectare at 2574 kg/ha in 2004-05 is much less compared to states like Punjab (3943 kg/ha), Haryana (2941 kg/ha), Andhra Pradesh (3111 kg/ha) and Karnataka (2712 kg/ha). The overall yield of foodgrains is also less than states like Punjab and Haryana. However, comparison of the agriculture inputs statistics of West Bengal with other agriculture developed states in India gives an intriguing scenario. The proportion of area under irrigation at 37.9 per cent in 2003-04 is much below the national average of 42.2 percent. Fertilizer consumption per hectare is well above the national average and is the highest in this region of the country. Rural indebtedness figures from the 59th round of NSSO shows that 50% of the farmer households are indebted in rural West Bengal. In West Bengal 50% of land is held by 80.5% of farmer household with an average area of less than 1 hectare, an outcome of aggressive land-reforms. Even when the average size of marginal holdings[5] (0.51 ha) in the state is well above the national average (0.40 ha) for the same size-group of land (GOI, 2007; p. 211), almost 88% of the total indebted farmer households in the state have a land size of less than 1.0 hectare. This shows that rural indebtedness have concentration around marginal farmers.

The net earnings from cultivation was not adequate enough to meet of the consumption needs of the farmer households having a land size of less than 2 hectares was reported from the 2003 NSSO survey. A later NSSO survey (61st round) in 2004-05 showed that 45.8% of the total work-forces in the state were dependent on agriculture. The bulk of agriculture output in the state is produced by the marginal and small farmers through labour intensive methods of production. This is a feature of the small peasant based agriculture production system. That the pace of growth in agriculture production in the state has been dependent on the use of high doses of fertilizer and labour, which has in fact increased cost of production substantially over the years. This makes farming in such small land holdings rather less remunerative economic activity.

The rate of increase in cost of production of most crops has exceeded rate of increase in the price of almost all crops. Farm Management Studies (1999-00 to 2000-01) showed that while the value of the product increased by 5.22% the cost of production has increased by 22.02% during the period. The corresponding figures for the period 2001-02 to 2004-05 were 21.6% and 30.13% respectively (GOWB, 2006a). This has been the general trend during the last many years. Also, increase in population will further increase fragmentation of lands making agriculture an unviable economic activity in near future. The health of the agriculture sector in the state can be improved only when, (i) agriculture yield is increased and (ii) returns from agriculture is adequate for a farmer household to improve their net well being. Sustainable growth in agriculture requires judicious use of resources like water and also keeping in check unmindful use of fertilizers that may hinder future growth of the sector.

Regional Variation in Agriculture of West Bengal

Warm and humid climate along with vast stretches of fertile plain lands have caused the agriculture to be developed as the most significant economic activity of West Bengal. Almost 61% of the total land area of this state is used for cultivation. Agricultural sector is the most important employment generating sector of the State. It also indirectly generates employment by promoting agro-based industries and other agriculture-related activities. West Bengal covers 2.7 % of India's physical area and accounts for 7.8 % of the country's population as per 2001 Census. The State has 7.5 % of the fresh water resource of the country which is becoming increasingly scarce due to the uncontrolled increase in use for domestic purpose, irrigation and developmental needs. The State, which was described as an area of with sufficient water, now suffers from acute scarcity of water during the lean months. Large regional variation in rainfall in the State causes the twin threats of flood and drought. Thus, development of irrigation and drainage potential has been given utmost importance in this state for agricultural activities.

Regional diversity due to difference in soil and agro-climatic condition in different region of the state, manifest itself in inter-regional variation in the performance of agriculture sector. The soil varies from the fertile plains of the Ganges to red laterite dry zone in the west. Climate varies from moist tropical in the southeast to dry tropical in the southwest and from subtropical to temperate in the mountains of the north. Annual rainfall varies from 900 mm in southwest to about 500 mm in parts of the north. The temperature ranges from sub zero in the hills during the winter to about 46^0C in southern parts during the summer. Large variation thus exists in the performance of agriculture sector in the State (GOI, 2005).

Broadly the districts of West Bengal have been clubbed into three different regions, namely Gangetic West Bengal[6], Paschimanchal[7] and Uttarbanga[8] . Of these the two identified economically backward regions Paschimanchal (83.05%) and Uttarbanga (85.84%) have a very high proportion of rural population who are engaged in the agriculture sector. The overall density of rural population in West Bengal is 676, and the corresponding figure for Paschimanchal, Uttarbanga and Gangetic is 560, 587 and 911respectively (Census, 2001). Cropping intensity is 158 in Purbanchal, 176 in Uttarbanga and 206 in Gangetic plains (GOWB, 2007). It is natural that cropping intensity will be high in Gangetic plains. The relatively low cropping intensity in Purbanchal districts especially in Purulia and Bakura is due to soil condition in this region. Compared to Gangetic plain districts, the share of primary or agriculture sector in GDP of other two regions are substantially high. The secondary or manufacturing sector is the weakest in Uttarbanga region as seen from the figures in Table 1. As a result labourers from this region often migrate in search of livelihood to other parts of the country. The number of labourers who migrate seasonally from Cooch Behar, Uttar Dainajpur, Dakshin Dinajpur and Malda district of Uttarbanga region is quite significant (Bagchi, 2010). The per capita income in these three districts is among the lowest in the state. This is not surprising as these districts have an overwhelming presence of the primary sector.

Besides the regional variation in District Gross Domestic Product (DGDP) as well as the share of primary sector in DGDP, there are other major differences in the performance of the agriculture sector as well amongst the region. Significant regional variation in productivity of rice exists between the regions. Except Malda the yield of rice is well below the state average for all the districts of Uttarbanga region. In Purbanchal region Purulia and Bakura has a much lower yield of rice as compared to Burdhwan and Gangetic plains districts. An initial comparison between yield of crops and irrigation shows that districts with low rice yield have very small area under irrigation as compared to districts with relatively high rice yields.

The role of irrigation in food crop production in West Bengal has been challenged by scholars like Maity and Chatterjee (2010), who have estimated that for the period 1969-2003 foodgrain output in the state has been highly responsive to use of HYV seeds, followed by fertilizers, pesticides and irrigation in order of importance. As against this, Saha and Swaminathan (1994) have considered the effect of HYV seeds on food crop productivity in West Bengal to be minimal or simply non-existent. The HYV was a package programme and it suited the rich and large farmers initially. In this state the size of land holdings is small and only with technological innovations, in terms of machineries and irrigational facilities to suit the needs of small scale farming did HYV seeds start to make an impact.

These studies examine the role of institutional and non-institutional factors in agriculture production but fail to understand the nature of input used in such production function. The nature of all the above inputs considered in food crop production is not same; irrigation is an essential input whereas, others are not. In absence of adequate irrigation crop production will fail and it is not possible to substitute irrigation with any other inputs.

In West Bengal *aman* rice, *boro* rice and wheat is entirely cultivated with HYV seeds. In case of *aus* rice it is well above ninety percent. Therefore, improvement in agriculture output through expansion of HYV seeds has reached its saturation

Table 3: Development Indicators of Agriculture for Districts of West Bengal

District	*Cropping Intensity 2005-06*	*Fertilizer kg per ha of GCA 2005-06*	*% of GCA irrigated 2005-06*	*% of GCA irrigated by Govt Canals (ha) 2005-06*	*Yield Rate tri annual average 2004-05 to 2006-07 (kg/ha)* Rice	*Boro rice*	*Food grains*	*% share of Primary sector in DGDP 2004-05*	*Composite Index*	*Rank*	*HDI 2004*
Burdwan	181.35	153.50	38.54	34.39	3042.00	3059.33	3029.33	32.73	0.5884	5	5
Birbhum	160.80	124.30	56.72	31.08	2987.33	3200.33	2862.00	39.51	0.6204	9	14
Bankura	147.16	110.90	55.39	35.70	2726.67	2554.67	2704.67	40.44	0.7372	15	11
Purba Midnapore	175.24	166.50	40.57	12.34	2295.00	3099.00	2268.67	27.24	0.4500	1	7
Paschim Midnapore	168.90	90.70	32.62	7.09	2580.33	3059.00	2550.33	37.06	0.5710	4	7
Purulia	106.80	131.10	21.88	9.19	2304.67	2295.33	2188.33	35.33	0.9018	18	16
Purbanchal	159.40	127.11	40.68	24.58	2656.00	2877.94	2600.56				
Uttar Dinajpur Dinajpur	184.04	80.70	29.70	0.52	2396.33	2921.00	2431.33	43.10	0.6359	10	13
Dakshin	159.55	152.00	9.42	0.00	2469.67	2954.33	2453.00	46.31	0.7290	14	13
Malda	198.53	140.20	28.51	0.00	3002.00	3639.33	2669.67	37.20	0.6063	8	17
Jalpaiguri	166.89	119.30	16.66	10.39	1625.33	2102.33	1641.00	36.80	0.7860	16	10
Darjeeling	169.12	152.30	3.73	1.01	1645.00	1950.33	1679.67	28.29	0.8333	17	4

Cooch Behar	207.49	136.10	20.79	0.33	1854.67	2480.33	1873.00	47.62	0.6904	13	11
Uttarbanga	181.56	125.70	20.01	2.55	2165.50	2674.61	2124.61				
Howrah	209.42	372.65	30.16	20.76	2219.67	2710.67	2210.67	11.38	0.6010	7	2
Hooghly	241.60	197.90	63.39	18.88	2796.67	2953.00	2784.33	24.71	0.4931	2	6
24-Parganas (N)	190.34	164.40	31.40	1.51	2596.33	3019.67	2516.00	18.46	0.6363	11	3
24-Parganas (S)	137.05	139.90	21.58	8.85	2208.67	3051.00	2170.33	24.40	0.6801	12	8
Nadia	250.16	94.00	29.16	0.00	2712.00	3357.33	2394.33	37.62	0.5145	3	9
Murshidabad	233.65	71.30	21.82	3.51	2820.00	3521.00	2469.67	38.43	0.5910	6	15
Gangetic West Bengal	207.50	135.38	31.73	6.54	2558.89	3102.11	2424.22				
West Bengal	177	129.66	31.98	12.30	2558.67	3082.33	2472.33	27.32			

level. Hence, differences in agriculture development in different districts are an outcome of other factors that contribute in agriculture development. Following Narain *et. al.* (1991) a composite index of agriculture development has been estimated for all districts of the state. Further, the districts have been clubbed into four levels of development as given in Table 4.

Table 4: Classification of West Bengal Districts in Various Categories of Agriculture Development

Level	*Criteria*	*Districts*
High Developed	Less than or equal to (Mean – Standard Deviation) of Composite Index	Purbo Medinipur, Hooghly and Nadia
Developed	Between (Mean – Standard Deviation) and Mean of Composite Index	Paschim Medinipur, North 24-Parganas, Murshidabad, Malda, Uttar Dinajpur, Howrah, and Birbhum
Less Developed	Between Mean and (Mean + Standard Deviation) of Composite Index	Cooch Behar, South 24-Parganas, Dakshin Dinajpur and Bankura
Least Developed	Greater than or equal to (Mean + Standard Deviation)	Jalpaiguri, Darjeeling and Purulia

Table 4 classifies the districts in four categories of agriculture development. Comparing the rank estimated from the Composite Index with HDI rank 2004 for the state of West Bengal shows that there is no consistent relation between the two. For example Darjeeling district which is higher in the HDI rank is in the low category of agriculture development. Murshidabad and Malda which were in the lower rank of HDI are placed in the high middle level of agriculture development index. But this does not in any challenge the HDI method of classification of districts, as both use different indicators of development.

The less agriculture developed districts in general and least developed districts in particular suffer from low level of agriculture productivity, poor irrigation and low cropping intensity. From the inter-correlation matrix given in Table 5, we see that irrigation is significantly related to foodgrain productivity.

Table 5: Inter-correlation Matrix of Variables for Agriculture Development in West Bengal

	Variables	1	2	3	4	5	6	7	8	9
1	Cropping Intensity	1.000								
2	Rice yield	0.251	1.000							
3	Boro rice yield	0.444*	0.797**	1.000						
4	Foodgrain Yield	0.155	0.961**	0.684**	1.000					
5	Fertilizer input	0.132	-0.150	-0.164	-0.073	1.000				
6	Percentage of Gross cropped area irrigated	0.171	0.625**	0.329	0.712**	0.085	1.000			
7	Percentage of surfaced Roads	0.304	0.042	0.158	-0.022	0.296	-0.056	1.000		
8	Agriculture credit per ha of gross cropped area	0.173	-0.081	-0.182	0.000	0.420*	0.088	0.384	1.000	
9	Agriculture wage rate for male field labourers	0.562**	-0.327	-0.010	-0.333	0.457*	0.013	0.516*	0.469*	1.000

** Correlation is significant at the 0.01 level

* Correlation is significant at the 0.05 level

The negative correlation between irrigation and rainfall which is significant has an interesting interpretation. In areas where rainfall is high there has been less expansion of irrigation. That cropping intensity has increased due to expansion of HYV especially *boro* rice is also evident from the table. Foodgrain yield is heavily dependent on rice yield is shown by the high correlation value which is also significant. Agriculture credit bears a significant relation with fertilizer, which implies that use of marketable inputs is possible only when agriculturist have access to credit. Since larger numbers of farmers are marginal or small landholders in the state, it is difficult for them to access intuitional credit for agriculture activity. The relation between agriculture wages of male field labourers with cropping intensity, fertilizer input, extent of surfaced road and agriculture credit is interesting. Increase in cropping intensity, use of fertilizer and better communication increases demand for labour in the rural areas, and subsequently increase in labour wages. Increase in agriculture credit leads to increase in agriculture activity which positively affects the wages.

Conclusion

The possibility for increase of foodgrains yield through expansion of HYV has been fully exhausted, and any further increase is possible only through increase in cropping-intensity. This requires expansion of irrigation facility through increase in state investment in the agriculture sector. Private investment in agriculture leads to a growth of private water market, and proliferate through exploitation of ground-water. A large component of mechanisation of agriculture in the state has been largely of pump-sets and shallow tube-wells. This has happened more in the Gangetic plains region of the state.

Large intra-state variations in agriculture development of the state need to be minimised. Priority need to be given to those districts that are agriculturally less developed. That Uttarbanga region of the state is agriculturally backward is evident as four out of six districts are in the less developed category. In Purbanchal region only Purulia and Bankura are under less agriculture developed category. While in the Gangetic plain region only South 24 Parganas is identified as less developed agriculture district. This is because large areas of the district is affected by saline water and are deltas.

The backwardness of Uttarbanga districts needs careful examination. The districts of Uttarbanga have a low percentage of surfaced roads. Any increase in the road density along with surfaced road will certainly help to increase rural income. Better road means better scope for agriculture marketing. Improvement of rural infrastructure viz., irrigation systems, all weather roads, better storage facilities should be undertaken on a priority basis. Irrigation in Dakshin Dinajpur, Jalpaiguri and Coochbehar is in dire state. It is understandable that Darjeeling being a hilly district will have a lower rate of irrigation but, there is still ample scope to improve from a low irrigation figure of 3.73 % of gross cropped area. Even when the districts of Uttarbanga receive relatively more rainfall compared to other regions of the state, we cannot ignore or be complacent about irrigation in this region. Lack of water management results in huge run-off of water during monsoon and is associated with corresponding erosion of soil as well. Such losses of natural resources cannot be replenished easily. The districts of Uttarbanga region have the potential to increase agriculture output.

Comparing the three regions in respect of their irrigation sources shows vast regional variation exists. Net irrigated area through major/medium schemes is not only highest in Paschimanchal region but other regions hardly have any presence of large schemes. Only Jalpaiguri has 11 percent of its net area being irrigated by the Tista project. Minor irrigation dominates the irrigation scenario in West Bengal. Over 98 percent of the irrigation in Gangetic plains and Uttarbanga regions are done through minor schemes. The share of ground water irrigation as compared to surface irrigation is much higher in these two regions. Seventy percent in Gangetic plains and seventy seven percent in Uttarbanga of the net area irrigated are under ground water irrigation. This seriously threatens the viability of agriculture in the long run in the state. It is only in Purulia, Howrah, South 24 Parganas, Jalpaiguri and Darjeeling that the surface water irrigation is more compared to ground water irrigation. This is because of the geographical conditions in these districts. Groundwater exploitation cannot be allowed at the cost of long-run viability of agriculture production. When private interest is in conflict with desirable optimal outcome, state intervention becomes inevitable. However, this does not mean all private initiative has to be curtailed. What it requires essentially is government investment in irrigation expansion, engaging local panchayats, encouraging community management of water, etc. All these will naturally help to meet the challenge faced by agriculture sector in the state.

Note

[1] Method for estimation of composite index:

The variables considered in the construction of composite index were, cropping intensity, yield of rice, boro rice and foodgrains, percentage share of primary sector in District GDP, percentage of Gross Cropped Area irrigated, fertilizer consumption per hectare of Gross Cropped Area, and percentage of surfaced road in each district. Since these variables are recorded in different units of measurement, they are first standardised. If variables considered are X_{ij}, where $i = 1,2, \ldots n$ (number of districts) and $j = 1,2, \ldots m$ (number of indicators). The standardised variable is denoted as $Z_{ij} = \frac{X_{ij} - \bar{X}_j}{\sigma_j}$, where $\bar{X}_j$ = mean of the jth indicator and σ_j = is the standard deviation of the jth indicator.

From the Z_{ij} matrix we identify the best value of the indicator, which is selected depending upon the direction of impact of the indicator on the level of development. Let the best value be denoted as Z_{oj}, and then we calculate a new variable $P_{ij} = (Z_{ij} - Z_{oj})^2$. Next we calculate $C_i = \sqrt{\left[\sum_{j=1}^{m} P_{ij}/(CV)_j\right]}$, where coefficient of variation in X_{ij} for j^{th} indicator. The composite index of agriculture development is then estimated as $D_i = C_i/E$, where $E = \bar{C} + 3\sigma_{D_i}$. Smaller value of D_i indicates higher level of agriculture development.

REFERENCES

Bagchi, K. K. (2010): "Dynamics of Rural-Urban Migration in West Bengal: A Case Study of Two Districts", Project Report submitted to Indian Council of Social Science Research, New Delhi.

Chand, R., P. Kumar and S. Sinha (2003): "Impact of Agricultural Trade and Related Reforms on Domestic Food Security in India",

Report of the study done for FAO Rome, Institute of Economic Growth, Delhi.

Chand, R. (2003a): "Government Intervention in Foodgrain Markets in the Changing Context", *Policy Paper* 19, National Centre for Agricultural Economics and Policy Research, New Delhi.

Chand, Ramesh (2003b): "Minimum Support Price in Agriculture: Changing Requirements", *Economic and Political Weekly*, Vol.38 No.29, pp. 3027-3028.

Chowdhury, M. (2009): "Non-Land Inputs: Enquiring the Role of Minor Irrigation in Agriculture Productivity, Stability and Equity in Dakshin Dinajpur District of West Bengal", Unpublished M.Phil. Dissertation, North Bengal University.

Dhawan, B.D. (1988): 'Indian Irrigation: An Assessment', *Economic and Political Weekly*, Vol. 23, No. 19, pp. 965-971.

Dhawan, B.D. (1994): *Irrigation in India's Agricultural Development*, Commonwealth Publishers, New Delhi.

GOI (2005): *State of Forest Report*, Forest Survey of India, Dehradun.

GOWB (2005): *Statistical Abstract*, Bureau of Applied Economics & Statistics.

GOWB (2006): Economic Review, 2006-07.

GOWB (2006a): Directorate of Agriculture.

GOI (2007a): *Agricultural Statistics at a Glance* 2006.

GOI (2007b): *Economic Survey* 2007-08.

GOI (2008a): *All India Report on Agriculture Census* 2000-01.

GOI (2008b): *Economic Survey* 2008-09.

Gulati, A. and P. Sharma, (1990): 'Prices, Procurement and Production: An Analysis of Wheat and Rice', *Economic and Political Weekly*, Vol. 25, pp. A36-A47.

Hanumantha Rao, C.H. (2005): *Agriculture, Food Security, Poverty, and Environment*, OUP, New Delhi.

Haque, T. (2003): "Decent Work in Agriculture in India" In a Report of the Asian Regional Workshop 18th to 21st August 2003, International Labour Office, Bangkok edited by D.P.A. Naidu and A. Navamukundan.

Jha, U.M. (1984): *Irrigation and Agricultural Development*, Deep & Deep Publications, New Delhi.

Kanwar, S. (2004): *Relative Profitability, Supply Shifters and Dynamic Output Response: The Indian Foodgrains*, Working Paper No. 133, Centre for Development Economics, Department of Economics, Delhi School of Economics.

Ki· ın, K.P., Jayasheela and Basil Hans, V. (2008): "Indian Agriculture in The Post-Economic Reform Period", *Journal of Development Research*, Vol.1, No.1, pp.29-42.

Lahiri, A. and P. Roy, (1985): 'Rainfall and Supply Response: A Study of Rice in India', *Journal of Development Economics*, Vol. 18, pp. 315-334.

Maity, B and B. Chatterjee (2010): 'Returns to Scale of Foodgrain Production in India: An Empirical Test', *European Journal of Social Sciences*, Vol. 14, No 3, pp. 496-501.

Masood, H. & K. Tabassum (2007): 'Agriculture: Problem and Prospects', *Kurukshetra*, Vol. 55, No. 9, p.19.

Narayana, N.S.S. and K. Parikh, (1981): *Estimation of Farm Supply Response and Acreage Allocation, Research Report RR-81-1*, International Institute of Applied Systems Analysis, Laxenburg.

Saha, A. and Swaminathan, M. (1994): 'Agricultural growth in West Bengal in the 1980's: A Disaggregation by Districts and Crops', *Economic and Political Weekly*, 29 (13), pp. 2039-40.

Swaminathan, M.S. (2006): Report of Sub-Committee on *"More Crop and Income per Drop of Water"*, Advisory Council on Artificial Recharge of Ground Water, Ministry of Water Resources, Government of India October 2006.

Vaidyanathan, A. (1996): "Agricultural Development: Imperatives of Institutional Reforms", *Economic and Political Weekly*, 31(35/37) pp. 2451-2458.

NOTES

1. Haque T., (2003): "Decent Work in Agriculture in India" In a Report of the Asian Regional Workshop 18th to 21st August 2003, International Labour Office, Bangkok edited by D.P.A. Naidu and A. Navamukundan.
2. HYV or High Yielding Variety technology is more popularly known as Green Revolution.
3. Ratio of agriculture land available to agriculture population in India was 0.33 ha. in 1994 and declined to 0.30 ha. in 2004 (Agriculture Statistics, 2006; 141).

4. A resource is essential when production is not possible in its absence.
5. Land holding's less than 1 hectare.
6. It comprises the districts of Howrah, Hooghly, Kolkata, Nadia, Murshidabad, 24-Parganas (N) and 24-Parganas (S). However, Kolkata is not included in the analysis because it is an all urban district.
7. It comprises the districts of Burdwan, Birbhum, Bakura, Paschim Medinipur and Purulia.
8. It comprises the six northern districts, namely, Darjeeling, Cooch Behar, Jalpaiguri, Malda, Uttar Dinajpur and Dakshin Dinajpur.

19

Impact of Liberalization on Economics of Pepper Cultivation in India

S. Jeyarani

INTRODUCTION

India is traditionally known as the "SPICE BOWL OF THE WORLD" because most of the spices are native of our country. India is aptly known as the "LAND OF THE SPICES" because many spices originated from our country. The history of Indian spices was mostly instrumental in the exchange of ancient culture and civilization within and outside the country.

Pepper ranks the first in position, as regards to area and production among the perennial spice crop in the country. Black pepper *(Pipernigrum L)* commonly known as 'KING OF SPICES' and 'BLACK GOLD' is one of the earliest known spice crops of India originated from Western Ghats of our country for centuries.

India accounts for one-fourth of the total world production of pepper. There are four varieties of pepper known as black pepper, white pepper, green pepper and red pepper. Of these three varieties the black pepper is the most significant and largely produced and consumed variety in India. The total area under pepper cultivation in India was 2,15,000 hectares and the production was 51,000 tonnes during the year 2004-05.

TABLE 1

Economics of Cultivation of pepper in India

Year	*2000-01*	*2001-02*	*2002-03*	*2003-04*	*2004-05*
Area (ha)	213860	218220	223060	206902	215000
Production (T)	63760	61460	70600	56842	51000
Productivity (kg/ha)	298	282	317	275	237
DomesticPrice (Rs)	174.24	80.39	88.32	74.11	69.08
ExportPrice (Rs)	174.45	89.04	82.78	82.00	75.00
Export(T)	21830	22877	21609	17363	28750

In India, pepper cultivation is mainly confined to the Southern States of Kerala, Karnataka and Tamil Nadu. Kerala continues to enjoy a near monopoly in area and production of pepper, accounting for 97 percent in production in the country and 94.31 percent of the total area under pepper cultivation, while Karnataka accounts for about 3.79 percent and the rest of about 1.90 percent is from Tamil Nadu, Andhra Pradesh and north eastern states especially Assam.

In Kerala, pepper cultivation is mainly concentrated in the various districts such as Idukki, Kottayam, Cannanore, Calicut, Wyanad etc. The important varieties grown in these areas are Panniyur – 1, Karimunda, Kottanaden, Kuthirarvaly and Pala.

Statement of the Problem

The average annual yield of spices in our country is only 18 per cent of the world's average. The major reason is that the majorities of the holdings in India are small and are cultivating old plants with regard to spices. Although Kerala is the largest producer of black pepper in India, there are fluctuations in the production and productivity. India's share in the total world production of pepper has fluctuated between 1970 and 1990 against the increasing and declining shares of Indonesia and Malaysia respectively[1].

India accounts for 54 per cent of total area under pepper in the world but its share of production is only 26.6 per cent whereas in other countries like Brazil, Indonesia, Malaysia account for lesser percentage of area but with more share in total production due to their higher productivity. According to the time series data from 1950-57 to 1989-90, pepper area has increased by 0.97 per cent per annum whereas the productivity declined by 0.07 per cent per annum. Pepper being an export oriented crop there are fluctuations in the quantum of export, its value and share in the world export of Pepper[2].

The Productivity of pepper in India is low (310 kgs/ hec.) due to lack of awareness of improved varieties and poor management practices adopted in the pepper plantations. Although Kerala is the largest producer of Black Pepper in India, there are several problems associated with them. One of the major issues of production is the lower productivity of pepper in India compared to other countries in the world. There are also certain issues to be studied, as pepper is mostly grown as mixed cropping and inter cropping.

The important reason cited for this is the predominance of small growers engaged in the cultivation of pepper. Similarly, there are problems relating to the attack of pest and diseases, which is mainly responsible for the fluctuations in production.

Although pepper is the export-oriented spice, there are problems associated with the marketing and exports of pepper. There are fluctuations not only in the quantum of export of pepper but also in the export prices. India's production is not in relation to the growing global world demand for Black pepper. So, there is a significant need to study the price supply behaviour of the product.

In view of these significant issues arising from the cultivation of pepper in India State, the proposed study will be made with the following objectives.

Objectives of the Study

The objective of this paper is to analyze the impact of liberalization on Economics of pepper cultivation in India before and after liberalization.

Methodology of the Study

An attempt is made to analyze the impact of liberalization on Economics of pepper cultivation in India during the Pre-liberalization period (1970-71 to 1989-90) and Post-liberalization period (1990-91 to 2004-05).

In order to analyze the trend and growth rate of Economics of pepper cultivation, log quadratic function has been applied.

$$\log Y = a + b_t + c_t^{\,2} + u$$

In order to estimate the structural changes in the growth rate of Economics of Pepper cultivation during the pre and post liberalization period, Kinked Exponential function has been applied

$$\log Y = a + b\,(D_1 t + D_2 k) + c\,(D_2 t - D_2 k) + u$$

Impact of Liberalization on Economics of Pepper Cultivation in India

Agricultural commodities are attached immense importance with the liberalization of trade in India during the nineties. However spices such as pepper, precisely black pepper, enjoy open trade status since the colonial period. As a result, such tradable constitute a significant proportion of total spices export from India; although the importance of spices in export composition has been on decline from 2.65 per cent in 1960-61 to 0.72 per cent in 1990-91.

But after liberalization from 1990's onwards the international trade in spices has grown by nearly 4 per cent per annum in volume and 15 per cent in value. An estimated 50,000 tones of spices and herbs valued at 1500 million US dollars is now imported to various countries globally every year from different countries. An impressive 20.47 per cent of this supply comes from India, but the recent data shows that the share has declined to 7.5 per cent in the export of spice extracts has shown spectacular growth in global market with a short span of time. During the year 2002-2003, the exports quantity touched an all time high of 2.64 lakh tones. However, during 2003-04 spices export declined to 2.47 lakh tones valued at 415 million dollars. The decline was mainly due to the drop in export of mint products and also because of lower export of pepper coupled with the fall in international price of pepper.

Globalization and trade liberalization have posed unprecedented challenges to Indian spices, which is the major export-earning commodity. The world trade Agreement leading to the establishment of the world trade organization came into effect in January 1995. India has removed all quantitative restrictions on all agricultural and other trade related commodities in 2001.All these resulted in a unified world market without quantitative restrictions, strong competition among producing and exporting countries and demand of high standard of quality and sanitary on regulations by importing countries. In the pre era of World Trade Organization, there was only one – way movement of spices from producing countries to consuming countries. But after removal of quantitative restrictions, spice trade between producing countries, also came into existence due to restriction and reduction of import duties.

Under the EXIM policy, like any other commodity, pepper used to be imported into India form Sri Lanka and other countries, duty free for re-exports. If the imports were for domestic consumption normal rate of duty for pepper imports is 70 percent. However, during 2003-04, 4,383 tonnes of pepper was imported from Sri Lank, which include import for re-export under the EXIM policy as well as import for domestic consumption under bilateral agreement when compared to the Sri Lankan production of 8500 tonnes. Thus it is evident from this that pepper of other origin are coming into India in the guise of Sri Lanka pepper to take undue advantage of the duty-free status. This has greatly affected the interest of Indian pepper. In this background, UPASI has suggested that, on the lines of tea, quantity cap 5 per cent of Sri Lanka's pepper production should be prescribed for such imports. The tariff for import of pepper from Sri Lanka has been reduced to nil, due to bilateral agreement. This resulted in flow of low quality Sri Lankan pepper to the Indian domestic market, leading to low demand of high priced Indian pepper. As a result of free trade agreements, there is strong competition among exporting countries. This has lowered the price of major spices in the world market. Import duty from other countries is retained at 70 per cent. Recently Government of India abolished the system of advanced licensing where nil import duty was levied to facilitate export as value added item.

The Government of India has enacted "Geographical Indication Good Registration and protection Act" in 1999. As a major producer and exporter of spices, India has to gain from this act. Eligibility of GI registration is based on certain specific quality, Reputation (or) other characters including appearance of the commodity or goods, which are exclusively due to geographical elements. After 2004 clamp down on the input – output norms for export of value added pepper products; the DGFT took step on January 3rd 2006 to check the duty free import for the purposes of export production. Now the axe has fallen on import of all spices including pepper for export production. For the export of spices and spices products the exporting countries have to comply with the specifications laid down by the regulatory agencies in importing countries.

Before liberalization, exporters had to comply with the pre-shipment inspection and Quality control as per the Ag-mark Grade specification prescribed by the directorate of marketing and Inspection. Export Inspection Agency under the Export Inspection council of India also has the mandate for Pre- shipment Inspection and Quality control certification. With the liberalization, Pre-shipment Inspection and Quality control were withdrawn and the exporters are free to export spices and spice products as per the specifications prescribed by the importing countries.

There has been a structural Break in the area, production, productivity and export prices of pepper under Pepper Cultivation in India between the Pre-Liberalization and Post-Liberalization Period.

TABLE 2

Estimation of Structural Changes on the Growth Rate of Economics of Pepper Cultivation in India

Year	*Regression Co-efficient* A	b	C	R^2	*NGR*	*Growth rate (%)*
Area	11.489	0.02011 (0.004)*	0.03158 (0.006)*	0.81	Acceleration	2.41
Production	9.917	0.03373 (0.007)*	0.04135 (0.011)*	0.76	Acceleration	3.63
Productivity	5.355	0.01329 (0.004)*	0.008306 (0.007)*	0.44	Deceleration	1.16
Dom.Price	1.757	0.09613 (0.01308)*	0.10841 (0.02066)	0.87	Acceleration	10.06
Exp.price	1.979	0.08629 (0.01235)*	0.10295 (0.01951)*	0.85	Acceleration	9.23
Export	9.817	0.03083 (0.00841)*	-0.01505 (0.01329)	0.34	Deceleration	1.43

Source: Computed Data

*Indicates significance at 5 per cent level

The growth rate of area under Pepper has been accelerating from a significant growth rate of 2.01 percent per annum during the Pre-Liberalization Period to 3.16 percent per annum during the Post-Liberalization Period in India. The growth rate of Production of Pepper has been accelerating from a significant growth rate of 3.37 percent per annum during the Pre-Liberalization Period to 4.14 percent per annum during the Post-Liberalization Period in India. But the growth rate of Productivity of Pepper has been decelerating from a significant growth rate of 1.38 percent per annum during the Pre-Liberalization Period to 0.98 percent per annum during the Post-Liberalization Period in India.

Thus the Production of Pepper increased drastically after Liberalization. Since the area under Pepper Cultivation increased drastically, the Production of Pepper also increased to a greater extent. Hence, there has been a positive impact on the improvement of Production of Pepper after Liberalization. But the productivity of Pepper in India decreased from the Pre-Liberalization to Post-Liberalization

Period explaining the adverse effect of liberalization on the growth rate of Productivity Production of Pepper.

The growth rate of Domestic Prices of Pepper has been accelerating from a significant growth rate of 9.61 percent per annum during the Pre- Liberalization Period to 10.84 percent per annum during the Post- Liberalization Period. The growth rate of Export Prices of Pepper has been accelerating with a significant growth rate of 8.63 percent per annum during the Pre- Liberalization Period and 10.30 percent per annum during the Post- Liberalization Period in India. Thus the domestic and export prices of Pepper increased drastically after Liberalization.

But the growth rate of export of Pepper has been decelerating from a significant growth rate of 3.08 percent per annum during the Pre- Liberalization Period to -1.51 percent per annum during the Post- Liberalization Period in India The export of Pepper decreased to a greater extent because of poor competence power of export in the international market and India has encouraged more Import of Pepper from Vietnam and Srilanka for the purpose of re-export of Pepper. Hence, there has been an adverse Impact on the Export of Pepper in India after Liberalisation.

Conclusion

Though India is the homeland of many spices, productivity of many of the spices are low, when compared to other competing countries. As the international market become increasingly competitive, it is imperative to enhance production and productivity and bring down the cost of cultivation and price of the produce to make Indian spices globally competitive. Farm mechanization will be promising since there is shortage of agricultural labour in India and labour has become very costly.

Government of India should focus attention in the matters like Import of low grade and low priced spices from other country and re-export under Indian label may destroy the image of Indian spices. The recent intervention by the government by way of lifting the provision of advance licensing for spices is an encouraging decision in the direction.

REFERENCES

1. Dole.C.Dahl and Hamond, *Market and Price Analysis: The Agricultural Industries,* McGraw Hill Publications Pvt. Ltd.,New York,1977.
2. Frederio Rosengarten, Jr., *What are Spices and Herbs, the Book of Spices,* Part I, Pyramid Books, New York, 1973.
3. Giriappa, S., *Plantation Economy in India,* M.D. Publications Pvt. Ltd, New Delhi, 1990.
4. Kumar, N.m *Introduction to Spices Plantation Crop, Medicinal and Automatic Plants,* Oxford University, IBM Publishing Pvt. Co. Ltd., New Delhi.
5. Loomis, R.A. and G.T. Barton, *Productivity in Agriculture United States, 1870-1958,* Technical Bulletin, United States Department of Agriculture, New York, 1961.
6. Wells. O.V, *Marketing Year Book of Agriculture,* V.S.D.A., 1954.

Journals

1. Alagappan V.and M.Manoharan, "Economics of Pepper Production", *Spice India,* Spices Board, Cochin, Vol.14, No.3, March 2001.
2. Alagappan V. and M. Manoharan, "Production of Pepper in India - A Global Perspective", *Spice India,* Spices Board, Cochin, Vol.14, No.1, January 2001.
3. Chandran C. et.al., "Resource use Efficiency in Pepper Cultivation", *Spice India,* Spices Board, Cochin, Vol.14, No.10, October 2001.
4. Global Pepper Production to go up", *Spice India,* Spices Board, Cochin, Vol.10, No.10, October 1997.
5. Jeromi, P.D. and N.Nagarajan, "Prices Competitiveness of India's Agricultural Export: A Case Study of Pepper", *Indian Journal of Agricultural Economics,* Vol.49, No.3, July-September 1994.
6. Jeromi, P.D "Growth of Pepper Economy of Kerala", *Agricultural Situation of India,* Vol. 48, No.11, 1994.
7. Jeyarani, S., Dhanabalan, M. and Sureshkanan, S., "Indian Export Share of Black Pepper in World Trade, *Peninsular Economist,* 23rd Annual Conference of Association for Economists of Tamil Nadu, 2003.
8. John, T.D. "Pepper Cultivation in Karnataka", *Spice India,* Spices Board, Cochin, Vol.XII, No.12, December 1999.

9. Koshy John, "The Gallery of Spices and Herbs Commemorative", Vol.I, *Spice Fair*, Cochin, 1989.
10. Koshy John, et.al., "Seasonal Climatic Influence in Pepper Production-Idukki District", *Spice India*, Spices Board, Cochin, Vol. XII, No. 12, December 1999.
11. Menon, M.K.K."Trends in Black Pepper – Production, Processing and Marketing", *Indian Spices*, Spices Board, Cochin, Vol.35, No.2.
12. "Pepper Output in '89 put at 1.55 to 1.60lakh MT", *Spices India*, Spices Board, Cochin, November 1988, Vol.1, No.5.
13. Radhakrishna, S. "A Study on Regional Productivities of Agriculture Inputs, *Indian Journal of Agricultural Economics*, Vol.19, No.1, 1964.
14. Rajesh, S.R. and N.Raveendaran and N.Ajjan, "Economic Analysis of pepper exports", *Spice India*, Vo.15, No.8, August 2002.
15. Reddy G.V., Nagarajan G.N. and Venkatram, J.V., "Economics of Production of Banana in Bangalore District, Karnataka", *Agricultural Banker*, Vol.2, 1984.
16. Saikat Sinharnoy and Sanjith R. Nair, (1994), "International Trade and Pepper Price Variations: A Co-Integration Approach", *Indian Journal of Agricultural Economics*, Vol.49, No.3, July-September.
17. Sandhu, H.K. "India's Export Share of Black Pepper in the World Trade – An Econometric Analysis",*The Indian Economic Journal*, Vol.40, No.3, 1990.
18. Seemanthini Ramadas and M. Kader Mohideen, "An Overview of Pepper Cultivation in Tamil Nadu", *Spice India*, Spices Board Cochin, Vol. 21, No.1, January 1988.
19. Senthilkumaran P.and V.Vadivel, "Prospects of Pepper in India", *Spices India*, Spices Board, Cochin, Vol.13, No.5, May 2000.
20. Shenoy J.R. and T.C. Ravindran, "Fluctuations in the Prices of Pepper in Recent Year", *Indian Cocoa, Arecanut and Spices Journal*, Vol.3, No.1, 1989.
21. Suseelappan, M.S. "Medicinal uses of Pepper in Ayurveda International Pepper" *News Bulletin*, April–June 1991.
22. Tamilselvan, M. et.al., "Marketing of Spices in India", *Indian Journal of Arecanut, Spices and Medicinal Plants*, Vol.1, No.2, April-June, 1999.
23. Taranath Shet, T."Marketing Perspective of Pepper", *Spice India*, Spices Board, Cochin, Vol.I, No.4, October 1988.

Unpublished Thesis

1. Bindu Padmini, "An Economic Analysis of Pepper Cultivation Under Different Cropping Systems in Kerala", M.Sc Project in Agricultural Economics, Department of Agricultural Economics, Center for Agricultural and Rural Development Studies, Tamil Nadu Agricultural University, Coimbatore, 1997.
2. Geetha, "The Supply Response of Pepper in Kerala" Unpublished M.Phil. Dissertation to Department of Economics, University of Kerala, Trivandram, 1982.
3. George Amballor, "Supply Response of Pepper in Kerala" Unpublished M.Phil Dissertation submitted to Department of Applied Economics, Cochin University of Science and Technology, Cochin, 1989.
4. Jeromie, "Economics of Pepper Production in Kerala", Unpublished M.Phil. Dissertation to Department of Economics, University of Kerala, Trivandrum, 1991.
5. Krishna, M. "Trends in the Export of Spices with special reference to Kochi Port", M.Phil. Dissertation, Department of Commerce, Madurai Kamaraj University, Madurai, 1999.
6. Mohan, K. "Production, Marketing and Price Behaviour of pepper in Vazhoor Block of Kerala State", Unpublished M.Sc (Agri), Project submitted to Tamil Nadu Agricultural University, Coimbatore, 1973.

News Papers

1. *The Economic Times,* "Commodities/Trade", Chennai, 29th September 2006.
2. *The Economic Times,* "Commodity / Trade", Chennai, 7th October 2005.
3. Ratna Ganguli, "Pepper Export Price 16 Per Cent as Regular Buyers Return (High Output Brings Price Down to Attractive Levels), *The Economic Times,* Commodities/ Trade, Chennai, 25th October 2005.
4. HO Binh Minh, "Vietnam's Pepper Output to dip 10 per cent", *The Economic Times,* Chennai, Commodities / Trade, 30th December 2005.

Reports

1. Peter, K.V., "Makings of a Global Leader", *The Hindu Survey of Indian Agriculture,* 1999.

2. Report of the National Commission on Agriculture, Part XII, Supporting Services and incentives, Government of India, Ministry of Agriculture and Irrigation, New Delhi. 1976.

3. Studies on Economics of Management in Coimbatore District, Tamil Nadu.

4. *Directorate of Economics and Statistics, 1971-72,* New Delhi.

5. Studies on the Economics of Farm Management in Tanjore, Report for the year 1969-70, Directorate of Economics and Statistics, Ministry of Agriculture and Irrigation, Government of India, New Delhi, 1974.

Website

1. www.peppertrade.com
2. www.spice India.com
3. www.indianspices.com
4. www.gerente@pepper trade.com.br
5. www.FAO stat Data base.com
6. www.infoline.com
7. www.ipsta.com
8. www.worldspice congress.com
9. www.global_secure_ex_in_service.us
10. www.Indiainfoline.com
11. www.mdg.org
12. www.mcxindia.com
13. www.hinduonnet.com

NOTES

1. Saikat Sinharnoy and Sanjith R. Nair, (1994), "International Trade and Pepper Price Variations: A Co-integration Approach", *Indian Journal of Agricultural Economics,* Vol. 49, No.3, July-September, p. 417.
2. Saikat Sinharoy and Sanjith R. Nair, (1994), "International Trade and Pepper Price Variations: A Co-Integration Approach", *Indian Journal of Agricultural Economics,* Vol.49, No.3, July-September, p. 418.

20

Credit and Agricultural Development

V.R. Deshpande

Introduction

Agriculture plays a crucial role in the development of the Indian economy. It accounts for 21 per cent of GDP and about two-thirds of the population is dependent on the sector. The importance of agricultural credit as a critical input to agriculture is reinforced by the unique role of Indian agriculture in the macroeconomic framework and its role in poverty alleviation. Recognizing the importance of the agricultural sector in India's development, the government and the Reserve Bank of India (RBI) have played a vital role in creating a broad-based institutional framework for catering to the increasing credit requirements of the sector. Agricultural policies in India have been reviewed from time to time to maintain pace with the changing requirements of the agricultural sector.

Agriculture in India has always been heavily dependent on the monsoons and has hence been an inherently risky activity. Because of the high risk inherent in traditional farming activity the prevalence of high interest rates was the norm rather than the exception, and non-committing exploitation and misery often resulted. Development of rural credit systems has therefore been found to be intrinsically very difficult and, as we will see, an issue of continuing official concern for over a century.

On the eve of the 1991 reforms, the rural credit delivery system was again found to be in a poor shape.

Agricultural credit has played a vital role in supporting agricultural production in India. The green revolution characterized by a greater use of inputs like fertilizers, seeds and other inputs, increased credit requirements which were provided by the agricultural financial institutions. Though the outreach and the amount of agricultural credit have increased over the years, several weaknesses have crept in which have affected the viability and sustainability of these institutions. Furthermore, antiquated legal framework and the outdated tenancy laws have hampered the flow of credit and development of strong and efficient agriculture credit institutions.

The objectives of this paper are:

1. To enquire into the problems of Agricultural Credit.
2. To Study the sources of Agricultural Credit.
3. To review the growth of Agricultural Credit.
4. To evaluate the government and RBI policies for Agricultural Credit

Credit Needs of Indian Farmers

The financial requirements of the Indian farmers can be classified into three types depending upon the period and the purpose for which they are required.

Farmers need funds for short periods of less than 15 months for the purpose of cultivation or for meeting domestic expenses.

The farmers require finances for medium period ranging between 15 months and 5 years for the purpose of making some improvement on land, buying cattle, agriculture implements, etc.

The farmers need finances for the purpose of buying additional land, to make permanent improvements on land, to pay off old debt and to purchase costly agricultural machinery.

There can be further classification of the credit requirements of farmers into two types - productive and unproductive loans. The former include loans to buy seeds, fertilizers, implements, etc.

Besides these, the Indian farmers often borrow for unproductive purposes too, such as for celebration of marriages, births and deaths, & for litigation etc.

Sources of Rural Credit

Broadly, there are two sources of credit available to the farmers-institutional and private. Non- institutional or private sources include money-lenders, traders and commission agents, relatives and landlords, institutional sources consist of the Government and co-operatives, commercial banks including the Regional Rural Banks, (RRBs).

Non-institutional sources — money-lenders landlords, trades etc. accounted for 93 per cent of the total credit requirements in 1951-52 and institutional sources including the Government accounted for only 7 per cent of the total credit needs in that year. The All India Debt and Investment Survey (1981) estimated that the share of non- institutional sources had slumped to about 37 per cent in 1981, money lenders accounting for barely 16 percent; the share of institutional credit, however, had jumped to 63 per cent- co operatives contributing 30 per cent and commercial banks about 29 per cent.

Non-institutional Sources

Money-Lenders

There are two types of money-lenders in rural areas. There are rich farmers or landlords who combine farming with money-lending. There are also professional money-lenders whose only occupation or profession is money-lending.

The cultivators depend upon the money-lenders for their requirements of cash. The Government and the Reserve Bank of India have been propagating that the importance of the money-lenders as suppliers of loans to the farmers has been declining rapidly. However, there are many reasons for the preponderance of the village money-lenders in rural areas even now.

Reasons are as follows:

a) The money-lender freely supplies credit for productive and non-productive purposes, and also for short-term and long-term requirements of the farmers.

b) He is easily accessible and maintains a close and personal contact with the borrower, often having relations with family extending over generations.

c) His methods of business are simple and elastic.

Traders and commission agents supply funds to farmers for productive purposes much before the crops mature. They force the farmers to sell their produce at low prices and they charge a heavy commission for themselves. This source of finance is particularly important in the case of cash crops like Cotton, Groundnut, Tobacco, etc., and in the case of fruit like Mangoes.

Farmers often borrow from their own relatives in cash or kind, in order to tide over temporary difficulties. These loans are generally contracted in an informal manner, they carry low or no interest and they are returned soon after the harvest. Farmers Particularly small farmers and tenants, depend upon landlords and others to meet their financial requirements. Relatives - this source of finance has all the defects associated with money lenders, traders and commission agents. Interest rates are exorbitant. Often the small farmers are cheated and their lands are appropriated. The landless laborers are forced to become bounded slaves.

Credit Delivery Mechanism In Rural Finance - Multi Agency Approach

Need for Institutional Finance

The need for Institutional credit arises because of the

weakness or inadequacy of private agencies to supply credit to farmers. Private credit is defective because.

i) It is based on profit motive and, therefore it is always exploitative.

ii) It is very expensive and is not related to the productivity of land.

iii) It does not flow into most desirable channels and to most needy persons.

iv) It is not available for making agricultural improvements.

Institutional credit is not exploitative and the basic motive is always to help the farmer to raise his productivity and maximize his income. The rate of interest is not only relatively low but can be different for different groups of farmers and for different purposes. Institutions also make a clear distinction between short-term credit and long-term credit requirements and give loans accordingly. Finally, Institutional credit is fully integrated with other needs of agriculturists. The farmers require not only credit but also guidance in the planning of their agricultural operations like the use of seeds, fertilizers, and pesticides etc., assistance in raising crops and in general, help for maximizing their income. Agricultural credit and agricultural improvement should go hand in hand and the farmers should be taught improved farming methods and also be provided adequate and cheap credit. In all developed countries, provision of credit facilities and extension services go hand in hand. This work can be done best by institutions like co-operative societies and commercial banks and not by rapacious money-lenders and commission agents.

National Policy and Objectives

Since independence, a multi-agency approach consisting of co-operatives, commercial banks and regional rural banks- known as institutional credit – has been adopted to provide cheaper and adequate credit to farmers. The major policy in the spare of agricultural credit has been its progressive institutionalsation for supplying agricultural and rural development programmes with adequate and timely flow of credit to assist weaker sections and less development regions.

The basic objectives of this policy are:

a) To ensure timely and adequate flow of credit to the farming sector.

b) To reduce and gradually eliminate the moneylenders from the rural scene.

c) To make available credit facilities to all the regions of the country, i.e. reduce regional imbalances; and

d) To provide larger credit support to areas covered by special programs like Pulses Development Program. Special Rice Production Program and the National Oilseeds Development Project.

Institutional credit, as mentioned earlier, refers to the funds made available by the Government, Co-Operative Societies, Commercial Banks and Regional Rural Banks (RRBs). The Government also set up Co-Operative Banks and Land Mortgage Banks. Much was expected from the co-operative credit movement as it was led by the farmers themselves. A survey or rural credit in 1950-51 showed that the co-operatives could meet barely 3.3 per cent of the total credit requirements of farmers, while the money-lenders accounted for 93 per cent of the credit needs of the farmers. The All-India Rural Credit Survey Committee (1954) stated: "Co-operation has failed, but Co-operation must succeed." It was the All India Rural Credit Survey Committee (1969) which recommended the adoption of "Multi-agency approach" to finance the rural sector. For the first time, the Government openly accepted that rural credit could not be met by co-operative societies alone and that commercial banks should play an important role in the rural sector.

In 1969 14 leading banks were nationalised. This was followed by the setting up of Regional Rural Banks (RRBs) Thus; the multi-agency approach of institutional credit to agriculture was evolved over a number of years.

While RBI was helping the co-operative sector directly. It was felt that the multi-agency approach to rural finance required a special banking institution to coordinate and help all the Institutions specializing in rural finance. It was for this reason that NABARD was set up as the apex bank for rural finance in 1982.

Growth of Institutional Credit for Farmers

The extent of institutional credit for farmers in recent years is given in Table 1.

(Rs. in crores)

Year	*Co-operative Banks (Rs.)*	%	*RRBs (Rs)*	%	*Commercial Banks (Rs.)*	%	*Total Institutional Credit (Rs.)*	%
1984-85	3,440	55	-	-	2790	45	6230	100
1997-98	14,090	44	2040	6	15830	50	31960	100
2002-03	24,300	34	5470	8	41050	58	70810	100
2005-06	39,400	22	15220	8	125860	70	180480	100

Table 1 shows that total agricultural credit from institutional sources had steadily increased from Rs. 6230 crores in 1984-85 to Rs. 1, 80,480/- crores in 2005-06. The contribution of co-operatives was 55 percent of total institutional credit in 1984-85 but was only 22 percent in 2005-2006. Correspondingly commercial banks including RRBs have raised their share from 45 percent to 70 percent during this period.

The Tenth plan (2002-07) projected a substantial jump in institutional credit flow to the agricultural sector to the tune of Rs. 736400/- crores – almost three times, as compared to the Ninth plan) and the annual average credit flow would be Rs. 149123/- crores – as against Rs. 46000/- crores during the ninth plan.

The many new institutions created by the Government and the vastly extended facilities of rural finance provided by these institutions have generally been appropriated by the top 30 percent of middle and affluent farmers in the country.

Even those credit facilities exclusively credited for marginal and small farmers and for economically backward classes do not reach the target groups but are misappropriated by more affluent farmers through collusion with government officials and politicians.

Little is being done for the weakest of the rural population consisting of bonded laborers, landless agricultural laborers, tribal, scheduled castes and scheduled tribes, etc. These people, constituting about 25 to 30 per cent of the total rural population, continue to be cruelly exploited by the high cast Money Lenders and Landlords.

There has been a steady declining trend in the share of co-operative banks in the flow of institutional credit over the years – from 55 % in 1984-85 to 40 % in 1999-00.

There was no coordination between different agencies operating in the same area and as a result, there was multiple financing, over financing in some area and under financing in others.

Despite the adoption of lead bank scheme and district credit plans, the different agencies often failed to formulate and develop meaningful agricultural credit programs in given blocks and districts.

There were practical problems in the recovery of loans. The major problem faced by the leading institutions, particularly the cooperatives, is the most unsatisfactory level of over dues. The ratio of over dues to demand is around 40 to 42 percent in the case of cooperatives and 47 percent in the case of regional rural banks.

The share of various sources in rural credit by earners reveals that the share of money lender in total credit is 70 percent. In absolute terms, it is of the order of Rs. 67000/- crores. The share of public sector banks is 10 percent followed by cooperative societies at 9 %. The share of self help groups (SHGs) is 1 percent. Government loans also account for barely 1 percent and other sources account for 9 percent.

The hold of money lenders in total rural credit has bounced back to 70 percent and PSU banks and cooperatives banks have trailed behind at merely 19 percent. This shows the failure of institutional credit to meet the needs of farmers, landless laborers and wage earners in rural India.

The financial condition of small and marginal farmers was pitiable. The farming community, all over the country has been seething with anger and dissatisfaction about the falling interest rates of banks not reaching them and being force to borrow at exorbitant rates from the money lenders. There were a series of suicides among farmers in Andhra Pradesh, Maharashtra and Punjab.

The UPA government realized the need to enhance credit flow to agriculture. In consultation with RBI, NABARD and commercial banks, the UPA government announced a package for agriculture. The initiatives announced in June 2004 include; stepping up agricultural credit from all leading institutions cooperative banks, RRBs and commercial banks from about Rs. 85000/- crores to Rs. 105000 crores (30 percent increase– this would continue year after year.)

Primary Agricultural Credit Society

Primary agricultural credit societies (PACs) are the grass root level arms of the short term cooperative credit structure. PACS deal directly with farmer borrowers, grant short term and medium term loans and also undertake distribution and marketing functions.

The usefulness of PACs has been rising steadily. In 1950 – 51 it advanced loans worth Rs. 23 crores this rose to Rs. 200 crores in 1960-61, and to Rs. 34520/- crores in 2000-01. The PACS have stepped up their advances to the weaker sections particularly the small and marginal farmers. This progress has been quite spectacular but not adequate considering the demand for finance from farmers. However, the primary credit society has continued to remain the weakest link in the entire cooperative structure.

Shortcomings of PACS: The cooperative credit system makes credit available to the farmers at convenient distances and has intimate knowledge of the local conditions and problems. But it is organizationally and financially weak and hence, in practice, its ability to support credit to the agricultural sector is considerably limited. The All India rural credit review committee brought out the following weaknesses of the primary credit societies.

a. Cooperative credit still forms a small portion of the total borrowings of the farmers.

b. Tenants and small farmers find it difficult to satisfy their need for funds fully from PACS alone.

c. Most primary credit societies are weak and are unable to meet fully and production oriented credit need of farmers.

d. Overdues at all levels are increasing alarmingly indicating the failure of Cooperative credit institutions and

e. PACs have not been able to ensure adequate and timely credit for the borrowing farmers.

District Central Cooperative Banks

Many of the cooperative central banks act as intermediaries between the state cooperative bank on the one hand and the village primary credit societies on the other.

They provide credit for a variety of purposes such as redemption of old debts, improvement of land, purchase of costly agricultural equipments, and construction of wells and erection of pumps and so on. At one time, the redemption of old debts was the most important and, in a sense, the only purpose for which the farmers approached the land development banks. In recent years, however, farmers have been borrowing from DCCB mainly for the purpose of land improvement and development including sinking of wells (56 percent and purchase of agricultural machinery 30 %.

Problems of Central Co-op. Banks

1) Problem of overdues.
2) Lack of trained manpower.
3) Diversification of loans.

RBI Guidelines for the Financing of Agricultural Credit by Commercial Banks

As far back as 1970, RBI circulated among all commercial banks a circular titled Guidelines for the financing of agriculture by commercial banks. So that the rationale, the policies and procedures for making agricultural loans might be clear to commercial banks.

- Credit norms and scales of finance.
- Margins of security.
- Securities against loans to cultivators.
- Recovery of defaults.
- Need for coordination
- New RBI guidelines on farm credit, 1998.

The Reserve bank of India set up in December 1997 a high level committee on agricultural credit, chaired by Mr. R.V. Gupta, a former Deputy Governor. The committee submitted its report in April 1998. Important recommendations of the Gupta Committee are as follows.

a. Free interest rates on farm loans.
b. Scrap 18 % target for agricultural lending.
c. Modify service area approach: RBI should modify the service area approach and allow banks to operate outside their areas and the agricultural borrowers should be free to go to any branch.
d. Offer farmers a composite credit package. The banks should formulate and offer a composite credit package to satisfy all their short term credit needs.
e. Devise a liquid savings package: It is well known that farmers tend to invest in land and gold. The banks should devise a liquid savings package for the farmers.

Special Agricultural Credit Plans

Public sector banks (PSBs) were advised to formulate Special

Agricultural Credit Plans (SACP) since 1994-95 to fix targets for agricultural lending for each year.

Since February 1988 a new strategy for rural lending, viz., "Service Area Approach" (SAA) under which each semi-urban and rural branch of commercial bank was assigned a specific area comprising a cluster of villages within which it would operate, adopting a planned approach for its economic growth.

The implementation of the Service Area Approach involved five stages, viz,

- Identification of the service area for each branch in the rural and semi-urban centers,
- Survey of the service area for assessing the potential for lending for different activities and selection or identification of beneficiaries.
- Preparation of credit plans on an annual basis.
- Co-ordination on an on-going basis for the effective implementation of credit Plans.
- A continuous system of monitoring the progress in the implementation of the plans.

Problems Faced in Service Area Approach (SAA) Strategy

(a) Allocation of Villages - The initial allocation of villagers under the service area approach was not always acceptable to all bank branches. In some cases, villages previously well-served by certain bank branches. In some cases, villages previously well-served by certain bank branches, were allotted to other bank branches which were new and which could not provide the same service. This was, however, a short period problem which could be solved over a period of time.

(b) Under-utilization of staff.

(c) Tribal and Hilly areas. Tribal and hilly areas in North Eastern States, Orissa, South Bihar etc. are under-developed and under-banked. Under the system of SAA, as many as 50 to 100 villages were allotted to be served by a single bank-branch. Such allocation does not serve any useful purpose.

Regional Rural Banks (RRBs)

The main objective of the regional rural banks is to provide credit and other facilities particularly to the small and marginal farmers, agricultural laborers, artisans and small entrepreneurs so as to develop agriculture, trade, commerce, industry and other productive activities in the rural areas.

RRBs have an important role to play in our rural economy as they have to act as alternative agencies to provide institutional credit in rural areas. In course of time, they are intended to eliminate money-lenders altogether. However, they were not set up to replace co-operative credit societies but to supplement them. In the last 30 years, RRBs have been active participants in programs designed to provide credit assistance to identified beneficiaries under the new 20-point programme, IRDP and other special programs for scheduled castes and tribes. They are also implementing differential rate of interest (DRI) schemes for the weaker sections, physically handicapped persons who are gainfully employed, can secure finance from RRBs for purchase of artificial limbs, hearing aids, wheel chairs etc. subject to a maximum of Rs. 2,500/- per borrower.

NABARD and its Role in Rural Credit

A National Bank for Agriculture and Rural Development (NABARD) was, therefore, set up in July 1982 by an Act of Parliament to take over the functions of ARDC.

NABARD has continued to follow the policy earlier laid down by the Reserve Bank in regard to sanction of medium credit limits for approved agricultural purposes. It also grants long-term credit to State Governments for contribution to the share capital of co-operative credit institutions.

NABARD provides two types of refinance. The first is extended to RRBs, Apex Rural Credit Institutions. viz., State Cooperative Banks and State Governments. The second type of refinance is extended to provide resources for ground level deployment of rural credit.

Agricultural and Rural Debt Relief Scheme, 1990

Agricultural and Rural Debt Relief Scheme also called the loan waiver scheme. The scheme came into force from May 1990. The Scheme provided debt relief up to Rs. 10,000 to the borrowers of public sector banks and RRBs. The borrowers include those engaged in agricultural and allied activities and artisans engaged in any activity of rural development relating to cottage and village industries, handicrafts, weaving, etc.

Comprehensive Crop Insurance Scheme, 1985

Agriculture is highly susceptible to such risks as drought, flood etc. It is necessary to protect the farmers from natural calamities and ensure their credit eligibility from the next season. Towards this purpose, the Government of India introduced a comprehensive crop insurance scheme throughout the country from Kharif 1985 covering major cereal crops, oilseeds and pulses. Farmers availing of crop loans from cooperative credit institutions, commercial banks including RRBs were covered under this scheme. The sum insured equal to crop loan disbursed subject to a maximum of Rs. 10,000 per farmer the premium charged was at the rate of 2 % for rice, wheat and millets and 1 % for pulses and oilseeds.

Recent Developments in the Field of Rural Finance

Micro - Finance

Micro credit or micro finance is a novel approach to "banking with the poor". In this approach, very successfully tried in Bangladesh, bank credit is extended to the poor through Self Help Groups (SHGs), Non-Government Organizations (NGOs) , credit unions, etc, Micro credit attempts to combine lower transaction costs and high degree of repayments. The SHG- bank linkage programme, introduced and encouraged by NABARD, is now being implemented vigorously by more than 30,000 branches of commercial banks, RRBs, and cooperative banks in over 520 districts in 30 states and Union Territories. It is estimated that, at the end of March 2004:

a) 17 Million very poor families were brought within the fold of formal banking services

b) The notable feature was the active women participation; more than 90 per cent of the groups linked with banks were exclusive women groups:

c) There was strong repayment performance- at more than 95 per cent of the loans disbursed;

Micro- finance initiatives have shown that banking with the poor is a viable proposition. Micro-credit has been hailed as the best method of creating additional employment and removing poverty. NABARD has been playing a catalytic role in terms of promotional support to NGOs and also in nurturing quality SHG's.

Weaknesses of Micro-finance

(a) Nearly 70 per cent of poor families are yet to be covered. (b) At present, Andhra Pradesh accounts for 40 per cent of SHGs linked to bank credit. The next three States, viz. Tamil Nadu, Karnataka and Uttar Pradesh, together accounted for only 30 per cent of SHG's linked to bank credit.

Kisan Credit Cards

Another notable development in recent years is the introduction of Kisan Credit Cards (KCC) in 1998-99. The purpose of the KCC scheme is to facilitate short term credit to farmers. The scheme has gained popularity and its implementation has been taken up by 27 commercial banks, 187 RRBs and 334 Central Cooperative Banks. Since its inception till the end of March 2004, more than 41 million KCCs have been issued and total loans sanctioned amounted to Rs. 97,710 crores. The KCC scheme has become very popular with farmers KCC holders are also provided personal accident insurance cover of Rs. 50,000 for death and Rs. 25,000 for disability.

The Government introduced in 1999-2000 a new scheme titled "National Agricultural Insurance scheme" or "Rashtriya Krishi Bima Yojana". The new Scheme (NAIS) envisages coverage of all food crops (cereals and pulses). Oilseeds, horticultural and commercial crops. It covers all farmers (both loanees and non loanees, under the scheme. The premium rates vary from 1.5 per cent to 3.5 per cent of sum assured for food crops.

Livestock Insurance

Since 1993-94, the Government of India has been implementing the Livestock Insurance Policy through the General Insurance Corporation of India (GIC). Under this policy, cover is provided for the sum insured or the market value of the animal at the time of death, whichever is less. Animals are normally insured up to 100 percent of their market value. Annually around 19-20 million animals are insured and the total premium collected has ranged between Rs. 131 crores to Rs. 145/- crores between 1994 and 2002.

Conclusion

A review of the performance of agricultural credit in India reveals that though the overall flow of institutional credit has increased over the years, there are several gaps in the system like inadequate provision of credit to small and marginal farmers, paucity of medium and long-term lending, limited deposit mobilization and heavy dependence on borrowed funds by major agricultural credit purveyor. These have major implications for agricultural development as also the well being of the farming community. Efforts are therefore required to address and rectify these issues.

Suggestions

1) Nationwide major mission programme is needed for different activities.
2) Expert teams will have to be formed for each agro climate zone, focusing on the relevant activities there. These teams can then design the package that needs to be put together in each place. The basic ingredients of each package can be similar provision of technology inputs, infrastructure, extension services, and

arrangements for the supply of inputs and the corresponding credit model.

3) Much greater involvement of region-specific market participants, private sector suppliers in all these activities and credit suppliers ranging for public sector banks, co-operative banks, the new private sector banks and micro-credit suppliers, specially self-help groups.

21

Credit and Empowerment of Small Farmers—A Study in Mysore District

M.S. Narasimhan & K. Sivachithappa

Introduction

In the wake of introduction of economic reforms in India since 1991 with emphasis on globalization and liberalization, financial sector reforms have assumed considerable importance. The basic objective of reforms in the financial sector has been to improve the efficiency, competitiveness, transparency and productivity of financial system as a whole. Under the process of financial sector reforms, Government of India gave considerable financial help to Public Sector Banks as also RRBs. However, cooperative banking sector have been denied this pattern of financial assistance despite the fact that the cooperative banks were engaged in the vital task of transforming rural economy of the country.

It is known that cooperative credit sector including agriculture and rural development banks constitutes an important segment of Cooperative Movement and is playing a critical role in financing short-term, medium-term and long-term agriculture operations including investment oriented projects for promoting rural development.

Keeping in view the importance of cooperative credit sector in the context of socio-economic development of the rural areas, the common minimum programme of the present Government has emphasized on the need to nurse back the weak cooperative credit sector to health and it has been proposed to double the flow of rural credit in the next three years so as to ensure that the coverage of small and marginal farmers by institutional lending is expanded substantially.

It is known that the financial position of a few State Cooperative Banks and a large number of District Central Cooperative Banks and PACs leave much to be desired. It is also known that at the operational level, cooperative banks have suffered losses for last many years due to their implementation of government sponsored policies and programmes. The interference by the government in the recovery process as also the relief and concessions announced by the government on account of natural calamities, floods and drought in different parts of the country have increased their losses. The Agriculture and Debt Relief (ARDR) Scheme of 1990, sponsored by Government of India did an irreparable damage to the climate of loan repayment culture traditionally prevailing in the rural areas.

Recently, Government of India has announced its decision to provide crop loan to the farmers at 7 percent rate of interest per annum with effect from 1-4-2006. In this context, Government has also promised to provide interest subvention (subsidy) at 2 percent per annum to the public sector banks and RRBs on the credit loans provided by them out of their own funds. As against this, no such interest subvention has been promised to the cooperative credit institutions who are expected to provide crop loans from out of their own funds which are being raised by them at a high cost of 9-10percetn per annum. As a matter of fact this 2 percent interest subvention is not sufficient for cooperative banks.

The average loan recovery levels for various rural cooperative banks at all India level stood at 68% during 2003-04 which was lower than that observed during 2002-03. It is possible that widespread drought conditions which prevailed in many states during 2003-04 and 2004-05 would have adversely affected these loan recoveries. Further, there are reports that deficiency in loan appraisal mechanism and inadequate follow-up and supervisor in the utilization of loans coupled with political interference have also adversely affected the loan recovery scenario. In view of this, it is imperative that greater emphasis needs to be laid in the coming years on scientific appraisal of loan applications and on the follow-up of utilization of loans sanctioned for specified objectives. In this context, it is pertinent to conduct in-depth study on the role of cooperative banks in the empowerment of farmers

Objectives of the Study

1. To identify the extent of finance lent by the institutions in the study area.
2. To assess the viability of the financial assistance extended to the small farmers.
3. To trace out the utilization of the institutional credit by the small farmers.
4. To find out the impact of the institutional loan on the socio-economic conditions of the farmers.
5. To study the extent of the relief from the moneylenders.
6. Identify the problems faced by the farmers and suggest the measures to overcome the problems of small farmers.

Methodology

The study is based on primary data. Survey conducted through administered questionnaire on the selected small farmers agricultural loan beneficiaries. 350 farmers were selected for the study. 50 farmers from each taluk, Mysore district encompass of seven taluks namely, H.D.Kote, Hunsur, K.R.Nagar, Mysore, Periyapatna, Nanjangud and T.Narasipura. The primary data was collected by interview method with the farmers in the village selected for the study through personal contacts. The Sample size consisting of all the taluks of the district those who have borrowed loan from the various institution agencies in the study area.

Discussion and Results

Annual Income: Analysis of income of sample farmers reveals the purchasing power and credit worthiness of a borrower. The details of annul income of the respondents are presented in the Table- 1.

Table - 1

Talukwise Annual Income of the sample farmers in Mysore district

Name of the Taluks	*<50000*	*50001-100000*	*100001-150000*	*Total*
H. D. Kote	46(92.0%)	4(8.0%)	0(0%)	50(100.0%)
Hunsur	46(92.0%)	4(8.0%)	0(0%)	50(100.0%)
K.R. Nagar	24(48.0%)	22(44.0%)	4(8.0%)	50(100.0%)
Mysore	28(56.0%)	22(44.0%)	0(0%)	50(100.0%)
Nanjangud	48(96.0%)	2(4.0%)	0(0%)	50(100.0%)
Periyapatna	16(32.0%)	26(52.0%)	8(16.0%)	50(100.0%)
T. Narasipura	20(40.0%)	30(60.0%)	0(0%)	50(100.0%)
Total	228(65.1%)	110(31.4%)	12(3.4%)	350(100.0)%

Source: Field Survey.

The Table 1 reveals the taluk wise Annual Income of farmers in the district. Total sample size is 350 respondents. Out of that the 65% per cent of the farmers earned below Rs.50,000 as Annual Income. 31.5 per cent of the respondents gained annual Income between Rs.50,001-1,00,000. 3.4 per cent sample farmers earned between Rs.1, 00,001 – 1, 50,000 annually. The Nanjangud Taluk found to be highest with 96 per cent of annual income of the farmers followed by 46 per cent both in Hunsur and H.D. Kote. Where as, T. Narasipura Taluk has 60 per cent of the farmers earned between Rs.50,001–1,00,000 of their annual income next to Periyapatna both in Mysore and K.R. Nagar with 52%, 22% & 22% respectively. Where as, Periyapatna Taluk has 16 per cent of sample farmers earned annual income between Rs.1,00,001 – 1,50,000. Income is one of the basic indicators, which shows the status and standard of living of a family.

Purchase of Bullock Carts: In the study area Co-operatives, Cauvery Kalpataru Grameena Bank (RRB), and Commercial Banks are main financial institutions for providing credit for purchasing of Bullock carts of farmers through borrowing of loan in the district.

Table - 2

Taluk-wise Purchase of Bulluckcart by credit in Mysore District

Name of the Taluks	*Commercial banks*	*Cooperative banks*	*Cauvery grameena bank*	*Non-institutions*
H.D.Kote	35(70%)	2(4%)	7(14%)	6(12%)
Hunsur	40(80%)	1(2%)	2(4%)	7(14%)
K.R.Nagar	40(80%)	8(16%)	2(4%)	0(0%)
Mysore	35(70%)	5(10%)	10(20%)	0(0%)
Nanjangud	39(78%)	11(22%)	0(0%)	0(0%)
Periyapatna	39(78%)	0(0%)	11(22%)	0(0%)
T.Narasipura	42(84%)	0(0%)	1(2%)	7(14%)
Total	270(81%)	27(6.3%)	33(6.6%)	20(5.7%)

Source: Field Survey.

The Table 2 reveals that the purchase of Bullock cart by credit in various institutions in the district, it is observed that amount borrowed from the commercial bank is the highest percentage of loan amount with 81.4 per cent followed by Cauvery Grameen Bank & Co-operative Bank i.e., 6.6 per cent & 6.3 per cent, 5.7 per cent credit needs are met by non-institutions. The Table also indicates that the Mysore taluk has accessed highest percent of loan borrowed in which 100per cent followed by T. Narasipura K.R. Nagar and Hunsur with 84per cent, 40 per cent and 40 per cent respectively. 22 per cent respondents obtained loan from the Co-operative Banks in Nanjangud taluk, followed by K.R.Nagar and H.D.Kote in the share of 85 per cent & 4 per cent respectively. Cauvery Kalpataru Grameena Bank provided to the sample farmers nearly 22 per cent respondents borrowed in Periyapatna taluk, followed by Mysore and H.D.Kote with 20 per cent and 14 per cent respectively. In Nanjangud respondents are not accessed loan from Cauvery garmeena Bank. In Hunsur and T.Narasipura taluks respondent's access loan from non-institutions with 14 per cent each. There are no facilities to avail loan from non-institutions in the taluks of K.R.Nagar, Mysore, Nanjangud and Periyapatna.

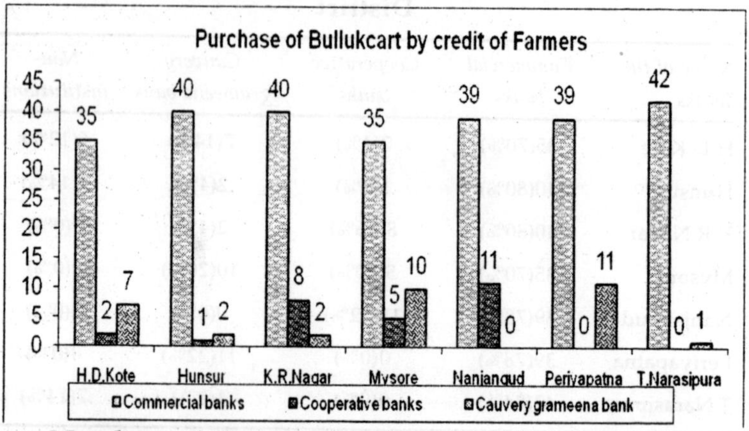

Members of Co-operative Societies: Farmers are getting membership in Co-operative societies in the form of shares in different denominates in the study area . The details of Taluk wise Membership of Cooperative Societies are presented in Table 3.

Table-3: Taluk-wise Membership of Cooperative societies in the study area

Name of the Taluks	*No*	*Yes*	*Total*
H.D.Kote	27(54.0%)	23(46.0%)	50(100.0%)
Hunsur	40(80.0%)	10(20%)	50(100.0%)
K.R.Nagar	24(48.0%)	26(52.0%)	50(100.0%)
Mysore	20(40.0%)	30(60.0%)	50(100.0%)
Nanjangud	40(80.0%	10(20%)	50(100.0%)
Periyapatna	32(64.0%	18(36.0%	50(100.0%)
T. Narasipura	16(32.0%	34(68.0%)	50(100.0%)
Total	199(56.8%	151(43.2%)	350

Source: Field Survey.

The Table-3 indicates that the members of Co-operative societies in the study area. Out of 350 sample farmers to the extent of 80 per cent of respondent are not getting membership of Cooperative societies in both the taluks of Hunsur and Nanjanagud followed by Periyapatna and H.D. Kote in which 64 per cent highest per cent found in T. Narasipura and 68 per cent respondents obtained the membership of Co-operative societies. But only 20 per cent of sample farmers have obtained membership from Co-operative societies in Hunsur and Nanjangud taluks respectively. The same is represented in the graph.

Membership of Cooperative Societies of farmers in the study area

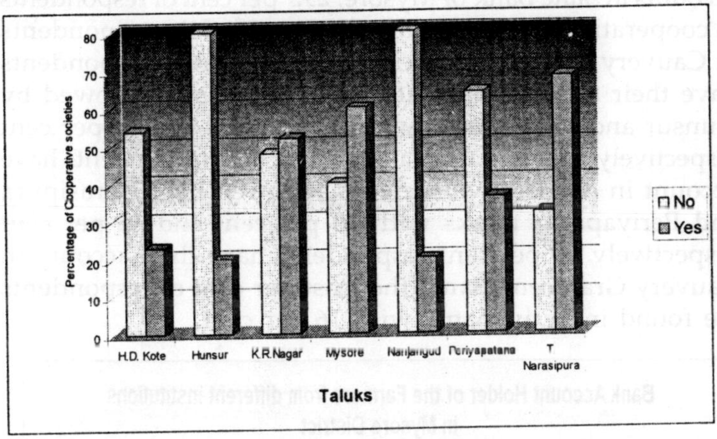

Bank Account: Farmers are having Bank Account in various banks in the study area. Taluk wise bank account holders of the respondents are presented in Table 4.

Table -4

Talukwise bank account holders of the farmers in Mysore District

Name of the Taluks	*SBM*	*Co-operative Society*	*Cauvery Grameena Bank*	*Total*
H.D.Kote	29(58%)	10(20%)	11(22%)	50(100%)

Hunsur	25(50%)	7(14%)	18(36%)	50(100%)
K.R.Nagar	15(30%)	21(42%)	14(28%)	50(100%)
Mysore	21(42%)	11(22%)	18(36%)	50(100%)
Nanjangud	18(36%)	17(3%)	15(30%)	50(100%)
Periyapatna	24(48%)	18(36%)	8(16%)	50(100%)
T. Narasipura	10(20%)	20(40%)	20(40%)	50(100%)
Total	142(40.6%)	104(29.7%)	104(29.7%)	350

Source: Field Survey.

From the Table 4 it can be noticed that the bank account holder of sample respondents in the district. Out of 350 respondents about 40.6 per cent respondents, have their accounts in State Bank of Mysore, 29.7 per cent of respondents in cooperative societies and 29.7 per cent of the respondents in Cauvery Grameen Bank. The 58 per cent of respondents have their accounts in State Bank of Mysore, followed by Hunsur and Periyapatna with 50 per cent and 48 per cent respectively. In K.R.Nagar taluk, 42 per cent respondents have account in cooperative societies followed by T.Narasipura and Periyapatna taluks with 40 per cent and 46 per cent respectively. 40 per cent respondents have their account in Cauvery Grameena Bank, the least per cent of respondents are found in Periyapatna with 16 per cent.

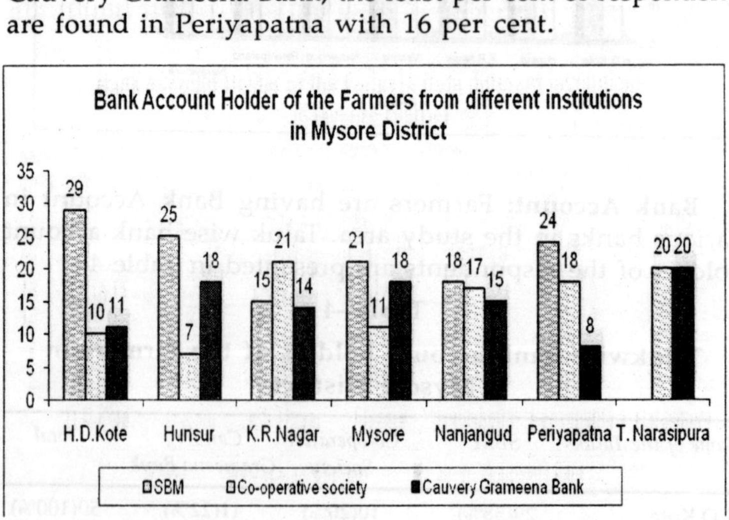

Bank Account Holder of the Farmers from different institutions in Mysore District

Major Findings of the Study

The most important findings of the present study may be briefly stated as follows:

1. Major finding is that 81per cent respondents have utilized the finance to productive purposes such as purchase of fertilizers, seeds, land development, purchase of agricultural implements etc. Nearly 19 per cent of respondents spent on unproductive purposes such as, celebrate ceremony, marriage etc.
2. It is noticed that, 51.7 per cent of respondents had paid interest from 6 to 10 per cent charged by the Institutional Agencies.
3. Non-institution sources have charged the high rate of interest. In the field study we observed that 90.9 present of the respondent observed the same opinion.
4. It was observed that 93.4 per cent respondent's status after availing the loan from the institutional finance has been increased.
5. Repayment by the beneficiaries is some what better, nearly 40.6 per cent respondents have repaid the loan in installments.
6. Around 48.8 per cent respondents responded they did not have sufficient water facilities. 44.6 per cent respondents said that increase in their loan amount and infrastructure facilities.

Suggestions

1. To liberate the rural farmers from the clutches of moneylenders the entire rural credit should be institutionalized. The Cooperatives and Commercial Banks have to play a more effective role in this respect.
2. In order to make the cooperative credit structure more efficient, government control over co-operative societies should be minimized.
3. There are no particular schemes for small farmers, all benefits are utilized to the big farmers. However,

there must be specific schemes for small farmers .Though, these schemes extended to the small farmers also.

4. Proper initiation should be taken to release the short-term loans as an essential inputs such as seeds, fertilizers when ever is required to the small farmers.
5. Crop insurance is provided to the Commercial crops only. These facilities are extended to the food crops also and small farmers land holding is very small when comparing to the big farmers. However, the facilities are used only by big farmers. Therefore these facilities also extend to the small farmers also.

REFERENCES

Aravindakshan, K. R (2006): "National Commission on Farmers on Credit and Cooperatives – A View Point" National Conference on Rural Cooperative Credit and Banking Institutions, Souvenir, New Delhi.

Deshpande R.S. and Nagesh Prabhu (2005): Farmers Distress, *Economic and Political Weekly,* October 29, pp.4663-4665.

Ramanujam.K.N. (2007): Crop Insurance Need of the Hour, *Kisan World,* September, 2009.

Reddy, Y.V. (2004): Rural Credit: Status and Agenda, *RBI Bulletin,* December, pp. 1087-1089.

Sasi Rekha, K. N. and J. Rani Ratna Prabha (2008): "Agricultural Credit in India in Pre and Post-reform Period", *Southern Economist,* October 15, 2008.

Singh (1983): *Agricultural Credit in India,* Atlantic Publishers and Distributors, New Delhi.

Subramanyam, B. (2006): Rationalization of Interest Rate Structure for Cooperative Credit Institutions, NAFSCOB, Souvenir, Mumbai.

Umesh. C. Patnaik and Ananthj K. Roy (1998): *Co-operation and Co-operative Management,* Kalyani Publishers, Ludhiana New Delhi p. 4.

22

Agricultural Development Through Regional Rural Banks—A Case Study of Mysore District in Karnataka

K. Sivachithappa

Introduction

Rural development remains an uphill task due to the complexity of problems existing in the rural sector. The rural sector requires a multi-dimensional approach to reach cost-effective solutions to these problems. The rural areas suffer from poor infrastructural facilities. The villages are yet to emerge as the main centres of production activity. The productivity is to produce goods in urban areas, even to meet the basic needs of rural consumers. This apart, the rural population requires not one but a few inputs and services. These have to be provided at the right time and in the right sequence. This demands the right kind of co-ordination amongst agencies extending help to the rural sector .

Rural economy is weaker sector of the national economy and even in the rural economy, a major segment is not only weak but in a miserable state. Regional Rural Banks seem to be the only hope in injects strength and accelerate the growth of rural economy and ensure the development of rural areas. Rural development in India is recognized as a sine qua non for faster economic development and welfare of common masses. Rural development in not merely development of rural areas but also the development of the rural peoples into self-reliant and self-sustaining modern little communities. Rural development is, therefore the development of rural areas in such a way that each component of rural life changes in a desired direction and in sympathy with the other components .

In Indian economy rural sector plays a significant role. It affects directly or indirectly almost all the economic activities in the country. It employs the maximum number of people. It is also the most important source of national income in India. It also supplies food for the survival of the entire population of India. It also supplies materials necessary for the major industries of India. A large part of the revenue of the government is also obtained from rural sector. In short, rural sector can be rightly considered as the backbone of our economy. In spite of the significant role of the rural sector, it continues to be neglected. The magnitude of poverty, illiteracy, and ill health is of higher order in the rural areas as compared to the urban areas.

The rural sector requires institutional credit to take up economically viable projects. But it needs to be noted that credit alone cannot deliver the goods. There is what is called the credit absorption capacity of the region. This depeds on the implementation of economically viable schmes. Hence, the formulation of economic plans should precede the preparation of credit plans. There are certain agencies like the co-operatives, regional rural banks and farmers service societies which are most appropriate to serve the rural population, but their performance needs to be toned up. Of course, cheap credit needs to be discouraged.

Majority of the rural fold are not able to meet their day-to-day requirements from their own sources of income not to speak of investigating in other productive enterprises for improving their economic conditions. Therefore, they have to depend on various financial agencies for getting funds for making investment. To bring about the overall development in the rural areas, financial assistance to the rural poor, particularly institutional assistance for the development of agriculture needs no emphasis. Finance is an essential requirement for almost every activity. If required finance is not available out of ones own income then one needs credit. In rural areas of India, credit requirements are more pressing. Rural credit in India is a part and parcel of its economic development. Rural population is composed of agricultural producers, tenant cultivators, village artisans and landless labour. All these categories are in need of credit. To provide the credit requirements to these categories regional rural banks play very significant role .

Objectives of the Study

1. To study the role of Regional Rural Banks in agricultural development.
2. To assess the effectiveness of various schemes of the RRBs in the light of a case study of Cauvery Grameena Bank in Mysore district.
3. To make suitable policy recommendations concerning the role and working of the RRBs so as to make them contribute more to the agricultural development of the region.

Research Methodology

The present study is based on simple random sampling method. Hence, the study is depending up on primary data. Information relating to the periods before and after the loans was collected from the 250 borrowers selected for the study. The study has been carried out in Mysore district.

Results and Discussion

To meet the credit requirements of rural people in Mysore district, Cauvery Grameena Bank was established. Cauvery Grameena Bank has so far been able to achieve the objective of helping the weaker sections despite the constraints. Cauvery Grameena Bank within the reasonable limits has been doing its best to maximize the lending to small entrepreneurs and persons engaged in service sector. The main objective of this bank has been to provide credit and other facilities especially to the small and marginal farmers, agricultural labourers, artisans and small entrepreneurs in rural areas. The numbers of accounts have also been increased rapidly.

Bank's credit operations are closely inter-linked with IRDP/SGSY programmes and allied programmes and thereby it is able to make significant contribution to rural development. Cauvery Grameena Bank's record in mobilization of savings, disbursement of advances as well as recovery of loans is impressive with its wide coverage in the district.

Nature of Loan Provided by Grameen Bank

Table – 1 provides the details of the nature of loan provided by the Cauvery Grameena Bank for the farming community in Mysore district. Nature of loan of farmers includes three categories;

1. Short-term loans;
2. Medium-term loans;
3. Long-term loans.

Out of 250 respondents, 70 percent of the respondents provided short-term loan; 18 percent of the respondents provided medium term loans and only 12 percent of the long term loans in the study area. It is pertinent to note that all type of loans have been provided by the grameen bank in the district.

Table- 1

Nature of loan provided by Cauvery Grameena Bank

Sl.No.	*Mode of loan*	*Respondents*	*Percent*
01	Short-term	175	70.0
02	Medium-term	45	18.0
03	Long-term	30	12.0
	Total	250	100

Source: Field Survey.

Amount of Loan Required

The details of the amount of loan required by sample respondents have been given in table – 2. Out of 250 sample respondents 40 percent reported the loan required amount of Rs.25,000 and 60 percent of the respondents reported Rs.50,000 loan amount. In all, 72 percent loaners are recipients of loan for an amount not exceeding Rs.20,000. This is perhaps because agricultural loans up to Rs.20,000 are advanced without any mortgage of property as security of loan; moreover under most of the loans sponsored by various agencies, the project cost does not exceed Rs.20,000.

Table - 2

Distribution of respondents according to amount of loan

Sl.no	*Amount of loan required*	*Respondents*	*Percent*
01	Rs.25,000	100	40.0
02	Rs.50,000	150	60.0
	Total	**250**	**100**
	Amount of loan received		
03	Rs.up to 20,000	195	78.0
04	Rs.up to 35,000	55	22.0
	Total	**250**	**100**

Source: Field Survey.

Reasons for Seeking Bank Loans

Out of the 250 sample respondents covered under study, 40.8 percent respondents took bank loans for starting the activity; this is the major reason was given by respondents. For the 32.8 percent respondents the intention to expand the scale of activity was another major reason for taking the bank loans. And another third major reason was the attraction of low interest on loans under the social purpose lending schemes (i.e.15.6 percent respondents). The fourth reason was to avoid taking loans from intermediaries (i.e. 10.8 percent respondents). The details can be seen in Table – 3.

Table – 3

Reasons for Seeking Bank Loans

Sl.no	*Reasons*	*Respondents*	*Percent*
01	To start activity	102	40.8
02	To expand the activity	82	32.8
03	To avail of low interest finance	39	15.6
04	To eliminate intermediary	27	10.8
	Total	**250**	**100**

Source: Field Survey.

Inadequacy of Bank Loan

Inadequate amount of loan affects its proper utilization to a great extent. This inadequacy often either leads to unproductive spending and in the long run, may turn out to be counter-productive and defeating the very objective of financing or compels the poor respondents to knock at the door of the professional money lenders. To save the weaker sections (poor farmers) from falling into the clutches of the private money lenders, it would be necessary for the banks to provide adequate amount of loan.

Table 4

Inadequacy of bank loan amount

Sl.no	*Particulars*	*No.of respondents*	*Percent*
01	Adequate	102	40.8
02	Inadequate	148	59.2
	Total	250	100

Source: Field Survey.

Table 4 depicts that in 59.2 percent cases the amount of bank loan was found to be inadequate for the activity and in only 40.8 percent cases it was adequate. This opinion is usually opined by small farmers, this amount is enough to maintain their activity. But in the case of large farmers or those who are intends to go for digging wells and purchasing bullock cots this amount is not adequate.

Impact of Bank Credit on Farming Community

Creation of employment opportunities and generation of adequate income for the beneficiaries is the theme of all social banking programmes. The endeavour is to lift the weakest among the weaker sections of the society above the poverty line on a permanent basis. This part is devoted to the analysis of the impact of bank credit on the income level of the beneficiaries, and to gauge the extent to which financing under various social banking schemes, programmes were successful in fulfilling the objectives laid-down before the banking industry.

The increase in income level and there by improvement in the economic conditions of the beneficiaries, after the bank loans, was possible due to the favourable changes in the arrangements for procurement of inputs. The bank loans enabled them to become independent and to realize higher profit margin for their product.

It is evident from the table- 5 that average amount of post-loan income is substantially higher than pre-loan income for all the activities under study. In this sector, average pre-loan income is Rs.4096.15, which has risen to Rs.6144.23 in the post-loan period. There are 21 respondents with pre-loan income range between Rs.3000 to Rs.5000 who were not able to improve their income. There is one beneficiary in the income Rs.5500 who is able to improve his income in post-loan period. The number of loaners in the income ranges Rs.6500 to Rs.9000 is 30 in the post-loan period. There is increase in the number of respondents in the higher income levels in the post-loan period. Median income of agricultural loaners indicates that 58 percent of the loaners of this sector are getting income above Rs.7000 in the post-loan period. The dispersion in income of the loaners is slightly higher in the post-loan period as compared to the pre-loan period.

Among the agricultural sector respondents, increase in income actually represents the saving of interest amount by availing bank credit and paying interest at a lower rate than they would have paid, had they borrowed the same amount from agricultural money lenders. The beneficiaries of tractor loans, on the other hand, were able to increase their income to a great extent.

A significantly positive correlation between pre-loan income and post-loan income establishes the point that those who had higher pre-loan income had higher income in the post-loan period as well. It can be inferred that those respondents who were using their own resources in the best possible manner and getting higher income were also in a position to earn a lot by using bank assistance.

Table – 5

Crop Loan Respondents Pre-loan Income

Sl.No	Amount (Rs.)	Respondents	Percent
01	3000	10	20.00
02	3500	3	6.00
03	4000	14	28.00
04	4500	12	24.00
05	5000	11	22.00
	Total	50	100.00

Average amount of increase in income: 9Rs.) Mean: 4095.14

Median: 4000

Crop Loan Respondents Post- loan Income

Sl.No	Amount (Rs)	Respondents	Percent
01	3000	7	14.00
02	3500	2	4.00
03	4000	4	8.00
04	4500	2	4.00
05	5000	5	10.00
06	5500	2	4.00

07	6500	2	4.00
08	7000	6	12.00
09	7500	4	8.00
10	8000	3	6.00
11	8500	7	14.00
12	9000	6	12.00
	Total	**50**	**100.00**

Average amount of increase in income: (Rs) Mean: 6143.20

Median: 7000

Impact on Respondents of Tractor Loaners

In this activity, above 70 percent of respondents pertain to tractor loans. Table – 6 indicates that, there are 15 respondents with pre-loan income range between Rs.5000 to Rs.7500 who are not able to improve their income after bank loans. The number of loaners in the income ranges between Rs.9000 to Rs.15000 is 34 in the post-loan period. This clearly shows that there is an increasing trend in the number of beneficiaries in the higher income levels in the post-loan period. Out of 50 beneficiaries selected under study 34 respondents have been improved their income. Median income of tractor loaners indicates that 70 percent of the loaners of this activity are getting income above Rs.10000 in the post-loan period.

Table – 6

Tractor Loaners: Pre-Loan Period

Sl.No	*Amount (Rs)*	*Respondents*	*Percent*
01	5000	18	36.00
02	6500	15	30.00
03	7500	17	34.00

Average amount of increase in income:

(Rs) Mean: 6271.82

Median: 6500

Tractor Loaners: Post-Loan Period

Sl.No	*Amount(Rs)*	*Respondents*	*Percent*
01	5000	11	22.00
02	6500	03	6.00
03	7500	02	4.00
04	9000	06	12.00
05	10000	14	28.00
06	12000	06	12.00
07	15000	08	16.00
	Total	**50**	**100.00**

Average amount of increase in income:

(Rs) Mean: 9615.56

Median: 10000

Impact on Beneficiaries of Dairy

It has been observed during the course of the study that in cases of direct financing by banks for the purchase of two buffaloes giving a gap of six months of the beneficiaries were able to get a continuous flow of income, resulting in repayment of loans and better income effect on the beneficiary.

The dairy loans sponsored by animal husbandry department were found to have impressive effect on the income level of the beneficiaries. It is possible because of training imparted to the borrowers before sponsoring their cases to banks for providing loans. Some beneficiaries took up another allied to agriculture, namely piggery. By and large, the beneficiaries of this activity earned a good return because of low cost for running the activity.

Table 7

Dairy Loaners: Pre-Loan Period

Sl.No	Amount(Rs)	Respondents	Percent
01	10000	15	30.00
02	12000	19	38.00
03	15000	16	32.00
	Total	50	100.00

Average amount of increase in income:

(Rs) Mean: 12256.80

Median: 12000

Dairy Loaners: Post-Loan Period

Sl.No	Amount(Rs)	Respondents	Percent
01	10000	10	20.00
02	12000	6	12.00
03	15000	4	8.00
04	17500	11	22.00
05	20000	11	22.00
06	25000	8	16.00
	Total	50	100.00

Average amount of increase in income:

(Rs) Mean:16942.85

Median: 17500

In this activity, average pre-loan income is Rs.12256.80, which has risen to Rs.17500 in the post-loan period. Median income during pre-loan period of this sector was Rs.12000. hence it is clearly shows that Rs.5500 is the incremental income after obtaining the bank loan.

Impact on Bullock Carts Beneficiaries

Table – 8 would enable us to appreciate the role played by regional rural banks in improving the income levels of the loaners of bullock carts. It can be observed that a beneficiary, irrespective of age, family size, number of literate in the family, debts of the family, amount of loan and supplementary investment in the activity, can be successful in this activity. In this activity, average pre-loan income is Rs.12255.81 which has risen to Rs.16941.86 I the post-loan period. Median income of this activity loaners indicates that 65.2 percent of the loaners of this sector are getting income above Rs.17500 in the post-loan period. Median income during pre-loan period of this sector was Rs.12000. hence it is clearly shows that Rs.5500 rupees are the incremental income after obtaining the bank loan.

Table – 8

Bullock Carts Activity Loaners: Pre-loan Period

Sl.No	*Amount(Rs)*	*Respondents*	*Percent*
01	10000	15	30.00
02	12000	17	34.00
03	15000	18	36.00
	Total	50	100.00

Average amount of increase in income:
(Rs) Mean: 12255.81
Median: 12000

Bullock Carts Activity Loaners: Post-loan Period

Sl.No	*Amount(Rs)*	*Respondents*	*Percent*
01	10000	10	20.00
02	12000	5	10.00
03	15000	4	8.00
04	17500	12	24.00
05	20000	12	24.00
06	25000	7	14.00
	Total	50	100.00

Average amount of increase in income:

(Rs) Mean: 16941.86

Median: 17500

Impact on Digging Wells activity

Out of 50 respondents, there were 24 loaners in the income range Rs.12000 to Rs.17500 in the pre-loan period and between in post-loan period also. On the other hand, there was a rise in the number of cases in the higher income levels i.e., from Rs.20000 to Rs.27500 in the post-loan provided as compared to pre-loan period. Average amount of income rose from Rs.15127.27 to Rs.19372.73 and median income jumped up from Rs.15000 to Rs.20000 in the post loan period.

Table- 9

Digging Wells Activity Loaners: Pre-loan Period

Sl.No	*Amount(Rs)*	*Respondents*	*Percent*
01	12000	21	42.00
02	15000	19	38.00
03	17500	10	20.00
	Total	50	100.00

Average amount of increase in income:

(Rs) Mean: 15127.27

Median: 15000

Digging Wells Activity Loaners: Post-loan Period

Sl.No	*Amount(Rs)*	*Respondents*	*Percent*
01	12000	14	28.00
02	15000	3	6.00
03	17500	7	14.00
04	20000	10	20.00
05	25000	11	22.00
06	27500	5	10.00
	Total	50	100.00

Average amount of increase in income:

(Rs) Mean: 19372.73

Median: 20000

Major Findings of the Study

It was found that the bank officials were keen to extend the facility of KCC to farmers. In most of the places, it is the bank personal who informed the farmers about the scheme and its benefits. All the respondent farmers indicated that obtaining KCC from banks is very easy. Further banks are not maintaining any minimum credit limit while issuing cards. Similarly the banks are not charging any fees on card holders for obtaining KCC. Since the banks are not maintaining any minimum credit limit, the marginal and small cultivators who require small loans are not deprived of KCC facility.

Cauvery Grameena Bank helps agriculture development by giving crop loans for meeting part costs of cultivation of crops repayable after the crops are raised and marketed.

Crop loans are advanced with the object of providing financial assistance to small and marginal farmers to purchase seeds. Chemical fertilizers and manure, pesticides, diesel and oil, to hire tractors, threshers and to pay wage the Labourers. This is production oriented loan and helps in raising the crop and thereby development of agriculture.

Cauvery Grameena Bank also contributes to agriculture development by giving loans to allied activities such as for purchase of bullocks and others.

Suggestions

1. The branches should provide credit assistance not only to their existing borrowers but also to other eligible persons within their command area provided they are not covered by any other financial agency. Immediate assistance would be needed for protecting and regenerating standing crops, repairs and protection of livestock sheds, for implements and for storage structure etc.
2. In addition to the general schemes to be adopted by all the RRBs specific area wise schemes should also be formulated to suit the socio-economic conditions prevalent in the area of the Regional Rural Bank.

3. To avoid under interference of local leaders it is suggested that the local should not be permitted to act as intermediaries for the identification of applicants or to pressurize the bank officials for sanctioning loans. They may be allowed to force the bank officials to permit loans to un-credit worthy applicants.

REFERENCES

Agarwal, R.K. (1991): *Evaluation of the Working of Regional Rural Banks*. Mittal Publications, New Delhi.

Agarwal, R.N.(1976): *Rural Banking in India,* Oxford and I.B.H Publishers, New Delhi.

Angadi, V.B. (1983): "Banks" Advances to priority sectors- an enquiry into the causes of concentration", *Economic and Political Weekly,* Vol. XXVIII, No. 13.

Batra, J.D. (1977): Rural Banks for the Rural Poor. *Kurukshetra,* 26 (2), 16 October.

Bhatnagar, R.C. (1982): "Recovery of Agricultural Loans". *State Banks of India Monthly Review,* Vol.XXI, No.2, pp. 43-48.

Biswajit Chatterji and Amit Kundu (2001): *Rural Banks in India's Agrarian Economy – New Agenda for Reforms,* Deep and Deep Publications, New Delhi.

Bose, A. (1982): "Commercial Banks and Rural Finance" *State Bank of India Monthly Review,* Vol.XXI, No.6, pp. 211-16.

Chatterji, Biswajit and Amit Kundu (1999): "Rethinking Rural Financial Institution", paper presented in the 35th Annual Conference of the Indian Econometric Society at Jaipur, March.

23

Primary Agricultural Cooperative Societies as a Strategy for Regional Development—A Study in Mysore District

Krishnappa Madival & K. Sivachithappa

Introduction

The cooperative organization in our country has developed and spread its activities and functions in all spheres of economy like agriculture, poultry, dairy, fisheries, handlooms, banking, sugar, spinning, consumer cooperatives and what not?. That is why this sector has emerged as an important and vital sector of our economy. The cooperatives have 207 million members embracing 100 percent villages and 67 percent of household in its fold in the country.

Today the India's cooperative scene presents a mixed picture. On the one hand, the cooperative movement has grown, membership has increased, it has become more diversified, there has been great deal of regional dispersal and there are numerous examples of cooperatives in India's landscape where it has made spectacular achievements. On the other hand, a large number of cooperatives are languishing, and considering the numbers of cooperatives are languishing, and considering the number of weak elements in the society, such elements cannot legitimately be said to belong to the cooperative fold.

One marked change in the cooperative movement that has surfaced in recent years is that several cooperatives have become big and more cooperatives have started making departures from the practice of cooperative principles enunciated by International Cooperative Alliance (ICA), particularly in raising capital by use of joint stock company methods. They had challenged the relevance of the existing principles, particularly limited interest on capital which they considered as the devil of the peace hampering the growth of the movement.

At the global level concern has also been expressed at increasing government intervention in the management of cooperative societies in many developing countries. Governments in these countries are using cooperatives as a tool of planned programme for achievement of planned targets. India is the land of cooperatives. The largest numbers of cooperatives are there in our nation.

Objectives of the Study

The following are the main objectives of the study.

1. To examine the performance and growth of primary agricultural cooperatives in Karnataka.
2. To evaluate the impact of primary agricultural cooperatives in development of agriculture in Mysore district.
3. To offer suggestions for the further improvement of the role of cooperatives in the development of community in each and every nook and corner of the society.

Methodology of the Study

The study is based on both primary and secondary source of data. This study is confined to Mysore district of the Karnataka State. To gauge the impact of primary agricultural cooperative societies on farming community in Mysore district 30 farmers have been interviewed. The secondary data has been collected from Cooperative Societies, Mysore district, Cooperation Journals and District Statistical Outline, Mysore district. The data has been collected up to 2006-07.

Results and Discussion

The history of cooperatives in India could be traced back to as early as 1891, when the first cooperative society was started in Punjab for controlling the common land of the village. However, the first official step to formalize the cooperative organization was taken in July 1901 and it got its final shape in 1904 when the first Cooperative Societies Act was passed. The Cooperative Credit Societies Act 1904 was restrictive in its scope as it permitted only primary credit societies and kept non-credit and federal societies out of its purview. The Cooperative Societies Act of 1912 removed many of these short comings and served as a model for subsequent Acts passed by various Governments when Cooperative Societies became a transferred subject under the constitutional reforms of 1919.

The promotion of cooperatives has been accepted as a part of the state policy in the development of various economic activities, particularly those providing support to agriculture. This was the strong policy recommendation of the Rural Credit Survey Committee of 1954. The policy led to state partnership in the share of cooperative law 1955 appointed by the Government of India suggested a number of modifications in the cooperative legislation. For giving effect to the concept of the state partnership and accordingly various State Cooperative Societies Acts were amended which in effect also strengthened the government control on the cooperative institutions.

In Mysore district cooperative movement has undoubtedly lent unflinching support to the needy and common man. Cooperation never failed to assist agriculture in a vary big way which is the main occupation in the district. Primary agricultural credit cooperative societies and milk producers' cooperative societies are the back bone of the cooperative movement in Mysore district. Taluk agricultural cooperative marketing societies have thrived and created history, the performance of some of these institutions is really an unparalleled. Business development programme for cooperatives has been successfully implemented in the district. Besides PACs, some women multi purpose cooperative societies and a house building cooperative society have embanked upon banking activities in a big technology women society have started functioning and their performance is really encouraging. A district level horticultural producers' cooperative society is in existence for the last ten years which has successful in processing fruits grown by farmers and in helping them in getting a good price for the produce. Comparative growth of cooperative societies in the district for the last five years details are furnished in Table – 1.

Table 1

Comparative Growth of Cooperative Societies in the District for the Last Five Years

Types of cooperative Societies	*2002-03*	*2003-04*	*2004-05*	*2005-06*	*2006-07*
DCC Bank	01	01	01	01	01
PACs	245	200	230	223	225
PCARD Bank	07	07	07	07	07
Credit Cooperative Societies	48	49	13	13	15
Cooperative Union	01	01	01	01	01
TAPCMs	07	07	07	07	07
Processing Cooperative Societies	-	-	01	01	01
Live Stock Cooperative Societies	04	07	06	05	03
Co-operative Milk Union	01	01	01	01	01
Milk Producers Cooperative Societies	649	683	691	706	722
Lift Irrigation Cooperative Societies	-	-	12	11	06
Fishers Cooperative Societies	17	20	20	21	22

Weavers Cooperative Societies	35	24	21	20	18
Industrial Cooperative Societies	-	-	23	19	17
Consumers Cooperative Societies	92	89	80	70	69
House Building Cooperative Societies	36	34	37	37	35
Labour Contract Cooperative Societies	05	03	-	-	-
Multipurpose Cooperative Societies	-	-	24	23	25
Student Cooperative Societies	-	-	07	06	05
Mahila multipurpose Cooperative Societies	-	-	27	24	24
Tailoring Cooperative Societies	-	-	01	01	01
Water Consumers Cooperative Societies	28	33	19	40	43

Source: District Registrar Office, Cooperative Department, Mysore.

At present there are 1449 Cooperative Societies are functioning to cater the needs of the community thereby enhancing the life style in the society in Mysore district. The data clearly show that there is an increasing tendency in different Cooperative Societies in the district. This is actually a healthy development in the cooperative movement in the district. Loans sanctioned by the cooperative credit societies in Mysore district during 2002-03 to 2006-07 details are furnished in Table 2.

Table 2

Loans Sanctioned by the Cooperative Credit Societies in Mysore District

Particulars	*Type of loans*	*2002-03*	*2005-06*	*2006-07*
Loans given by agricultural credit cooperative societies	Short-term	7295	6329	2328
	Medium-term	16843	18	-
	Total	24138	6347	2328
Liquidated cooperative societies	Credit	6	9	11
	Non-credit	165	143	110
	Total	171	152	121

Non-credit cooperative societies	Marketing	7	8	8
	Housing	36	36	27
	Milk	271	249	241
	Others	308	290	579
	Total	622	583	855
Credit cooperative societies	Agricultural	230	243	237
	Non-agricultural	89	107	112
	Total	319	350	349
Other cooperative banks		77	236	235

Source: Mysore District at a glance.

Now let us explain the performance of primary agricultural cooperative credit societies in Mysore district, in terms of number of societies, total membership, total borrowers, share capital i.e., from members and from government, funds of societies, deposits, borrowings, total profit and total losses. The details of these particulars are depicted in Table 3.

Table 3

Details of Primary Agricultural Cooperative Credit Societies in Mysore District

Particulars		*2006-07*
No.of Societies		226
Total Membership		156301
Total Borrowers		33243
Share Capital	From Members	732.46
	From Government	202.59
Funds		419.64
Deposits		1577.66
Total Borrowings		5293.04
Total Profit		351.91
Total loss		59.90

Source: Assistant Registrar of Cooperative Union, Mysore district.

The success of credit institutions and the prosperity of cultivators mainly depend on productive utilization of agricultural finance. Misdirection of loan reflects adversely on the character of the cooperative institution and ultimately results in the stopping of the flow of credit to cultivators even for productive purposes. Proper end use of credit is more important than the provision of adequate credit itself. Proper utilization of loan is one of the prime factors in the filed of rural finance to boost-up production.

Once the credit is used for unspecific purpose, it's not only results in low production and indebtedness of the farmer, but also leads to the vicious circle of poverty. The diversion of loan to unproductive purpose has an equally adverse effect on the lending institution, that the recover of the loan become difficult and this result in decreasing the lending capacity of the bank.

Loans from Primary Agricultural Cooperative Credit Societies in Irrigated Area

In Mysore district nearly 58.11% of the loan has been sanctioned to all the three types of farmers against their requirements, remaining 41.25% of the loan is considered as credit gap. In case of small farmers 49.10 percent of loan has been sanctioned remaining portion of the loan considered as credit gap. Whereas 47.9 percent and 68.75 percent of the loan has been sanctioned for medium and big farmers respectively.

In the case of big farmers credit gap is little compared to the small and medium farmers. In other words, major portion of the requirements of the big farmers have been fulfilled compared to medium and small farmers. The details are furnished in the Table 4.

Table 4

Loans from the Primary Agricultural Cooperative Credit Societies in Irrigated Area 2002-2007

Types of farmers	*No. of farmers*	*Required*	*%*	*Sanctioned*	*%*	*Credit gap*	*%*
Small	10	224000	100	110	49.10	104	46.42
Medium	10	365000	100	175	47.94	195	53.42
Big	10	560000	100	385	68.75	175	31.25
Total	30	1149	100	670	58.15	474	41.25

Source: Field study, Mysore.

In the case of non-irrigated region it says that only 41.22 percent of the loan has been sanctioned, remaining 58.78 percent of the loan considered as credit gap. In case of small farmers only 45.12 percent of the loan has been sanctioned, whereas in case of medium farmers it is 45.97 percent. And nearly 37.56 percent of loan has been sanctioned in case of big farmers.

It is clearly shows that medium farmers get more loans compared to small and big farmers, but big farmers compared to small farmers get fewer loans. The details of loans sanctioned from the PACs in non-irrigated area since 2002 to 2007 are furnished in the Table- 5.

Table 5

Loans Sanctioned from the Primary Agricultural Cooperative Credit Societies in Non-Irrigated Area – 2002 to 2007

Types of farmers	*No. of farmers*	*Required*	*%*	*Sanctioned*	*%*	*Credit gap*	*%*
Small	10	195	100	88	45.12	107	54.87
Medium	10	235	100	108	45.97	127	54.04
Big	10	386	100	145	37.56	241	62.43
Total	30	816	100	341	41.22	475	58.78

Source: Field Study, Mysore.

End use of Loans in Irrigated Area

Normally farmers use loan for several purposes, such as purchase of seeds, fertilizers, pesticides, bullock carts, land improvements, digging well, pump sets, paying labour charges and other purposes like paying old bets education, house hold utensils. The details of end use of loan in irrigated area in Mysore district are depicted in Table- 6.

Table 6

End Use of Loans in Irrigated Area

Particulars	*Small*	%	*Medium*	%	*Big*	%
Seeds	42000	22.22	49	24.37	88	20.41
Fertilizers	47000	24.86	46	22.88	86	19.95
Pesticides	33000'	17.46	31	15.42	25	5.8
Land improvement	21000	11.11	20	9.95	51	11.83
Pump set	-	-		-	26	6.03
Labour	39000	20.63	37	18.40	96	22.27
Others	7000	03.70	18	8.95	59	13.68
Total	189000	100	201	100	431	100

Source: Field Study, Mysore.

It has been observed that, in case of small farmers 22.22 percent of the loans are used for purchasing of seeds, whereas 24.86 percent of loan is for purchasing of fertilizers, 17.46 percent for pesticides, 11.11 percent for land improvements, 20.65 percent for labour and for other purpose 3.70 percent of loan is used. In the same way, in case of medium farmers 24.37 percent of loans are used for purchasing of seeds, 22.88 percent for fertilisers, and 15.42 percent for pesticides, 9.9 percent for land improvements, 18.40 percent for labours and 8.95 percent for other purposes.

In the case of big farmers 20.4 percent of loans is used for purchase of seeds, 19.95 percent for fertilizers, 5.8 percent for pesticides, and 11.83 percent for land improvements, 6.03 percent for pump sets, 22.27 percent for labour and 13.68 percent for other purpose.

End use of Loans in Non-Irrigated Area

In Mysore district, in case of small farmers 13.03 percent of the loan is used for purchasing of seeds whereas, 15.57 percent for fertilisers, 14.75 percent for pesticides, 14.75 percent for land improvements, 15.57 percent for labours and 21.31 percent for other purposes.

In the case of medium farmers 25.37 percent of the loan utilised for purchasing of seeds, 10.44 percent for fertilisers, 11.10 percent for pesticides, 8.95 percent for land improvements, 15.65 percent for labours and 28.35 percent for other purposes.

In the case of big farmers in Mysore district, 13.13 percent of the loan is used for seeds, 13.63 percent for fertilisers, and 15.65 percent for pesticides, 18.68 percent for land improvements, 14.64 percent for labours and 24.24 percent for other purposes. The details of end use of loans of PACs in non-irrigated area in Mysore district are presented in table-7.

Table- 7

End use of loans of Primary Agricultural Cooperative Credit Societies in Non-Irrigated Area in Mysore district

Particulars	*Small*	%	*Medium*	%	*Big*	%
Seeds	22000	18.03	34000	25.37	26000	13.13
Fertilizers	19000	15.57	14000	10.44	27000	13.63
Pesticides	18000	14.75	15000	11.19	31000	15.65
Land improvement	18000	14.75	12000	8.95	37000	18.68
Pump set	19000	15.57	21000	15.67	29000	14.64
Labour	26000	21.31	38000	28.35	48000	24.24
Total	122000	100	134000	100	198000	100

Source: Field Study, Mysore.

On the basis of these two tables we can easily say that the farmers in non-irrigated area used more loans to other purposes like for education, paying old debts, marriage etc., compared to the farmers in irrigated area.

Repayment Performance of Primary Agricultural Cooperative Credit Societies

It is very interesting to say that, no farmers were found irregular in repayment of the loans availed from the PACs in Mysore district, it means all the farmers in Mysore district i.e., small, medium and big are regular in repaying the loans to the PACs. The details of loans obtained from the beneficiaries regarding repayment of PACs in the district are furnished in the Table- 8.

Table- 8

Repayment performance of Primary Agricultural Cooperative Credit Societies in irrigated area in Mysore District

Types of farmers	*No of farmers*	*Regular*	*Irregular*
Small	10	10	0
Medium	10	10	0
Big	10	10	0
Total	30	30	0

Source: Field Study, Mysore.

With concerned to non-irrigated area the situation is different, we may find irregular cases in all the types of farmers in Mysore district. In case of small farmers 50 percent of them are regular in repayment the loans to the PACs. Whereas remaining 50 percent of them are irregular in repaying the loans to PACs in the district. In case of medium farmers, 70 percent of the farmers are regular re-payers. And in the case of big farmers, 80 percent of the farmers are regular in repayment the loans, remaining 20 percent are irregular in the district. The details regarding repayment furnished in the Table 9.

Table 9

Repayment position of the Primary Agricultural Cooperative Credit Societies in Non-Irrigated Area

Types of farmers	*No of farmers*	*Regular*	*Irregular*
Small	10	5	5
Medium	10	7	3
Big	10	8	2
Total	30	20	10

Source: Field Study, Mysore.

The purpose of the loan taken is agriculture and consumption loan in case of the marginal and small farmers and in case of the medium and large farmers it is agriculture and business. In concluding remarks we can say that access to organized credit facility is very high in case of the medium and large farmers and it is less in case of their counterparts like marginal and small farmers. Therefore the marginal and small farmers trying to get loans from the money lender who have been exploiting them to a greater extent.

Major Findings of the Study

It has been observed that, in case of small farmers 22.22 percent of the loans are used for purchasing of seeds, whereas 24.86 percent of loan is for purchasing of fertilizers, 17.46 percent for pesticides, 11.11 percent for land improvements, 20.65 percent for labour and for other purpose 3.70 percent of loan is used. In the same way, in case of medium farmers 24.37 percent of loans are used for purchasing of seeds, 22.88 percent for fertilizers, and 15.42 percent for pesticides, 9.9 percent for land improvements, 18.40 percent for labours and 8.95 percent for other purposes in Mysore district. Hence under study the role of cooperative banks in advancing agricultural sector is quite satisfactory.

Policy Implications

The analysis of data and the researcher observations reveal that there are some lacunae for the development of agriculture through cooperative credit institutions. Therefore, few suggestions have been made to promote agriculture through cooperative credit.

1. PACS have to train and educate the farmers regarding the utilization of loan in a proper way and to adopt modern and scientific method of cultivation so as to enable the farmer to repay his loan amount within the stipulated period of time out of his earnings.
2. The prompt repayers should not be deprived by delaying the issue of loan and at the earliest possible

not exceeding a week after receiving his loan application, loan has to be sanctioned.

3. Loan is usually sanctioned before the sowing of karif season and not for rabi. But in some cases loan is required for second crop also which has to be considered by PACS and sanction the loan depending upon the prevailing conditions.

REFERENCES

Anegundi (1998), *Problems Of Urban Cooperative Banks In Karnataka,* Sapna Book House, Bangalore.

George, P. T., Mohanan N. and Rajgopal (1985), *Status of Cooperative Movement in India,* NIRD, Mimeo.

Hota, Sanjibkumar and Vinod Sharma (2001), "Cooperative Credit: Revamping Needed", *Yojana,* Vol.45 July 2001.

Mathur, B.S. (1983), *Cooperative In India,* Himalaya Publications, Bombay Revised Edition.

Memoria and Saxena, (1974), *Cooperative In India,* Himalaya Publishing House, Bombay.

Misra, R.V. (1998), Cooperatives for Empowerment of People, *The Cooperator,* Vol.37(5) Nov. P.195-197.

Mohanan, W. (1972), Cooperative Overdues and Small Farmers, *Indian Cooperative Review,* Vol.13 (3):241-249.

Nair, T. G. (1976), Deposit Mobilization by Cooperatives in India – A Review, *Indian Cooperative Review,* Vol.13 (3):241-249.

Nakkiran, .S, (1971), *Problems of Urban Cooperative Banks In India,* Anmol Publications, Ajmeer.

Nakkiran, S., (1986), *Cooperative Banking in India,* Rainbow Publishing House, Coimbatore.

Patnaik, Surendra (1999), Cooperative Banking in India, The Cooperator, Vol.37 (5). Nov.P 171-182.

Thanikodi (1998), "Central Cooperative Banks in India – Problems and Remedies" *The Cooperator,* Vol.42. No.12.

Contributors and Their Affiliations

Dr. S.K. Mishra - Associate Professor, Department of Economics, Sakaldiha P. G. College, Chandauli (Varanasi), U.P.

Shri Dewendra Pratap Tiwari - J.R.F. in Political Science, B.H.U., Varanasi.

Dr. Sib Ranjan Misra - Professor, Department of Economics and Politics, Visva- Bharati, Santiniketan, West Bengal.

Dr. R. Balasubramaniyan – Reader, Department of Economics, D. G. Vaishnav College, Arumbakkam, Chennai, Tamil Nadu. E-Mail: baladgv@yahoo.co.in

Dr. P. C. Tiwari – Associate Professor in Economics, Handia P. G. College, Handia, Allahabad, Uttar Pradesh.

Dr. C. Dhandapaṇi - Reader in Economics, Muthurangam Government Arts College, Vellore - 632 002, Tamil Nadu.

Dr. N. Suresh Babu - Reader, Post Graduate and Research Department of Economics, Presidency College, Chennai-600 005, Tamil Nadu.

Dr. S. N. Tripathy - Gokhale Institute of Politics and Economics, BMCC Road, Pune, Maharashtra- 411004. E-mail: sn_tripathy2004@yahoo.com

Dr. M. P. Singh - Professor, Department of Economics, B.H.U, Varanasi, Uttar Pradesh.

Dr. Vimal Shankar Singh - Reader & Head, D.A.V.P.G.College, Varanasi, Uttar Pradesh.

Dr. R. Kumar – Lecturer, Department of Economics, Presidency College, Chennai- 05, Tamil Nadu.

Dr. K. Ramesh – Reader, PG and Research Department of Economics, Presidency College, (Autonomous), Chennai – 600 005, Tamil Nadu.

Dr. Kakali Majumdar - Assistant Professor, College of Management, Shri Mata Vaishno Devi University, Jammu. Address for Correspondence: Shri Mata Vaishno Devi University, P.O. Kakryal, Katra, Jammu & Kashmir, PIN-182320.

Dr. Sudhansu Sekhar Nayak - Senior Faculty, Department of Commerce, R.N. College, Dura, Berhampur-10, Ganjam, Orissa.

Dr. G. Jayasankar - Lecturer in Economics, P.G. and Research Department of Economics, Govt. Arts College, Tiruvannamalai - 606603, Tamil Nadu. Email: jayashankar_cyr@yahoo.co.in

Dr. Pradeep Kumar Punjabi - HOD and Associate Professor, Department of Economics, MVS College, J.R.N. Rajasthan Vidyapeeth, Udaipur, Rajasthan. Email: p_punjabi@hotmail.com

Shri Ram Singh Rathore - Lecturer, Department of Management, Shekhawati College of Management and Information Technology, Sikar (Rajasthan). Residence: B-30, Shivpuri Colony, Kalwar Road, Opposite Anjali Motor, Jhotwara, Jaipur-12. Email: singh.raunak@yahoo.co.in

Dr. Sukhjeet K. Saran - Department of Economics and Sociology, Punjab Agricultural University, Ludhiana, Punjab.

Dr. Mini Goyal - Department of Economics and Sociology, Punjab Agricultural University, Ludhiana, Punjab.

Dr. Subhabrata Chakrabarti, Assistant Profesor; Kharagpur College; Kharagpur; West Bengal.

Dr. K. K. Bagchi - Professor, Department of Economics, University of North Bengal, Darjeeling, West Bengal.

Shri Anjan Chakrabarti - Assistant Professor, Dept. of Economics, St. Joseph's College, Darjeeling

Dr. Sanchari Roy Mukherjee - Professor, Dept. of Economics, North Bengal University

Shri Govinda Choudhury – Assistant Professor, Dept. of Economics, North Bengal University

Dr. S. Jeyarani - Assistant Professor, Department of Economics, The American College, Madurai, TamilNadu.

Dr. Mrs. V. R. Deshpande – Reader, Department of Economics, MES Abasaheb Garware College, Karve Road, Pune -411 004.

Dr. M. S. Narasimhan - Department of Economics, Government First Grade College, Sira, Tumkur District, Karnataka.

Dr. K. Sivachithappa – Assistant Professor, PG. Department of Economics, University of Mysore, PG Centre, Mandya – 571402, Karnataka.

Dr. K. Sivachithappa - Assistant Professor, Department of Economics, University of Mysore, PG Centre, Mandya – 571402, Karnataka.

Shri Krishnappa Madival - Dept. of Economics, Government First Grade College, Bantwal, D. K. District, Karnataka.

